IMMIGRANT MINDS, AMERICAN IDENTITIES

ORM ØVERLAND

Immigrant Minds,

American Identities

Making the United States Home,
1870–1930

UNIVERSITY OF ILLINOIS PRESS

URBANA AND CHICAGO

Publication of this book was supported by a grant from
the Ellis Island–Statue of Liberty Foundation.

Library of Congress Cataloging-in-Publication Data
Øverland, Orm, 1935–
Immigrant minds, American identities : making the United States home,
1870–1930 / Orm Øverland.
p.   cm. — (Statue of Liberty–Ellis Island Centennial series)
Includes bibliographical references and index.
ISBN 0-252-02562-8
1. Immigrants—United States—History.
2. United States—Emigration and immigration—History.
I. Title.
II. Series.
JV6451.O93   2000
305.8'00973'09034—dc21   99-006986

C 5 4 3 2 1

For Berge Jørn, Arve Peder, and Sverre Orm

I have been repeatedly impressed by immigrants telling me or writing to me how they felt when they first glimpsed the Statue of Liberty: how tears filled their eyes, how they wanted to fall on their knees, how they lifted their children to see the goddess. These immigrants were Americans before they landed. They were part of the same movement, the same surge toward freedom, that brought over the Pilgrims. Their stories seem to me intensely exciting literary material and a source of inspiration for freedom and democracy. The inscription on the Statue of Liberty remains significant.

—Louis Adamic, *From Many Lands* (1940)

Contents

Acknowledgments

MANY HAVE HELPED ME to make this book. A sabbatical from the University of Bergen and a grant from Norsk forskningsråd (the Norwegian Research Council) in 1997–1998, and grants from the Longfellow Institute of Harvard University, where I was John E. Sawyer Fellow for six weeks during the spring term of 1996 and the academic year of 1997–1998, gave me the time and means for research and writing. Grants from L. Meltzers Høyskolefond (the L. Meltzer Foundation), the Department of English at the University of Bergen, and the Norsk faglitterær forfatterforening (Norwegian Association of Nonfiction Authors) have subsidized travel to archives, libraries, and conferences.

I have had the privilege of drawing upon the rich resources of the Widener Memorial Library at Harvard University. The Immigration History Research Center at the University of Minnesota has been invaluable, not least because of the helpfulness of its excellent staff. Visits to the Beinecke Rare Book and Manuscript Library of Yale University and the archives of the Norwegian-American Historical Association at St. Olaf College were also very useful. The friendly and competent people of the Inter-Library Loan Division of the University of Bergen Library have again made it possible for me to write at an institution with scant resources for the study of the United States.

I was encouraged at an early stage of my work by invitations from Maya Koreneva of the Russian Academy of Sciences, Harald Runblom of Uppsala University, Sølvi Sogner and Per Winther of the University of Oslo, and Waldemar Zacharasiewicz of the University of Vienna to present some of my ideas at conferences. I presented drafts of chapters for discussion at the Warren Center of Harvard University, the Immigration History Research Center of the University of Minnesota, and the Department of English and the International Migration and Ethnic Relations (IMER) Program at the University of Bergen. Questions and criticism at these sessions were both supportive and helpful.

The generosity of colleagues in my department at the University of Bergen made it possible for me to complete this book during the winter and spring of 1998–99. In rewriting my first draft, I benefited enormously from the insights and constructive criticism of Allan Winkler and the two readers for the University of Illinois Press, John Bodner and Jon Gjerde.

Contact with colleagues at home and abroad is a continuous education. Many have assisted me in my work with this book in more specific ways, offering valuable suggestions and giving me encouragement. They include Rosalind Beiler, Caryn Cosse Bell, Dag Blanck, John R. Chávez, Ruth Crane, Roger Daniels, Knut Djupedal, Paul Fessler, Victor Greene, Asbjørn Grønstad, Øyvind Gulliksen, Edward Ingebretsen, Matthew Frye Jacobson, Rob Kroes, Odd S. Lovoll, Štépánka Magstadtova, Karen Majewski, Jay Martin, Todd Nichol, Einar Niemi, David E. Nye, Peter J. O'Connell, David J. Olson, Irena Ragaisiene, Ian Richmond, (the late and missed) Timo Riippa, Peter Rose, Marc Shell, Werner Sollors, Maya Thee, and Rudolph J. Vecoli. Without the love and support of Inger, very little would have been possible.

Prologue:
Homemaking in America

IN COMMON AMERICAN USAGE the noun *foreigner* has had one meaning not registered in major dictionaries of American English: *an American or a resident in the United States who is not of British origin.*[1] To be characterized as foreign has been central to the experience of so many first- and second-generation Americans who came from a European country other than the United Kingdom that one can only wonder why lexicographers of a nation of immigrants have not noted this meaning of the word. Migrations in the nineteenth and early twentieth centuries made European immigrants foreigners in an absolute sense. Should immigrants return home to, say, Italy or Norway, they would be regarded as foreigners by Americans of British origin on their departure and considered American on arrival in their native village. On either side of the Atlantic their formal citizenship would not be germane to the identity bestowed upon them by other residents. By the time of the Second World War, the United States had become more open and welcoming to its non-Anglo-Saxon population, as evidenced, for instance, by the 1938–39 series of radio broadcasts sponsored by the U.S. Office of Education: *Americans All . . . Immigrants All.*[2] The subject of this book is how European immigrants in the late nineteenth and early twentieth centuries responded to their status as foreigners in their chosen land.

An immigrant's name, dress, customs, food, language, and religion were among the factors that Anglo-Americans—or native Americans, as they were called until quite recently—could regard as foreign.[3] One obvious response to this was to try to shed all that made one a foreigner and to become a new person, an American. Such attempts were seldom successful and rarely led to an enthusiastic welcome into the American family. Another response was to affirm the Old World identity and to insist that it too was American. Neither response was without problems. Although the first could alienate individual immigrants from their own identities, the other could alienate them from their progeny. Immigrants who deliberately denationalized themselves in their attempts to become "real" Americans were less reliant on the immigrant community and its many organizations, institutions, and publications than those who felt more comfortable with what we now call an ethnic identity. Because I am focusing on how organized groups responded to the problem of being considered foreigners, this book examines the latter and not the former response.

Many descendants of immigrants have continued to celebrate their forebears' Old World identities without any sense of conflicting loyalties or divided hearts. Consequently, the national celebrations of some European nations have become the occasion of ethnic celebration in the United States.[4] Here, however, their function has become quite different. In the United States such celebrations serve to bolster both nationalism and ethnicity. The ethnicity that is celebrated has European roots but has taken on American characteristics. The nationalism that is confirmed and celebrated is unabashedly American. There is nothing foreign about such celebrations.

At least one European day of celebration has transcended ethnicity: on March 17 many Americans with no trace of genetic Irishness playfully claim an Irish identity. Green beer on St. Patrick's Day is an American, not an Irish, custom. The rather general Americanization of the celebration of St. Patrick's Day is not a recent phenomenon. The editor of the Chicago Czech-American newspaper *Denní Hlasatel* (Daily Voice) seems to have missed the point in his editorial of March 19, 1903. He noted, "This year, as in other years, our patriotic youth took it upon themselves to decorate their breasts with green ribbons, shamrocks, and other symbols of the Irish people on the occasion of St. Patrick's Day. Although in most cases it was done in a jocular manner, nevertheless it was a sad manifestation." The editor admonished his readers against making "sport of the struggle of the Irish" but was obviously more concerned with the dignity and honor of the Czechs: "Our Bohemian nation with its culture, its maturity and history surpasses by far the Irish nation, and our children, American born perhaps, have no reason to be ashamed of their Bohemian origin and to try to pass themselves off as Irish."[5] These young

Americans of Czech descent, however, were playing out their *American* identities by joining other Americans in celebrating St. Patrick's Day.

Columbus Day, now the second Monday of October, is also a day of ethnic American celebration. Although Italian Americans—whose claim to Columbus is by no means uncontested— have appropriated the day, it has no meaning in the European homeland of their ancestors. Most of those who celebrate Columbus Day have European roots; the day and its celebration, however, are indigenous to the United States. By celebrating Columbus, Italian Americans are affirming not their foreignness but their special right to a home in America—their right by discovery. In Norway the Seventeenth of May takes second place only to Christmas as a day of celebration, and, like Christmas, the celebrations focus on children. In that northern European country it is a national holiday, celebrating independence and the signing of the constitution in 1814. It is a day of excessive nationalistic exuberance. In the United States, Americans of Norwegian descent also celebrate the Seventeenth of May. These celebrations have not transcended ethnicity to the same extent as the celebrations of St. Patrick's Day. Nevertheless, the Seventeenth of May has become a day for the celebration of American ethnicity and American nationalism rather than of European nationalism.[6] Jon Gjerde has noted that in the late nineteenth-century Midwest "celebrations of national holidays . . . consolidated images of both the European past and the American present." He gives several illustrations of expressions of what he calls "multiple loyalties":

> Irish immigrants in Dubuque merged an 1883 Fourth of July celebration with advocacy of the Irish National Land League and of independence for Ireland. Swiss Americans saw no incongruity in incorporating the history of Switzerland into their Fourth of July observance in 1876. Their centennial parade float contained representations of Helvetia and Columbia surrounded by images of the Swiss cantons with their coats-of-arms. Members of a rural German community six years later celebrated American life by reading the Declaration of Independence and listening to a speaker discuss the role of Germans in the Revolutionary War, "a chapter in American history," reported a German-language newspaper, "too little known." . . . And Roman Catholic newspaper mastheads juxtaposed portraits of George Washington and Pope Pius X, a clear illustration of the importance and compatibility of allegiance to both church and state.[7]

Ethnic celebration in the United States, then, is primarily a celebration of the American identity of immigrants and their descendants. The affirmation and celebration of ethnicity is a way of affirming and celebrating that a particular ethnic group has a home in America. Paradoxically, to celebrate being Irish on St. Patrick's Day, being Italian on Columbus Day, or Norwegian on the Seventeenth of May is to celebrate being American.

In Sioux City, Iowa, May 17, 1926, was celebrated in a Lutheran church on the following Sunday, with festive meetings in the afternoon and evening and with ethnic food served in the church basement in between the two more formal events. The speaker both afternoon and evening was a professor from St. Olaf College in Minnesota, Ole Edvart Rølvaag. One year later he would achieve literary success and great renown with his best-selling novel *Giants in the Earth.* According to a contemporary report on the festivities in Sioux City, Rølvaag's text for his speech was, "You are the salt of the earth. You are the light of the world." Not surprisingly, given the chauvinistic mood of such celebrations, he suggested that these words were an appropriate characterization of the Norwegian "race."[8] With a major newspaper as his source, Rølvaag could reveal that Norway had given the world more geniuses—six in all—than any other country in the preceding generation. Such a gift, the speaker admonished his listeners, places a special obligation on our people.

This was quite a heady dish to serve up on a day of ethnic celebration, and what followed was no less likely to bolster the pride of the Norwegian Americans of Sioux City: "He gave an outline of the social system in ancient Norway and demonstrated how our people from as far back as we have historical records had a fully developed popular democracy in self-governed counties. This is precisely the same democracy that the Norwegians brought with them to England, either directly with the Vikings or indirectly through the Normans, and that the Pilgrim fathers in their turn brought with them to America. Later research has disclosed that the early colonists came from those parts of England that had been settled by the Vikings."

We have every reason to believe that these sentiments were well received by the audience. "The most important 17th of May speech I have heard in a long time," one well-informed member of the audience told the reporter. In the evening Rølvaag addressed himself more specifically to the special situation of a European immigrant group in the United States. There may have been too much veneration of tradition and the old ways in the former homeland, he acknowledged, but added, "*Here—*in the new land—no tradition restrains progress; but nor are there any firm footsteps to follow in. This is America's strength, but also its weakness." He admonished his listeners not to listen to the voices that urged them to "tear down" the memorials to their own pioneer past in America and expressed the hope that later generations of Norwegian Americans would be able "to afford to have forefathers and that the faith and works of the fathers would become a source of strength for the race."

In the afternoon Rølvaag had not spoken to his listeners' pride as Norwegians but to their pride as Americans of Norwegian descent, just as he in the evening did not speak to them about nostalgia for the ways of the old country but admonished them to use their American immigrant traditions to achieve both success and a meaningful life in the new one. In both instances, however, he may today seem to have been insisting a little too much on the value of belonging to the Norwegian race. In his 1998 book, *Whiteness of a Different Color,* Matthew Frye Jacobson reminds us that when Americans in the nineteenth and early twentieth centuries spoke of race, they were not simply using another word to speak of ethnicity and nationality. Of special relevance in the present context is his observation that racism "is a theory of who is who, of who belongs and who does not, of who deserves what and who is capable of what."[9] According to Rølvaag, the reasons Norwegians belonged in America were both ideological (they were *the* source of American democracy) and racial (through the Viking settlement of England and Normandy they were closely related to Americans of English descent). Because he had so often been characterized as a "foreigner" in his homeland, he felt the need to argue these points, however, and to convince other Norwegian Americans of their right to their American homeland. A few years earlier, in 1922, he had published a volume of polemical essays in response to the Americanization hysteria of the war years. He was especially concerned with the need for immigrants and their descendants to recognize their immigrant history, have it recognized as part of American history, and to regard their own language and traditions as American rather than foreign. "Here mother and father are mere *foreigners,* or such close descendants of them that the odor still clings. Our young people do not feel that their fathers' history ties them closer to the history of this country and its people."[10] Rølvaag's insistence, then, on his people's right to a home in America was triggered by a collective experience of dismissal as foreigners.

Historian Victor Greene has observed that in their celebration of St. Patrick's Day, Irish Americans "complemented their identity as Americans. Doing homage to St. Patrick became an important ritual for all immigrants, partly because it reminded them of the compatibility and basic similarity of being both Irish and American." Rølvaag argued that Norwegian Americans' ancient tradition of democracy was what gave them a special right to be at home in America. Similarly, Greene has observed that one function of the celebration of St. Patrick's Day has been to weld "together the Irish and American national struggles. Both peoples had been English colonials who had suffered British tyranny, and both sought freedom and democracy or, as they called it, 'republicanism.'"[11] Thus two different European national celebrations have in the United States become American ethnic celebrations with rather similar functions of affirming a unique relationship between the ethnic inheritance and the mainstream American tradition. The affirmation, however, is exclusive in the sense that this relationship is not claimed for all Americans. The basis for this kind of affirmation is precisely the unique character of the relationship between a specific ethnic group and the dominant American group, the Anglo-Americans: Irish Americans claiming the bond of a common British adversary in their struggle for common ideals, Norwegian Americans claiming blood relationship with the Anglo-Americans and that Norway was the source of American democracy. Note, however, that although the pleading is special, Irish and Norwegian Americans both claim that a tradition of freedom and democracy is what makes each group uniquely qualified for a home in America. Note too that the affirmation has not traditionally been reciprocal: Americans of British descent have not been overly eager to affirm their relationship with Americans of other origins. The lack of reciprocity has made the need for such affirmation all the more strongly felt in the many other ethnic groups.

Some years after Rølvaag insisted on the essentially American character and tradition of his people, Michael Musmanno, then twelve, fell in love with an immigrant girl in his class at a country schoolhouse in Stowe Township, Pennsylvania. Penelope Worthington had recently come from England with her family and, as Musmanno later told the story, "it was not long until I was accompanying her home, carrying her books, and writing her notes of adoration. One day I decided that when I grew up, Penelope Worthington should be my wife." He asked a friend to act as go-between, and the next day the friend reported, "I talked to Penelope and she said she loves you. . . . But she says she can never marry you because you are a foreigner." "I was born in America; she had been here seven months," the adult Musmanno muses. "She was an American, I was a foreigner. . . . I did not even attempt to argue the question with her because I accepted what everybody said and believed. Italians were foreigners."

Musmanno, a justice of the Pennsylvania Supreme Court, tells this story in the opening chapter of his popular history, *The Story of the Italians in America*. Here he presents the standard litany of early achievements found in so many amateur histories of U.S. immigrant groups, beginning with Columbus and other Italian explorers. Musmanno's childhood memory interrupts his narrative and implicitly reveals his motivation for writing the book. He not only tells of the earliest explorers, such as Christopher Columbus, Giovanni Caboto, and Giovanni da Verrazano, but also demonstrates that Italians were part of society in the British colonies and that they played important roles in the early Republic. Equally important are the stories of how Italian blood was sacrificed for the new nation in the Revolutionary War. And all this is in rebuttal to Penelope Worthington. "But they were not foreigners in the eyes of the founders of our country," Musmanno says of the Italians in eighteenth-century America. Indeed, they were one of the nation's charter peoples.

Musmanno draws upon one of the first historians of the United States to argue his point: "As early as 1789 the historian David Ramsey wrote: 'The Colonies which now form the United States may be considered as Europe transplanted. Ireland, England, Scotland, France, Germany, Holland, Switzerland, Sweden, Poland, and *Italy* furnished the original stock.' Nor did the Italians themselves look upon America as a foreign land," Musmanno adds.[12] In his next chapter, "Crusading for American Freedom," Musmanno tells the story of Philip Mazzei, the Italian whom Benjamin Franklin met in London and who settled in Virginia just before the War of Independence. There Mazzei became involved in the cause of the colonies as a pamphleteer and may have had an influence on Thomas Jefferson. Mazzei's ideas, Musmanno suggests, became part of the foundation of the new republic: "It is certain that some telling language in Mazzei's articles strikingly resembles phrases immortalized in the Declaration of Independence."

The stories Musmanno tells are not myths in the sense that Columbus, Verrazano, and Mazzei are not well-documented historical characters. Columbus's voyage in 1492 did open up the Americas to European exploitation and settlement; Mazzei did write for the cause of American independence and probably had an influence on Jefferson. The stories about them become mythic in the way they are made part of a twentieth-century Italian-American story of belonging in America. Although Mazzei was a real person who took part in the events leading up to the break between the colonies and Britain, the claimed relationship between eighteenth-century Mazzei and twentieth-century Musmanno may not be imaginary but is nevertheless imagined. The manner in which Musmanno evokes these stories to exorcise the ghost of Penelope Worthington places them in the realm of myth. Historians may not dispute the stories of the exploits of Christopher Columbus and Leif Erikson. But when these and similar stories become part of an argument about why Italian Americans or Norwegian Americans have a special and natural right to a home in the United States, the home of their choice, Columbus and Erikson become mythic figures and their stories have mythic uses.

Such myths may be called "homemaking myths" because they have had the function of claiming the United States as the rightful home of many immigrant groups. They are closely related to the kind of amateurish history writing that has been called "filiopietistic" because it invariably tells of the past excellence or greatness of a particular nation. These myths, however, can occur in a variety of contexts and always to demonstrate why a particular immigrant group should not be considered foreign. They have been the vehicles for a vision of an imagined America where a privileged immigrant group had an exclusive right to belong. Although such myths were pervasive and have been told in most groups, each one is exclusive rather than inclusive. Each group created the stories anew and based them on myths and traditions of the old home country or on the real or imagined group experience in the new one.

The grammatical change from the third person singular to the first person plural in two statements—"He was here first" and "We were here first"—illustrates the modulation from history to myth. Through their exploits, contributions, and sacrifices the early visitors and settlers from Italy made America their own and thus also made it the land of their descendants. The myths insist on family relationships across the centuries and on continuities where historians see few if any connections. The historian David Mauk, for instance, sees interesting parallels between the "chronologically separated" maritime migrations of Norwegians to New Amsterdam in the 1630s and to New York in the midnineteenth century. A narrator of what I would call a Norwegian-American myth, however, would have it that "we" have been here since the 1630s. The historian Marcus Lee Hansen saw parallels between seventeenth-century New England Puritans and nineteenth-century immigrants. He was struck by how the restrictive policies of the Puritans "must have been typical immigrant reactions." Consequently, it should not be surprising that later immigrants responded in a similar manner. Immigrant homemaking myths, on the other hand, have claimed a genetic or ideological relationship with the New England Puritans to argue the special right of a particular group to be recognized as Americans.

The large number of Italians who emigrated at the turn of the nineteenth century, writes Musmanno, "were going to America, the America of Columbus, of Amerigo Vespucci, of John Cabot, of Philip Mazzei, the America of their fellow townsmen who had just returned after working in New Jersey, Delaware, Pennsylvania, and New York." The mythic character of Musmanno's vision is evident in the manner in which he links the future promise of America with ancient glory. The roads followed by the Italian immigrants "into the future of dignity and freedom from want" were the roads that "traveled back to the days of majestic, invincible, and enlightened Rome. . . . These were the roads the immigrants followed on their way to the seaports to board the vessel that would transport them over the route traversed by their original countryman Cristoforo Colombo and his sons and their descendants."[13] As the descendants of Columbus, these immigrants were not going as foreigners to a foreign land but as his heirs to their rightful home.

Although homemaking myths were related as part of an argument for a unique status in the American home for the members of a particular group, the plots and themes of the stories share so many characteristics that they must be considered an American phenomenon rather than one peculiar to individual ethnic groups. The claims they made to an American home were not only exclusive; they often became competitive, as when several groups had their special stories to prove that they were the first to arrive in America. It should be noted that this competition was not with the dominant founding group, the Anglo-Americans. The immigrants claimed a place in the American home equal to that of the Anglo-Americans, and in making that claim they were competing with each other. The home imagined in these myths could not accommodate all immigrant groups, at least not in the same style. In his 1981 book Patrick J. Gallo tells of "a lone individual at a recent Columbus Day parade in New York City holding a placard which carried the declaration, 'Leif Erikson was here first.' Another person, obviously an Italian-American, exclaimed, 'They are even trying to rob us of that?' He shook his head in disgust."[14]

The competition, however, was not only between the heroes of different ethnic traditions but also for the appropriation of such heroes. When Columbus was chosen as one of two American heroes to have their names attached to the federal capital and when his name was given to so many places and institutions in America, the intention was not to honor an American ethnic group. Even as late as 1893, Italian Americans did not have a significant role at the World's Columbian Exposition in Chicago. It was years before the Italian Americans were able to appropriate the Columbus story and make it theirs in the early decades of the twentieth century, and their right to the story is still not undisputed.

Indeed, counterclaims have been made with far greater force than that offered by the lonely Norwegian-American protester observed by Gallo. For some years New York City has had two Columbus Day parades: one

Italian (celebrating the ethnicity of the navigator) and one Hispanic (celebrating the ethnicity of the monarchy that sponsored the expedition). In New York the Italian-American event, on the second Monday of October, is by far the largest and the one that makes the greater stir. An organizer of the 1996 Hispanic parade in New York explained to a *New York Times* reporter: "We don't understand what the Italians celebrate. Everybody knows the discovery was a thoroughly Spanish event. Just look at us, what language do we speak. What do we look like? Italy had nothing to do with it." The response of the chairman of the Italian parade: "I understand why the Hispanics want to associate themselves with Columbus. Some people also say he was Jewish. I think just about the only ones who have not claimed him are the Russians. But the fact of the matter is that he was Italian." And how could the issue of the national identity of a sailor who crossed the Atlantic in 1492 be of importance to Americans in 1996? As the *New York Times* observed, "Columbus remains someone to celebrate, a source of pride and of cultural and ethnic identity."[15]

That the question of whether the 1492 expedition should be identified by the explorer's place of birth or the land of his financial backers could be so important in 1996—both for descendants of peoples who fought to liberate themselves from Spanish colonialism and for descendants of late nineteenth and early twentieth-century immigrants from an Italy that did not exist in 1492—demonstrates that the Columbus they celebrate is a mythic character. Of course, all the heroes of European-American foundation myths may be equally irrelevant to African Americans and Asian Americans, who have their own and no less American homemaking arguments to make. My interest here is not in the relative importance of the voyages of Leif Erikson and Christopher Columbus but in how they have had and continue to have symbolic importance to Americans claiming different European heritages and in how they have entered into the formation of American ethnic identities. This way of looking at American myth making neither can nor intends to replace the Anglo-American myths of foundation, mission, and sacrifice. It does, however, insist on a view of American mythology that includes the myths of Americans of Greek, Jewish, and Italian origin as well as of those whose ancestors came from the British Isles.

All American foundation stories have not necessarily had a function as homemaking myths. Of interest here is the manner in which they have been used. And their use has been intimately related to a perceived need in immigrant groups to argue that they were not foreigners in the United States. Thus the stories of the Welsh expedition to America under the leadership of Prince Madoc, presumably in 1170, of so-called Welsh Indian tribes, and of a Welsh influence on North American Indian languages have interested many antiquarians and amateur historians but did not, to my knowledge, arise because of attempts to exclude the Welsh as foreigners.[16] As fascinating and valuable as accounts of ancient journeys from Europe, Africa, and the Pacific are, this book is concerned with the use of foundation stories as parts of the homemaking arguments of immigrants from Europe.[17] That America got its name from the Italian mariner Amerigo Vespucci is central to the stories Italian Americans tell about themselves and their right to a home in the United States. Vespucci, however, is not the only contender for this honor. Some have claimed that the new land, which John Cabot believed was an island, was named for the Welsh merchant Richard Ameryk, a main investor in Cabot's second expedition.[18] But neither Anglo-Americans, who have had little need for stories to prove that they have a right to be American, nor, to the best of my knowledge, Welsh Americans have made a Richard Ameryk story the centerpiece in a homemaking argument. Therefore, apart from this brief appearance, he will not be a character in this book.

Although the image of the United States of America as land of promise is largely a European invention, homemaking arguments are not limited to Americans of European descent. An awareness of the differences in the myths of immigrants from Europe and those created by Americans of, say, Mexican and African origin may further our understanding of the different obstacles confronted by those whose paths into America have other points of departure. It may also deepen our appreciation of the crucial factor of race for acceptance in the American home.

Unlike so many immigrants from European countries, the original Mexican Americans of the Southwest were not attracted to the United States by a dream of improving the quality of their lives. In fact, the first Mexican Americans were not immigrants to the United States in any sense of the word, yet their status as Americans was surely as marginal as that of immigrants. Mexicans in the northern regions of their country abruptly found themselves living in the United States after the Mexican-American War of 1848. Faced with the pressures of the growing number of Anglo-Americans, and with isolation from the cultural and political centers of Mexico, some began to mythologize their rootedness in the region they claimed as their home. This process led to the "increasingly popular belief . . . that the region was their homeland," primarily because Mexican Americans had preceded the Anglo-Americans in the region but also because they were descended from the indigenous people of the Southwest, the residents of mythic Aztlán, from where they had migrated to create the Aztec Empire. In his study of the Chicano image of the Southwest, *The Lost Land*, John Chávez explains that Mexican Americans developed such a myth to "lend credibility to the Chicanos' image of themselves as indigenous to the Southwest, their homeland, both ancient and modern."

By the end of the nineteenth century, most Mexican Americans had come to regard Mexico itself rather than the American Southwest as their homeland, and in this way of thinking they may more easily be compared to immigrant groups. Chávez explains that then, in the early decades of the twentieth century, another myth gained ascendance. Although it may seem to have made the exact opposite claim of the earlier one, the new myth too was a response to marginalization. What we may call the Spanish myth of Mexican Americans did not insist on their right as descendants of the indigenous inhabitants but served to create an image of Mexican Americans as Europeans, as pure-blooded Spanish, indeed, as a people who were more Spanish than the Spanish themselves and were therefore the true inheritors of the one-time greatness of that European nation. In other words, as Spanish Americans they were at the very least the equals of the Anglo-Americans as bearers of a great European tradition in America. The homemaking myths of marginal groups have seldom been noticed by those with a secure and central position in American society. Chávez, however, gives an interesting instance of the contemporary recognition of the Spanish myth, an article in *Harper's Weekly* in 1914 that claimed, "These Spanish people of New Mexico . . . are not of the mixed breed one finds south of the Rio Grande, or even Arizona. . . . Indeed it is probable that there is no purer Spanish stock in Old Spain itself."

If a claim to a status at least equal to that of the most prestigious ethnic group is to have an effect, it should include the corollary claim that you are different from those who by association may lower your status. The definition of your proximity to the elite must include a definition of your distance from those who are looked down upon by the elite. Rølvaag was not arguing for the acceptance of all immigrants as Americans but that Norwegian Americans as a group (indeed, a race) had a special right, which other immigrant groups did not have, to be included in the American family. The organizers of the two different Columbus Day parades in New York in 1996 could not accept each other's claims to prominence in the ethnic hierarchy. Similarly, the Spanish myth of the Southwest insisted on the distinction between "Spanish" Americans and more recent Mexican immigrants. A Chicano lawyer reminiscing about his immigrant childhood in Denver wrote about his experience of discrimination from "so-called Spanish-Americans [who] claimed direct descent from the original conquistadors of Spain. They also insisted that they had *never* been Mexicans, since their region of New Spain (later annexed to the United States) was never a part of Mexico. But what they claimed most vociferously—and erroneously—was an absence of Indian ancestry."[19]

A homemaking argument based on an account of descent from the original inhabitants of the land could hardly have been expected to make much of an impression in a nation where the indigenous peoples had always been seen as the absolute and defining Other. The Naturalization Act of 1790 limited naturalized citizenship to "free white persons," and the earlier colonial charters had defined the civilized and Christian communities in opposition to "the New World's 'barbarous' or 'savage' inhabitants." The United States has a tradition of recounting its history "in terms of race," writes Matthew Frye Jacobson, and the distinction of "'civilized' Europeans from 'savage' Indians and 'mongrelized' Mexicans" was clear.[20] In such a context a myth of Spanish origins would seem of greater efficacy than a myth of indigenous roots. But neither these Mexican-American homemaking myths nor those created by European immigrants made much impression on the dominant Anglo-American community, where they received little attention.

The late nineteenth-century homemaking myths of African Americans struck other themes and expressed different strategies, both because of a more problematic past and because of more extreme and more consistent experiences of exclusion and refusal than those experienced by European Americans. Nevertheless, in the early part of the period discussed in this book, the homemaking arguments of both groups were related to each other in interesting ways. European groups were basing some of their arguments on a shared whiteness, whereas some African-American representatives were basing theirs on a long-shared history with the Anglo-American elite and making explicit references to unreliable foreigners. Two examples, from Booker T. Washington and Paul Laurence Dunbar, show both similarities and differences in the myths involved in such arguments.

Washington later recalled that when he got up to speak to a mainly white audience at the Atlanta Exposition in 1895, "the thing that was uppermost in my mind was the desire to say something that would cement the friendship of the races and bring about hearty coöperation between them." For the two decades since the end of Reconstruction, the experience of Washington and other black southerners had been of an inexorable worsening year by year of their social, political, and economic conditions. They had little ground for optimism, and it is telling that Washington's homemaking argument was based on a myth of past service and common interest, both before and during the Civil War and a future vision of "a new heaven and a new earth" in a land held in common by its white and black inhabitants, "our beloved South."

He ended his address with that appeal to a shared love of a shared homeland of the two southern races, and he had opened it with the reminder that he spoke for a people who were as rooted in the South as the whites: "One-third of the population of the South is of the Negro race." In his second sentence he referred to African Americans as "this element of our population," and the implied and invited contrast is with another element that was getting increasing negative attention at the end of the century, the so-called foreign element. At a time when the whiteness of many European immigrant groups was being questioned, Washington based his argument on the contrast between a native and therefore known and trustworthy black population and a foreign immigrant population: "To those of the white race who look to the incoming of those of foreign birth and strange tongue and habits for the prosperity of the South, were I permitted I would repeat what I say to my own race, 'Cast down your bucket where you are.' Cast it down among the eight millions of Negroes whose habits you know, whose fidelity and love you have tested in days when to have proved treacherous meant the ruin of your firesides."

His appeal was to a sense of common ground and to a record of past performance: "As we have proved our loyalty to you in the past, in nursing your children, watching by the sick-bed of your mothers and fathers, and often following them with tear-dimmed eyes to their graves, so in the future, in our humble way, we shall stand by you with a devotion that no foreigner can approach, ready to lay down our lives, if need be, in defence of yours." As Washington perceived the situation, African Americans were pitted against immigrants in a competition for accommodations in the American home. History has proved him right in his analysis. History, however, has also shown that his analysis made no impression on his audience. At least not on their behavior.[21]

Paul Laurence Dunbar's story, "At Shaft 11" (1898), gives narrative form to the strategy Booker T. Washington outlined in his "Atlanta Exposition Address" in 1895. Dunbar illustrates the loyalty to be expected of African Americans, who, as Washington had put it, had served "without strikes and labour wars," as opposed to the treacherous behavior of the foreign Irish. In Dunbar's story the striking miners are unreliable and violent and have Irish names such as Tom Daly and "Red" Cleary. The steadfast foreman, Jason Andrews, has "sturdy, stubborn old Scotch blood that coursed through his veins," while Harold Crofton, the spokesman for the owners, is obviously an Anglo-American. Black strikebreakers, led

by "big Sam Bowles," are called in: "With the true racial instinct of col-
onisation, they all flocked to one part of the settlement. With a wisdom
that was not entirely instinctive, though it may have had its origin in the
Negro's social inclination, they built one large eating-room a little way
from their cabin and up the mountain side." The strikers become violent
and are eventually subdued by the timely arrival of an armed militia.
"Some of the strikers availed themselves of the Croftons' clemency and
went back to work along with the blacks," Dunbar writes. The faithful
Jason Andrews "was the admiration of white and black alike. He has
general charge now of all the Crofton mines, and his assistant and stanch
friend is Big Sam." The black workers achieve the protection of the Anglo-
American owners by behaving, as Washington had advised, like the "most
patient, faithful, law-abiding, and unresentful people that the world has
seen."[22] The story implies that, because of their loyalty to those at the
top of the racial hierarchy, the blacks are given a place in the hierarchy
below that of Scots but certainly above that of the Irish.

Although the myth created by Booker T. Washington looked back
with some pride to a past that included slavery and the Civil War where
"we have proved our loyalty to you," this myth was essentially one of
future promise, rather than one of a glorious conquistador past, as in the
Spanish myth of Mexican Americans. One myth looks forward to a desirable future, the other creates a desired past, but both concern themselves with the quality of the American home for a specific ethnic group
in the present. And both myths have the privileged Anglo-Americans as
their main group of reference, in the one instance not only with a plea
for protection in return for loyalty but also with a claim to a status just
below that of the sturdy Scot, and in the other with a claim to a status of
equality with the Anglo-Americans themselves. Note too the similarity
in the hierarchy implied in the African-American myth, as expressed by
Dunbar and Washington, where immigrants or foreigners appear as shifty
and untrustworthy, and the distinction drawn between Spanish Americans and Mexican-American immigrants in the Spanish myth.

One aspect that the homemaking mythologies of European immigrant groups have in common with those here identified as African
American and Mexican American is that they harmonize with a middle-
class ideology of uplift and the right to success and that they insist on
the validity of the American dream for a particular ethnic group. Such
notions were of course shrugged off, even scoffed at, by large numbers of
immigrants whose experience spoke to them more of the evils of class
divisions and the need for class solidarity across ethnic lines. For the
many Italians, Germans, Scandinavians, and Poles for whom labor unions

or Socialist Party locals offered a more meaningful community than middle-class ethnic societies, homemaking myths may have had little importance. Their concepts of rights were not based primarily on ethnic bonds but on a class-based internationalism. This difference came out clearly during the First World War when, for instance, nationalist Lithuanian-American leaders were, like their counterparts in all immigrant groups, eagerly promoting the purchase of Liberty bonds as proof of the loyalty of Lithuanian Americans. Meanwhile, socialist leaders of the same nationality were actively demonstrating against the war, arguing that "true patriotism should be demonstrated through concern for the welfare of one's fellow worker." This book explores the contexts and the expressions of the view put forward by many leaders of many immigrant groups that the members of a particular group were the best Americans because of their peculiar national traits and traditions. Germans are the best Americans, claimed many German-American narratives, because they were Germans. Not all German Americans agreed. Joseph Bruckner, who spoke in German at a "Workers' Fourth of July" celebration in Chicago on July 3, 1876, said, "Let us be socialists in the true sense of the word, then we will also be the best citizens of this republic . . . and we will not have celebrated the Centennial in vain."[23] His appeal was to a socialist ideology rather than to any race or ethnicity. Socialists, regardless of their nationality, made the best Americans.

The conflict between these two visions of the future, one of the United States as a haven of ethnicity, the other of the international dominance of the working class, may be illustrated by a report on "Croatian Day at South Chicago" in the *Danica Hrvatska* (Croatian Morning Star) of August 30, 1934. Many socialist Croatian Americans had protested against the celebration. "Handbills were distributed by some of the 'class-conscious' fighters for workingmen's rights. These leaflets were written after the school of Marx, Lenin and Radek, pointing out the Croatian Day to be an assault on your pocket and mind," the newspaper reported. The sharpness of the class and cultural divisions between members of the same American immigrant group to some extent mimicked the social and political situation in the European home country. Divisions were marked, for instance, among Americans from Finland, a country that experienced a bloody civil war in 1918. But even though so-called Church Finns and Labor Finns could disagree strongly and even though Norwegian-American socialists and republicans were relentless political adversaries, they usually recognized their ethnic bonds despite their differences. Although this book focuses on an America composed of a variety of ethnic groups, it is nevertheless important to keep in mind the America that was divided along class lines. Whereas class divisions may speak more clearly of social, economic, and political realities in the United States, ethnicity has often had a stronger hold on American imaginations.

Indeed, homemaking mythologies contain a considerable degree of naïveté. We may shake our heads at Norwegian Americans in Sioux City being told that all that made the United States good and great came from Norway, at the competition between Italian Americans and Hispanic Americans for Columbus as their particular hero, at Mexican Americans in New Mexico and Colorado who insist they are more Spanish than the Spaniards in Europe, or at African Americans being told that their loyalty to their owner during the Civil War or to their present employers in times of labor unrest will earn them a decent home in the United States. Not all immigrants subscribed to these stories. Other immigrants at the turn of the nineteenth century distanced themselves from the homemaking strategy of so much immigrant filiopietism. After attending a ball for Scandinavian immigrants in St. Paul in 1886, Andreas Ueland, a judge in Minneapolis, wrote sarcastically to Rasmus B. Anderson, then the U.S. minister to Denmark: "Prof. Olson's speech was much applauded. We had a right to this country, for we discovered it and we were the best people of the world, but too modest. . . . This is then the sentiment which is to lead the Scandinavians here! This shall make them prominent and useful in shaping the affairs of the country so as to secure lasting prosperity and greatness." To the historian Frederick Luebke the mythmaking stories are "grotesque distortions of the past." By looking at only one immigrant group, however, he takes such stories to be the expressions of "a few arrogant German-Americans."[24] But virtually all immigrant groups from Europe have stories that claim that a group was a founding group, that it fought harder and sacrificed more for American freedom and independence than any others, and that it was the foremost bearer of traditional American values. Any interpretation that assumes the homemaking stories are typical of members of any particular nationality rather than of the immigrant condition is distorting the past. If mirth, however wry the smile, or irritation are our only responses to immigrant myth making, we have not only cut ourselves off from an understanding of what these stories may tell us but have also closed our minds to the fact that we too live in a world of myths and wishful thinking, a world we have imagined or created, much in the way Norwegian Americans, Italian Americans, Greek Americans, and Polish Americans created theirs in the decades before and after 1900. Our ability to create our reality may be limited, but we do create our understanding of our world. Our understanding of our past is often a response to our experience of present needs and pressures.

The immigrant narratives that gave non-British immigrants central roles in the making of the United States must also be understood as responses to the dominant Anglo-Saxon historical narrative that prevailed throughout the nineteenth century and the beginning of the twentieth, a narrative often characterized as "Whig history." The United States described in the works of historians such as George Bancroft, Richard Hildreth, and John Gorham Palfrey was not the home of German Americans, Irish Americans, Italian Americans, Swedish Americans, or the many other immigrant groups that began to claim homes in increasing numbers just as these large-scale narratives began to appear. The popular historical narratives of the many immigrant groups may indeed be filiopietistic in the exaggerated and often shrilly made claims for their important contributions to the making of the country of their choice. But we must remember that the widely accepted Anglo-American historical narratives, which excluded these ethnic groups, were often no less self-congratulatory and filiopietistic.

In many respects the kind of filiopietistic history telling that is at the core of this book is part of what David Lowenthal has labeled "heritage," insisting that the distinction between it and history is "vital": "History explores and explains pasts grown ever more opaque over time; heritage clarifies pasts so as to infuse them with present purposes." However vital the distinction may be, it is not always clear. What may appear to be "history" in some contexts may be judged as "heritage" in others. To Lowenthal a distinguishing mark of heritage is that it is "responsive to present needs." But historical scholarship, such as that of the so-called Whig historians who were dominant in the period around the turn of the nineteenth century, was no less responsive to the needs of the present. History as filtered through the process of making texts for schools often comes out as heritage rather than history.

"Bias," writes Lowenthal, "is a vice that history struggles to excise; for heritage, bias is a nurturing virtue. Blind allegiance to nation, state, or faith remains the main aim of most school history." The version of American history to which immigrant children were exposed in the public school was what immigrant leaders were trying to counter with their historical narratives. Lowenthal quotes some lines from a school song from the 1960s: "Take a look in your history book, / And you'll see why we should be proud." But in *their* schoolbooks the children of immigrants found nothing to make them particularly proud, not even to make them feel comfortably at home. If the immigrant's homemaking narratives are "heritage masquerading as history," this may surely be said of the history to which they were reacting as well, a history from which they had been excluded. It may well be that "a mythic past crafted for some present cause suppresses history's impartial complexity," but immigrant leaders who found their peoples excluded from the mythic past of the land of their choice had good and present cause to craft a mythic past of their own.[25]

The characteristic homemaking myths of American ethnic groups of European origin may be grouped in three main categories: myths of foundation ("we were here first or at least as early as you were"), myths of blood sacrifice ("we fought and gave our lives for our chosen homeland"), and myths of ideological gifts or an ideological relationship ("the ideas we brought with us are American ideas"). The chapters that follow consider each category separately. To these could be added a fourth and more general group of stories of the contributions to America by what we may call ethnic heroes. Such stories of inventors, politicians, businesspeople, and all manner of successful immigrants, mainly men, are central to all filiopietistic and popular histories of immigrant groups. Except for those that belong in the thematic categories of foundation, sacrifice, and ideology, however, they will not be given special consideration here.

Earlier historians have of course been aware of main themes in immigrant filiopietistic history making. Oscar Handlin, however, misconstrues the widespread search for the early appearances of historical characters who have a shared nationality with a later immigrant group: "Some justified their Americanism by discovery of a colonial past; within the educated second generation there began a tortuous quest for eighteenth-century antecedents that might give them a portion in American civilization in its narrower connotation." As I will argue, the interest in discovering "a colonial past" was not so much to justify an immigrant's Americanism as to insist that immigrants from, say, Poland or Sweden were as much a part of the American past as were those from the United Kingdom. What was "justified" was an American multiculturalism, that the second part of the compounds Italian American, German American, and Jewish American was as valid as the "American" in Anglo- or English American and that the latter were no more "native" to the United States than the former. Nor was this an exercise limited to or even especially prevalent among members of the second generation. And it certainly did not imply "a rejection of their parents who had themselves once been green off the boat and could boast of no New World antecedents," as Handlin put it.[26] On the contrary, the very insistence on the unbroken connection over the centuries—between medieval, sixteenth-, and seventeenth-century characters and the nineteenth- and twentieth-century immigrant experiences—is what gives this historiography a mythic quality. Homemaking myths affirm the community between the first and second generations of immigrants and their claimed early American predecessors.

The three categories of homemaking stories are often woven together or combined, as when the Chicago rabbi Emil G. Hirsch gave the keynote address at Isaiah Temple in 1905 at the celebration of the 250th anniversary of the landing of the first Jews in New Amsterdam. Here he gave a forceful argument for regarding the Jews as one of the founding groups of European settlement in North America, asking his audience to "consider that [when] John Jacob Astor, the founder of the family which now occupies such a prominent position in social life[,] did not hesitate to work for the Jew, Hayman Levy, at $1 a day, it seems a strange perversion of history to see his posterity refusing to rub shoulders with people whose patrimony far antedates their own." But the Jewish claim to an American home did not rest on early arrival alone. "More than 6,000 Jews, twenty per cent of the total number in America, shouldered a musket to put down slavery," Hirsch continued. "In one of our Chicago cemeteries there is a monument to Colonel Speigel, whose body lies where it fell under the flag of his country." To these stories of foundation and blood sacrifice Hirsch added the vision of a common ideological heritage: "Judaism and fundamental Americanism are one. The puritans were Old Testament Christians. The reformed Jew can say that every American city is his Palestine." The occasion for Rabbi Hirsch's speech was the first of "twelve or more Chicago celebrations" of this 250th anniversary, and "the walls of the temple were covered with American flags. A large crowd breathed affirmative response to the sentiment *that because of their Judaism American Jews are better Americans.*"[27] The idea that members of a particular ethnic group are "better Americans" because of their early arrival, their blood sacrifice, and their peculiar ideological tradition—that they are better Americans *because* of their ethnicity—is the burden of all homemaking myths. The celebration of ethnicity in the United States is primarily a celebration of the American home of the ethnic group.

The homemaking myths or stories that are the subject of this book, then, had a function similar to that of ethnic celebration in the United States. They affirmed ethnicity and served to strengthen an ethnic identity and identification by offering individuals an ethnic home within a national home that was so large and included so many widely different families that a comfortable domesticity could be difficult without the creation of a more intimate, yet symbolic, living space. But because they could not take for granted the very right to be at home, the right not to be considered a foreigner in one's country of choice, even one's country of birth, these stories were also part of a homemaking argument. The intended function of homemaking arguments has been to convince the dominant and founding social and cultural group, the Anglo-Americans, of the unique right a particular group had to a place at their side and as their equals. But these arguments were hardly noticed by those they were meant to impress. In practice the function of homemaking arguments has been to strengthen the self-image and thus the cohesiveness of particular ethnic groups.

Homemaking myths are so commonly found in the writing and speechmaking of European immigrant groups in the last decades of the nineteenth century and the early decades of the twentieth that they should be considered an essential feature of American ethnicity in this period. These myths have been overlooked, however, because they represent an amateurish historiography that is discredited by professional historians and considered not only naive but potentially harmful.[28] But the need to create such myths, however naive they may be, must be taken seriously. Consequently, the myths themselves also deserve our attention as expressions of an American identity created in the face of Anglo-American denials of such an identity. Homemaking myths may be understood as particular constructions of ethnic memory to ensure and improve an ethnic as well as an American future. Not only did homemaking myths insist on a particular ethnic group's right to a home in America; they had a function similar to homemaking in the more common sense in being part of a process by which marginalized groups made a more comfortable and central space for themselves in the common American home. The point made by all homemaking myths was, as the motto for a German-American celebration in Milwaukee in 1890 had it, "Wir sind keine Fremden in diesem Lande"—We are not strangers in this country.[29] Chapter 1 explores why so many found it necessary to argue this point and insist on it again and again in the late nineteenth and early twentieth centuries.

1 Contexts and Contests: Where Is Home and Whose Home Is It?

THE LARGE MASS OF immigrants that entered the United States in the second half of the nineteenth century and the early years of the twentieth did not have clearly defined European national identities. Whether they came from Italy in the south, Scandinavian countries in the north, or from the ethnically diverse Austro-Hungarian Empire in between, they identified with regions, even villages, rather than with nations, many of which were yet to be formed. Local origin was often the more meaningful basis for the organization of European immigrants in American associations such as the Yiddish-American *landsmanshaftn* and the Norwegian-American *bygdelag.*[1] With the experience of migration came a new awareness of difference, which created a basis as well as a need for a more comprehensive national and ethnic identification. As early as 1915 Horace Kallen noted the development of a new national identity among immigrants. In his important essay, "Democracy Versus the Melting-Pot," he explains that "it is the shock of confrontation with other ethnic groups and the natural feeling of aliency reënforced by social discrimination and economic exploitation that generate in them an intenser group-consciousness." As Kallen saw it, two opposite factors in the process were the ethnic enclaves (the coming "to kin and friends who have gone before") and the immigrant's encounters with the Anglo-American, who dealt "with him as a lower and outlandish creature." Thus the immigrant who arrived in the United States "totally unconscious of his nationality . . . must inevitably become conscious of it."[2]

The making of such an identity, however, could be a slow and gradual process, as was learned by the organizers of a gift from Norwegian immigrants to their former homeland on the occasion of the centennial of the Norwegian constitution in 1914. They thought that the cathedral in Trondheim would be a rallying national symbol. It was, after all, both the shrine of the medieval patron saint, St. Olaf, and the church where the first king and queen of a Norway wholly independent for the first time in about five hundred years had been crowned less than a decade earlier. So many immigrants, however, objected to giving money to a church in a region with which they had no ties that the committee had to change its plans and create an alternative, a fund for the victims of natural calamities and poverty. Because the fund-raisers for various kinds of monetary gifts to the old country published lists of donors and donations in newspapers to ensure public control, it is possible to estimate how much money they collected and for what purposes. In the period that the sizable sum of 250.000 kroner, or about $65,000, was collected for the nationwide "memorial gift," a larger sum was collected for local projects, such as assembly halls, church organs, and old people's homes.[3]

Many who emigrated to the United States did not plan to remain. Their intention was to work here for a few years and then return to their homeland. Immigrants with vague notions of a European nationality could have at best vague notions of the implications of becoming citizens of the United States. The immigrant experience, however, brought about significant changes in attitudes and loyalties to both old and new homelands. Although many immigrants did in fact return to their old homeland after spending some years in the United States, many more changed their minds and remained to become citizens.[4] The process of identifying with the country of their choice was for most a far more natural one than that of identifying with the country—as distinct from the village or region—they had left behind. Indeed, the Old World identity developed in the United States was, for most, an *American* ethnic identity rather than a European national one. Again, the Norwegian-American celebration of the 1914 centennial is a good example. Although rallying Norwegian Americans in support of a national memorial gift had proved difficult, no one seems to have objected to the celebration of Norwegian-American ethnicity in Minneapolis and St. Paul initiated by the joint council of the many *bygdelag*. Approximately fifty thousand people took part in the celebrations based at the Minnesota State Fairgrounds in May

1914. They celebrated as Americans of Norwegian origin, not as Norwegians in the European sense of the word.[5]

Any attempt to study immigration and immigrant ideologies, however, must be based on an awareness of the significant differences in experience before and after the act of migration. One factor that was particularly important in the shaping of an ethnic identity in the United States was the national and political status of the European homeland. Members of the elite in some groups were as caught up in European nationalist causes as they were in the forging of an American future for their group. Indeed, Matthew Frye Jacobson has characterized some immigrants as exiles, people "for whom a lamentable absence from the Old World was among the most salient aspects of life in the New." Three groups that developed what he in his title calls a "diasporic imagination" were the Irish, Polish, and Yiddish Americans, who developed "a political culture based on ideas of injury and displacement." Their "allegiance to the old centers of experience translated into an emergent, New World zeal for Old World nationalisms: Irish nationalism, Polish nationalism, Zionism, and various brands of Yiddish labor nationalism." A telling illustration of how American freedom could be praised—not as a value in itself but for the opportunity it gave to work for the liberation of the Polish homeland—is a line from an early poem by the Polish-American writer Teofila Samolinska: "Here one is free to fight for the Fatherland." This 1870 poem, writes Jacobson, "set the tone for much of the literary production in Polonia in the following decades."[6] Polish Americans usually used the concept of Polonia to refer to the collective body of Poles abroad. Polonia, in the context of the turn of the nineteenth century, was the fourth Polish "region" (the other three were the parts of Poland under Russian, German, and Austrian-Hungarian rule). The word thus acquired its meaning and emotional punch from the predicament of the claimed but not realized European homeland.

When Norwegian Americans spoke of *Vesterheimen,* taking it (mistakenly) to mean "the western home," they were referring to their ethnic community in the United States. A nineteenth-century union with Sweden that was not dissolved until 1905 may have colored their cultural and political views, but their "western home" was inextricably in the United States and not an imagined region of the land they had left. The most commonly expressed nationalism of German-American leaders throughout the nineteenth century was a nationalism for Americans of German descent and focused on German culture and German contributions to the United States. Indeed, until 1870 Europe had no German national state, and pride in *Deutschtum*, or Germanness, could not be perceived to be in conflict with pride in being American. As the First World War began in Europe, the primary allegiance of immigrant groups from different parts of the large Austro-Hungarian Empire was to no small extent dependent on their perception of the effect of the outcome of the war on their European homeland, which was not yet independent.

Nevertheless, the various immigrant cultures exhibit a remarkable degree of shared rhetoric, themes, and strategies in their political and cultural writings. Indeed, it may be an error to distinguish too sharply between the Old World nationalism of some and the New World home-making efforts of other immigrant leaders. For instance, while much of the Lithuanian-American leadership at the turn of the last century may have had an "exile" outlook, Gary Hartman has observed that "Lithuanian-American support for the nationalist movement was not only about restoring Lithuania's sovereignty. . . . It was, in part, an attempt to validate the Lithuanian-American community itself."[7]

The individual experiences within an immigrant group were no less varied than were the differences between groups. For many immigrants the shifting of loyalties and the longing for the old home undoubtedly created emotional tensions. Making the transition from a Bohemian or Finnish peasant to an American farmer, artisan, or laborer was not always simple and easy. The majority of immigrants, however, were preoccupied with their daily lives in a new country rather than with sentimentalizing the conditions in the country they had left. For many, of course, survival was a struggle. Despite hardships, however, many were enjoying rewards from their labor that had been unimaginable in their former lives. Immigrants in general were a forward-looking rather than a backward-looking group, even though a superficial reading of immigrant letters and verse may give the impression that nostalgia was their dominant mood. Indeed, some scholars have concluded that immigrants had a "divided heart." One scholar, who has studied the work of Italian-American poets, claims that "it is a known fact that the immigrant is a living dichotomy. He has two souls."[8] Such a view is based on a misinterpretation of immigrant writing. Although immigrants may not have had time or inclination to think much of the old home in the course of a year, they would nevertheless easily slip into a nostalgic mood when writing the annual letter to aging parents. Either thoughts of those who had been left behind would crowd the writer's consciousness, or the writer may simply have deemed it unseemly to write joyfully of being far from parents or other family. The act of writing poems and stories is another situation in which men and women could become nostalgic, although they may have had little regret for having changed countries. The many instances of such situational nostalgia should not mislead us in our attempts to understand immigrants' emotional responses to their new land. Immigrants were on the whole more preoccupied with finding a place in their new society than with pondering the one they had left.

Instead of seeing immigrants as people crippled by divided hearts or confused by two souls, we should appreciate the potential emotional and intellectual bonus available to immigrants who could draw upon two traditions. We should see immigrants as relatively well-adjusted individuals who could spend their working day speaking English with a wide variety of Americans, including Anglo-Americans, and their personal time speaking Greek or German in their family or with friends and other ethnics in a saloon or at church. Jon Gjerde has usefully characterized the immigrant as possessing a "complementary identity" and observed that "faithfulness to an ethnic subgroup within a 'complementary identity' theoretically fostered a magnified loyalty to the United States."[9] In his autobiography Waclaw Kruszka, a Polish-American Roman Catholic priest, writes of becoming aware in the 1890s that his three loyalties as a Pole, an American, and a Roman Catholic were not contradictory.[10] An American ethnic identity should be understood, then, as an enriching supplement to an American identity, not as an emotionally crippling state of mind, as an asset rather than a liability. That the acquired American identity of the immigrant was challenged, however, and that this challenge could engender emotional and intellectual difficulties, is another matter.[11]

Still, there was an essential historical difference between ethnic expressions of nationalism in the United States (with the important exception of the national identities of indigenous peoples and also of some forms of African-American and Mexican-American nationalisms) and such expressions in European countries with a plurality of ethnicities. The filiopietistic rhetoric of immigrant and ethnic leaders contains no suggestion that the past glory and present excellence of their ethnic group in any way speaks for separatism. The goal, however distant, is not to establish an ethnic nation. On the contrary, the most fervent expressions of American ethnic nationalisms are for immediate entry into and eventual, preferably distant, merger with the larger and multiethnic American nation. One may speculate on whether the complementary ethnic identity of the individual immigrant was the cause of, was caused by, or was simply met by an American national identity that was correspondingly complementary. But whether we look at individual private expressions (as in letters and diaries) or at public rhetoric (as in speeches and newspapers), the essential characteristics of American ethnic nationalisms at the turn of the nineteenth century are that they are in harmony with, enhance, or are, each individually, the best version of the all-encompassing "nation" nationalism. As later chapters will demonstrate, the greatest praise for Poles, Czechs, Finns, or Norwegians as American ethnic groups was that they, each group individually, were the best Americans. Thus a Finnish-American nationalism and an all-American nationalism were not in conflict.[12]

The new American ethnic identity that developed with immigration was, as Kallen observed, in great degree based on the experience of difference. In many instances the process started with the quite natural attraction of people who found they had more in common in their new and foreign environment than they may have experienced before migration. "Chain migration" is the name given to the often studied phenomenon of concentrations of immigrants from the same region and even village in urban and rural immigrant neighborhoods. Gradually, however, as the new and shared experience of being ethnic Americans became more meaningful than the fading memories, the local point of departure in the old homeland gradually ceased to be the social glue of immigrant communities.[13]

To some extent, aspects of the immigrants' new American ethnic identity were the deliberate creation of an immigrant elite of writers, journalists, clergy, professionals, businessmen, and politicians. Dag Blanck has, for instance, demonstrated how a relatively small group of Swedish Americans in the Lutheran Augustana Synod in the years around the turn of the nineteenth century created a Swedish-American identity based on a blend of veneration of Old World traditions and values and a largely imagined New World history.[14] In their daily lives, however, many immigrants probably had as little concern for the romanticized image of the old homeland as they had for the ideological constructions of the relatively small elites in immigrant communities. Jerre Mangione's beautifully evocative memoir of life in a Sicilian immigrant family in Rochester, New York, *Mount Allegro*, says little about abstract Italian-American values and much about the joys and sorrows of American family life with roots in Sicily.[15] At the heart of immigrant communities in all parts of the United States, at the turn of the nineteenth century as much as at the turn of the twentieth, are men and women busy making ends meet and ensuring a better and American future for their descendants.

To some extent, however, the attitudes of common immigrant men and women, as well as of their children and grandchildren, were nevertheless shaped by the endeavors of an immigrant elite through the newspapers, churches, parochial schools, entertainments, and the many local and national ethnic associations that engaged immigrants to varying degrees in the language of their old homeland. As Kallen says, "The great ethnic groups of proletarians, thrown upon themselves in a new setting, generate from among themselves . . . their shopkeepers, their physicians, their attorneys, their journalists and their national and political leaders, who form the links between them and the greater American society."[16] Of course, many in this elite had status based on Old World class distinctions, education, or capital—or all three. It was primarily the better educated members of the immigrant elites who rubbed shoulders with Anglo-Americans and read English-language journals and books. This elite was consequently more exposed to a nativist and exclusive Anglo-American ideology than the rank-and-file. With their aspirations for social recognition the elites were also more easily rankled by rebuffs and rejections.

John Higham distinguishes between three overlapping kinds of leadership in ethnic groups: received leadership, where the basis of authority is in the structures of the Old World society; internal leadership, where authority is derived from the new situation in the United States; and projective leadership, a kind of leadership by example that uses successful individuals as ethnic symbols of achievement.[17] The first and second kind of leaders are of special interest here, in particular the leadership they exercised in the psychological rather than material aspects of group advancement. (This is one of four main tasks that Higham ascribes to ethnic group leaders.) One important function of immigrant leadership that stands out in Victor Greene's fine comparative study, *American Immigrant Leaders, 1800–1910*, is that of mediation between the immigrant group and the larger U.S. society; in this role immigrant leaders serve as the "agents of their groups' adjustment in America." He argues convincingly "that the groups' awareness of a new ethnic American identity was chiefly the result of the thinking of some of the group elite."[18] Higham has a similar view of the key role of immigrant leaders and has explained why it is important for historians to study their work: "Leaders focus the consciousness of an ethnic group and in doing so make its identity visible."[19]

One major concern of immigrant leaders in all groups in the late nineteenth and early twentieth centuries was the creation and promotion of an ethnic identity based on individual and collective self-respect and pride in origin. So pervasive was such concern in this period that lack of self-esteem and, indeed, a feeling of shame in regard to one's national or ethnic origin have clearly been central to the American immigrant experience. The often exaggerated claims of filiopietistic histories and festive speeches trumpeting the glories of American immigrant groups must always be understood in this context and held up against the Anglo-

American social and cultural forces that made it difficult for immigrants to identify themselves as Americans.

To accuse immigrant leaders of an exaggerated filiopietism, however, may be a misconstruction of history. Many leaders of the dominant Anglo-America were no less filiopietistic. Marcus Lee Hansen has pointed to the American "admiration for things English," explaining it partly with the increased influx of immigrants from England in the decades after the Civil War. "So far did the prestige of the country of origin go," he writes, "that . . . the tone of society was established by the usages that the English newcomer sanctioned." In 1915 Kallen made a similar point (but with no reference to English immigration) and, more specifically, compared the "throwing back of the Brito-American upon his ancestry" to immigrant filiopietism. After its various expressions in the creation of societies such as the Colonial Dames, the vogue of a genealogy that could establish colonial beginnings, the turning of ancient English homes "of the forbears of national heroes" into shrines, and the increased "public emphasis . . . upon the unity of the English and American stock . . . and 'Anglo-Saxon' civilization," he concluded: "If all this is not ethnic nationality returned to consciousness, what is it?"[20]

Ethnic leaders, intellectuals, and writers were dedicated to the creation of a similar kind of collective pride in the former homelands of their respective groups. To them it was evident that such pride was necessary both for the development of an ethnic group identity and for the collective entry of their ethnic group into the new homeland. From one perspective it may seem obvious that ethnic leaders have a vested interest in the maintenance of their ethnic culture and that for them the development of an ethnic identity also means securing a power base. For the many who were involved in journalism, creative writing, or publishing in the many languages other than English in wide use at the turn of the nineteenth century, the link between material self-interest and language maintenance was very close. Nevertheless, considering the brief life spans of most immigrant newspapers and the small audiences for books and journals of any pretense to quality, it should be evident that most members of this large group of immigrant leaders were more strongly motivated by ideology and interest in the welfare of their ethnic group than by self-aggrandizement. To disregard that idealism and a sense of being called to serve their people were the main motivations for most of these people would lead to serious misinterpretations of American ethnic and immigrant cultures. Throughout the history of U.S. immigration such leaders have urged the members of their group to enter the United States collectively and not simply to disappear in the great mass without bringing with them some contribution from the old homeland to the culture of their chosen homeland.

The immigrant or so-called foreign-language press has served many functions. Perhaps the most important one has been to introduce immigrants of diverse cultures, languages, and religions to American society and politics.[21] Immigrant shapers of opinion seem to have generally agreed that their various peoples had to enter the United States on their own terms. That is, they would become Americans not by losing their cultural identity and attributes but by contributing these very identities and attributes to their new country. In this process, it was thought, these identities and attributes would be transformed to American qualities. (Indeed, as we will see, there were frequent claims that the cultural baggage brought by immigrants was "American" to begin with.)

A prerequisite for such a positive Americanization process was a natural pride in origin, and the encouragement and promotion of such pride has been a constant theme in the immigrant press, as demonstrated by the English-language monthly, *Syrian World* (1926–34). Syrian immigrants were for the most part Christian and from what is now Lebanon. An editorial in the issue for March 1929 is, for instance, titled "Pride in Ancestry" and explains that "Syrians can take justifiable pride in their ancestry and can lay claim to one of the oldest and most advanced civilizations in history." In an article called "Our Pride in Our Ancestry," published in February 1932, the Reverend W. A. Mansur, a frequent contributor, "dwells on the achievements of the Phoenicians, ancestors of the Lebanese, in an effort to instill pride in your Lebanese Americans today."[22]

The most prominent and visible of all Syrian or Lebanese Americans in the 1920s was Kahlil G. Gibran, whose immensely popular *The Prophet* was published in 1923. For the first issue of *Syrian World* in July 1926, he wrote "Message to Young Americans of Syrian Origin"; its central theme is the instillment of pride in origin:

> I believe in you, and I believe in your destiny.
> I believe that you are contributors to this new civilization.
> I believe that you have inherited from your forefathers an ancient dream, a song, a prophecy, which you can proudly lay as a gift of gratitude upon the lap of America.
> I believe you can say to the founders of this great nation, "Here I am, a youth, a young tree, whose roots were plucked from the hills of Lebanon, yet I am deeply rooted here, and I would be fruitful." . . .

And I believe that it is in you to be good citizens.

And what is it to be a good citizen? . . .

It is to stand before the towers of New York, Washington, Chicago and San Francisco saying in your heart, "I am the descendant of a people that builded Damascus, and Biblus, and Tyre, and Sidon, and Antioch, and now I am here to build you, and with a will."

It is to be proud of being an American, but it is also to be proud that your fathers and mothers came from a land upon which God laid his gracious hand and raised His messengers.

Young Americans of Syrian origin, I believe in you.[23]

Lebanese were a small and relatively recent immigrant group in the 1920s. Moreover, their credentials as white were not above question. In 1914 a petition for citizenship by a Syrian immigrant, George Dow, was turned down in South Carolina where a court declared that only Europeans could be white, as required by the Naturalization Act of 1790. On appeal, however, a higher court in 1915 granted him whiteness and, consequently, citizenship, citing "the Dillingham Commission's *Dictionary of Races and Peoples*, which had asserted that Syrians 'belong to the Semitic branch of the Caucasian race, thus widely differing from their rulers, the Turks, who are in origin Mongolian.'"[24]

German Americans, on the other hand, were the largest non-English immigrant group. Moreover, their long and continuous history, first in the colonies and then in the United States, their powerful nationwide organizations, and the many German Americans in prominent social positions all spoke of influence and success and must have given them a more secure sense of home in America than that experienced by, for instance, most Lebanese Americans. Nevertheless, German-American leaders also saw lack of ethnic pride as a problem, as did Julius Goebel, a professor at the University of Illinois, when he reflected on the "future of Germanness in America" in 1913 and observed how "a submissive fear" characterized many "poor German souls" and criticized them for accepting derogatory names such as "Dutchman" and even "foreigner." Goebel saw a greater awareness of their German-American history as essential for German-American ethnic awareness and self-confidence.[25]

Pride was evidently not a characteristic prevalent among immigrants and their descendants. Although published proclamations of shame are few, we may infer the pervasiveness of shame from the large number of those who have born witness to the need to "instill pride" in members of all immigrant groups. One story of the consequences of an internalized shame of heritage—and, consequently, of self—was told by Jane Addams in her convocation address, "Immigration: A Field Neglected by the Scholar," at the University of Chicago in 1904. She related the "hideous story" of a young Jewish woman in New York, a stenographer and the daughter of immigrants from Russia. At the office she had met a young Jewish-American man and they became engaged, even though he had not yet met her family.

> She felt keenly the difference between him and her newly immigrated parents, and on the night when he was to be presented to them she went home early to make every possible preparation for his coming. Her efforts to make the menage presentable were so discouraging, the whole situation filled her with such chagrin, that an hour before his expected arrival she ended her own life. Although the father was a Talmud scholar of standing in his native Russian town, and the lover was a clerk of very superficial attainment, she possessed no standard by which to judge the two men. This lack of standard can be charged to the entire community, for why should we expect an untrained girl to be able to do for herself what the community so pitifully fails to accomplish?[26]

That the community—and Addams was speaking of the Anglo-American community—could fail the rural immigrant as well as the urban one is the burden of the story of an "old immigrant from Norway" whom Louis Adamic, himself an immigrant from Slovenia (then a part of Yugoslavia), had met north of Bemidji, Minnesota. The anecdote appears in the introduction to Adamic's 1945 book about the contributions of the many ethnic groups to U.S. history, *A Nation of Nations*:

> He told me of an "Americanization" campaign in that part of Minnesota around 1905. A poster appeared on walls in little towns and on tree-trunks by the roadsides. It was a picture of an elegant Uncle Sam and an outlandish yokel. In a loop coming out of Uncle Sam's handsome mouth was the word *Yes*, the loop from the yokel's wide-open mouth read *Ya*, and across the top in big letters was the admonition: "Don't say 'Ya'— say 'Yes'!" "That placard," said the old man, "it was as though pasted on a wall in our home and I couldn't pull it down. My oldest boy ran away. The children could not forgive their mother and me that we were 'foreigners.' They would not let us say anything in Norwegian to them— anything intimate. They held us away. It was years before that placard wore off enough for the runaway to come back."[27]

The articles on ethnic pride in *Syrian World* speak primarily of the need for such pride among the young, that is, among the descendants of immigrants. The accounts of the consequences of lack of pride in the Russian-Jewish-American family in New York and the Norwegian-American family in Minnesota are concerned with the lack of self-esteem among members of the second generation and the resulting disruptions of relations within immigrant families.

The need to counter such lack of pride and self-esteem among the descendants of immigrants is the motivation given by the two authors of a popular account of memorable Italians, *Italians: Past and Present*, published by the Staten Island Italian Historical Society as late as 1955. They tell of talking about their project while doing research in a library. A librarian, a young woman, listened to them and interrupted them with the words, "I'm sorry, but I don't agree with what you're saying. I'm Italian; I like Italy, but I don't like the Italians." When they asked her to explain what she meant, she specified, "It's not the Italians I don't like; it's the Italo-Americans." And she talked to them of her immigrant grandparents, their sacrifices, and their inability to enter America, and of her mother, who was torn between her desire "to become Americanized" and her Italian "heart." This granddaughter of immigrants felt she had no part in the "rich background" of Italy or of "colorful" America. "I have so little of both . . . I . . . I feel *so* inferior," she said as she left the two amateur historians. To demonstrate "how wrong she is," and "how very wrong are those who share the same sentiment," became the main purpose of their book: "Italo-Americans have inherited the wealth and civilization of two great nations."[28]

So often have leaders in a wide range of immigrant groups expressed their concern for a perceived lack of self-esteem among immigrants in the decades around the turn of the nineteenth century that it appears to have been a major problem in their communities and an important motivation for their work. In his history of the Order of the Sons of Italy, *L'Ordine Figli d'Italia in America*, Baldo Aquilano wrote in 1925 about the "state of moral inferiority" that was a result of the prejudices against Italians. He observed that it had "deep and disastrous repercussions," both in successful Italian immigrants and in those he called "the degenerate children of our fellow countrymen": "The first were ashamed to appear to be Italian and in several cases they would change their sonorous name by adding an Irish or a German ending. Sometimes they became fierce italofobics and the first to spread poison against Italy. The second, educated in the American schools where an exaggerated chauvinism is implanted . . . in the mind of the child, would often deny every tie of blood or sentiment, despising their parents, insulting their relatives, and holding the Italians in contempt."[29] Indeed, leaders of several immigrant groups often pointed to the public schools as a source of this problem.

In Ole E. Rølvaag's novel *Peder Victorious* the eponymous protagonist is sent to a school where both children and teacher are Norwegian

Americans because his mother fears the influence of his Irish-American friends at the school he had been attending. On his first day at his new school Peder sees on the blackboard, "written in a beautiful hand, '*This is an American school; in work and play alike we speak English only!*'" On reading it, "a feeling of shame came over him." This sense of shame is enforced when he opens "a geography book containing many illustrations" and finds a picture of "a combat between a man and an infuriated bear. The beast already had both its front paws on the man's shoulder; but the man looked undaunted; in his hand he held a sheath-knife, his arm drawn back; in a moment the steel would be buried in the breast of the bear. The title of the paragraph accompanying the picture was the single word: *Norway.* Under the picture someone had written in pencil: 'A Norskie.'" Peder reads the "paragraph about the land of his ancestors," the only "information he ever got about the land from which his people had come" in all his years in public school. He closes the book and decides, "When I am grown up I am going to go so far away that I'll never hear the word *Norwegian* again! He felt so sore of heart that he could have lain right down and bawled."[30]

After children internalized such negative images of themselves, parents could enforce the work of the public schools at home, which is ideally a source of strength for an individual's identity. A short story, "The Seventeenth of May" (1921), by the Norwegian-American writer Dorthea Dahl illustrates how parents themselves could be part of the process that created a lack of self-esteem in the immigrant communities. Here a member of the ladies' aid society of a western congregation seems to believe that any association with the old homeland implies that her status as an American is questioned: "We had ought to remember that we ain't Norwegians no more," she says, relating how her daughter had had to stand up for her 100 percent Americanism when her employer had spoken of what a fine country Norway was: "She wanted her to know that she wasn't no more Norwegian than anybody else."[31] Such attitudes and their effects are so often described in the fiction, memoirs, and historical accounts of members of immigrant groups that they may be characterized as a collective inferiority complex.

To the editor of the *Denní Hlasatel*, writing for the edition of June 22, 1904, the obvious remedy for the belief of many Bohemian Americans (or Czechs, as they would more commonly refer to themselves a few years later), that "our greatest good lies in quickly forgetting the cradle of our race and becoming Americanized," was to take "as their example the Americans [i.e., Anglo-Americans] themselves, whose English origin dates back to the long ago." Other immigrants too should practice the "racial patriotism" of the Anglo-Americans, the editor proclaimed. The poor self-esteem of the Bohemian American who appears to be ashamed of "his brother-immigrant" and considers "a Yankee closer to him" was, according to the editor, "due to faulty upbringing and insufficient schooling. The blame for this rests on their unenlightened parents, who often—we must admit with shame—are proud that their children do not know Bohemian and speak only English." Like many immigrant leaders in this period, this editor was insisting that Americans had many different origins and that, just as Anglo-Americans could cherish their English heritage, Bohemian Americans could and should cherish theirs.

These immigrant leaders agreed that their heritage should be respected as American in the same manner as that of the Americans of British descent. In his 1922 volume of polemical essays, Rølvaag was preoccupied with the effect of having one's own *American* past labeled as foreign: "Our young people do not feel that their fathers' history ties them closer to the history of this country and its people. . . . If the school system had the slightest bit of understanding of psychology, it would do everything it could to encourage ethnic pride in the children, instead of trying to break it down." One of Rølvaag's remedies was to have courses "in pioneer history, that is the *history of Norwegian immigration*" taught in Norwegian-American schools. This would open "the eyes of our own youth to the fact that we really do have a part in the history of America."[32]

An immigrant inferiority complex was a prerequisite for what Jane Addams, in her 1904 Chicago lecture, called "the American process of elimination," a negative process of Americanization wherein the important thing was not so much what you acquired as what you left behind and forgot. As an example of "how patriotism may not be taught" she told of a Civil War veteran who spoke at one of the Chicago public schools on Decoration Day (now Memorial Day) as part of a civic program to "instruct the children in the significance of Decoration Day and to foster patriotism among the foreign-born by descriptions of the Civil War." Inspired by the veteran's account of his personal experience in battle, "an eager young Italian broke out with characteristic vividness into a description of his father's campaigning under the leadership of Garibaldi." But such pride in a father's achievements or even such comparison between wars of unification in the United States and Italy could have no place in a U.S. school, and the visiting speaker

> somewhat sharply told him that he must forget all that, that he was no longer an Italian, but an American. The natural growth of patriotism upon respect for the achievements of one's fathers, the bringing together of the past with the present, the pointing out of the almost world-wide

effort at a higher standard of political freedom which swept over all Europe and America between 1848 and 1872 could, of course, have no place in the boy's mind because it had none in the mind of the instructor, whose patriotism apparently tried to purify itself by the American process of elimination.

Jane Addams expressed views that were representative of the settlement movement. In 1918 Mary McDowell, who worked in the University Settlement near the Chicago stockyards, warned against the policy of emptying the minds of immigrant children of their own language and traditions. The *Chicago Daily Tribune* quoted her as saying, "It is nonsense to say that we are impeding the progress of the immigrants if we permit them to perpetuate the traditions of the land of their birth and to keep their language alive. They can absorb new ideas only when the ideas are conveyed to them in the language they understand. When they have grasped the meaning of American ideas, they will naturally want to learn our language." The editor of the *Denní Hlasatel* had no doubt that the views of Mary McDowell went to the heart of the problem of the immigrants' negative self-image and that Americanization, as it was practiced, would create poor citizens: "Her words should permeate the thinking of the American people and should especially reach those who would like to make out of immigrants so-called 'Americans,' meaning people who would speak English, but would at the same time be ashamed of the spirit they had imbibed with the milk of their immigrant mothers—people who would have only a hazy concept of the real American spirit."[33]

Another immigrant journalist and writer who saw Americanization as a process of elimination that caused a sense of inferiority in immigrants was Waldemar Ager, who wrote short stories, novels, and essays; edited the weekly newspaper *Reform*, which was dedicated to the cause of prohibition; and ran his Fremad (Forward) Publishing Company, all in Norwegian, in Eau Claire, Wisconsin, from 1892 until he died in 1941.[34] To him the melting pot was the metaphor of a lethal instrument of destruction. So-called Americanization, he insisted, probably influenced by German-American leaders, sailed under a false flag in that the Old World traditions and language of the Anglo-Americans were no more "American" than the Old World traditions and languages of other immigrant groups. The melting pot metaphor had quickly caught the public attention after the opening production of the play, *The Melting-Pot*, in Washington, D.C., in the fall of 1908. Like the playwright (a British Jew), many spoke of the melting pot in glowing terms, the means of creating a new American (super) human being, different from and better than the many individual nationalities or races that had gone into it. But other more critical voices spoke of it as a metaphor for the sloughing off of all national traits and the acquisition of an Anglo-American veneer.[35] In his critique of the melting pot, Ager notes that the play and the metaphor became "exceedingly popular among those individuals in our population who above all others consider themselves true Americans" but that

> the self-designated American himself does not wish to mingle with the foreigners. He doesn't wish to assimilate with them or to absorb in himself the Russian, Pole, or Jew, but he wants these people to intermingle their traits with each other. . . . The major intent and the general understanding of Americanization is simply that the immigrant is to be denationalized. The taking on of the character of the "new man" is of secondary importance. Discarding the "old man" is by far the more significant issue. From an "American" point of view, the melting pot is thus not for "Americans." It is its function to denationalize those who are not of English descent.

Underlying Ager's criticism of Americanization is the view that there wasn't actually any such thing as an American culture: "We encounter a culture which is regarded as being American, but on closer examination we find that it is 'English' and that it has no more valid claim to be native here than the Norwegians' *norskdom* (Norwegianness) or the Germans' Germanness." Therefore the "new dress" the immigrant is supposed to take on "is made for others and by other measurements and does not fit us." Having cast off his old clothes, then, the immigrant is, "culturally speaking . . . naked."[36]

In his fictional treatment of this theme in his novel *On the Way to the Melting Pot*, Ager demonstrated that such cultural nakedness means spiritual death. The trajectory of the novel's male antagonist, Lars Olson, is similar to that of David Levinsky in Abraham Cahan's novel, *The Rise of David Levinsky*, also published in 1917. Lars acquires the ruthlessness and skills necessary to succeed in business but loses his soul. Assimilation, the road to the melting pot, is a process in which the immigrant discards all distinguishing traits, all vestiges of the culture of the old country, and becomes an empty shell, good for little but extinction in the melting pot. At the end of the novel Lars, as seen by the female protagonist, has been "melted down to money and prestige." She recognizes, however, that his fate is a common one and, moreover, a necessary preparation for entry into "the great melting pot":

> First they stripped away their love for their parents, then they sacrificed their love for the one they held most dear, then the language they had learned from mother, then their love for their childhood upbringing, for God and man, then the songs they learned as children, then their mem-

ories, then the ideals of their youth—tore their heritage asunder little by little—and when one had hurled from his heart and mind everything which he had been fond of earlier, then there was a great empty void to be filled with love of self, selfishness, greed, and the like. . . . Thus they readied themselves for the melting pot's last great test.

Ager's central thesis, that the melting pot is for the spiritually and culturally stunted and defective, is also brought out in an extended metaphor of an industrial process involving a melting of useless scraps and wrecked parts to make new patented machines. The manager of the factory where this work is done explains that "he could not recall having seen a single typewriter, an electric motor, a usable sewing machine or piece of farm machinery wander into the melting pot." The process used only useless scrap metal because it was the cheapest raw material available. The message is obvious: it did not make economic sense to melt down products that had a function and still could serve a purpose.[37]

The alternative to this deathly process of elimination promoted by leaders of widely different immigrant groups was the preservation and cultivation of the immigrants' Old World values and traditions and the instillment of pride in origin. One of the many who shared Ager's concerns and his vision was his friend and fellow novelist, Ole E. Rølvaag, who in his last novel, *Their Fathers' God* (1931), has one of his characters use a building metaphor to speak of the destructive effects of the melting pot: "We are ashamed of the age-old speech of our forefathers. And we find it embarrassing to admit our Norwegian ancestry. Such an attitude can never, I tell you, *never* build a nation. Like dead timber, we go into the building. We may harm, but we cannot be of much help."[38] In the final analysis, then, it was the strength and quality of the United States as much as the mental health of the individual immigrant that suffered from the immigrants' collective lack of self-esteem.

Outside of small but committed minorities in the many immigrant groups, however, the advocates of preserving the old ways and old language spoke to ears that were so attuned to the more enticing tunes of Anglo-America that they could hardly hear those who admonished them to stay away from the very culture that they had come to be part of. After reading Rølvaag's 1922 volume of polemical essays, a friend tried to warn him that his message might not appeal to young immigrants. Try to imagine, he wrote, a young man recently engaged and filled with love for his fiancée and with hope for his future life with her, who is then admonished to love his mother.[39] Neither Rølvaag nor most other immigrant leaders, however, were involved in a nostalgic retrograde activity. Rather, they were working to ensure an American future for their people (and, of course, their own positions of influence) by strengthening communal bonds through pride in history and tradition. Pride, they thought, was essential to the creation of a strong group identity that again would be the basis for a collective entry of the group into American society. Only then could an immigrant group have an influence on American culture, be more than "dead timber." The alternative to pride in origin was to have immigrants disappear one by one without leaving a trace.

This seemed obvious to the leaders of the Czech-American National Council who addressed an appeal in the September 2, 1914, edition of the *Denní Hlasatel* "To Bohemian Parents and Students": "It is our aim and desire to introduce into the rapidly developing American nation the very best elements of our race, and thus gain true merit for future America. This, however, cannot be achieved if our youth is ignorant of the best that is in our character and in our history. We want to merge with America, rather than get lost without a trace." For the editor of this newspaper it also seemed obvious that this could not be achieved without ethnic pride or, as he put it in an editorial, "For Czech Parents to Consider," on September 14, 1917: "To feed and clothe your children does not complete your obligations. There is one supreme duty which you must fulfill toward those of your own blood: to bring up your child to be a man in a moral sense—a man who loves not only his parents and companions, but also the nation in which his parents were born. For this reason it is necessary to inform your child about his nationality so that he will not ridicule or think lowly of the nation from which he is descended—or disavow the merits of our great men of art and science." Such admonitions were a frequent theme in the newspapers of many immigrant groups.

As early as June 1, 1866, in the editorial of the first issue of the Chicago newspaper *Skandinaven* (Scandinavian), Knut Langeland wrote of the necessity of having a history in order not simply to disappear in America. Langeland, who had started out as a pioneer farmer, had been the editor of two early Norwegian-American newspapers in Wisconsin around 1850 and was a lifelong critic of tendencies among his people to isolate themselves from American society. His goal, like that of so many other immigrant leaders, was the forging of an American ethnic group that would preserve the best traits in the Old World character and acquire the best traits in the American one. "No people can claim to be civilized unless it leaves behind testimonials to its history," he insisted in his 1866 editorial. He saw the immigration of his ethnic group in a global perspective and regarded its history as one of many contributions to the history of the United States. A history was, he thought, necessary for an identity—just as a group identity was necessary for the creation of a history. If

we are able to preserve and develop our identity, he wrote in his editorial, "we may be able to place our small contribution to the outcome of
the great migrations of the nineteenth century on the altar of our adopted fatherland with the conviction that though our contribution may be
small compared to that of other nationalities, it may yet in quality be the
equal of any."[40]

There is pride in that statement, and a measure of pride is necessary
for the process of a group collectively placing their contribution on the
altar of their adopted country. Note, however, that for Langeland this
pride leads to and is part of a sacrificial act. Surely Langeland's metaphor
of the altar is one of the more striking of the many metaphors that have
been used to express the great and as-yet-unrealized American idea of
making one of the many. Here the immigrant gift—a term used by both
Jane Addams and Frances Kellor[41]—is presented as a sacrifice at the
American altar, which suggests that immigration carries a price. Yet the
significance of the altar is surely also that something is asked in return
for the sacrifice, at the very least a blessing. The request made by the
immigrant at "the altar of our adopted fatherland" is that of acceptance
in and by the promised land.

Acceptance, however, was the crux of the problem facing the immigrant, and refusal of the sacrifice involved in the process of immigration
was the cause of the lack of pride and shame addressed by so many immigrant leaders. For even after taking off the "foreign" cultural clothing
and donning American clothes—ill fitting, as Waldemar Ager and other
immigrant spokesmen would have it, because they were made according
to English measurements—immigrants were not readily accepted as
Americans. Or, to return to Langeland's metaphor, both the immigrants
who exchanged their ethnic identity for an Anglo-American one and the
immigrants who offered their traditions as a gift to their new land had their
sacrifice refused and their request for acceptance denied. Indeed, not only
immigrants but also their descendants were met with this denial and refusal. The twelve-year-old American-born Michael Musmanno was far
from alone in making the discovery that he was a foreigner compared to
the most recent immigrant from the Anglo-American homeland. In the
nineteenth-century experience of another successful American, Hans
Mattson, a Swedish immigrant who served as an American diplomat in
India, "it may be safely said that it will on an average take two generations before the children of the non-English-speaking immigrants shall
cease to suffer more or less from these prejudices. Certainly the children
of immigrant parents, although born and brought up in this country, are
often subjected to sneers and taunts by their more fortunate playfellows,

even within the walls of the American public schools."[42] The problem for the Italian-American child in Jane Addams's anecdote was not only that he was asked, literally, to forget his own father but that if he had followed the veteran's demand, he would certainly have lost his pride in his origin but would nevertheless be as far as ever from acceptance as the veteran's American equal. The condition of shedding one nationality without having acquired another was what Ager called "cultural nakedness."

In 1922, in the last volume of his satirical trilogy about the Americanization of a Norwegian immigrant, first as a businessman in Minneapolis in the 1880s and then as a settler and political boss in the Red River Valley, Johannes B. Wist observes, "If you asked these young people of Norwegian descent what nationality they were, they would immediately answer—not without some indignation at being asked such a question—that they naturally were Americans. What else could they be? But if you asked a Yankee what kind of people these immigrant children were, they would always answer without hesitation that they were foreigners or Norwegians." Wist's wry comment on this predicament, with implicit reference to American nativism in general and its most concentrated expression in the Americanization drives of World War I in particular, was that "while it was your duty to be an American, you did not really have permission to be one."[43] The real Americans were Anglo-Americans. Indeed, the term "native American" has until fairly recently been a synonym for Anglo-American. The term never caused confusion even though, for instance, both African Americans and German Americans could be said to be as "native" as Anglo-Americans.

Benjamin Franklin was probably not the first American to express his anxiety at the threat of foreigners in the land. He was certainly not the last. American nativism, as described and analyzed by John Higham, has a long tradition and has found cruel expression.[44] Oscar Handlin may have exaggerated the uprootedness of immigrants at the turn of the nineteenth century and made them passive victims of a process in which they were the main actors. Nevertheless, his classic study of immigration, *The Uprooted*, is full of insight, and he was certainly aware of the effect of nativism on the immigrant psyche: "The memory of charges violently made lingered long after the charges themselves were no longer a threat. They left behind a persistent uneasiness. The foreign-born could not forget that their rights as citizens had once been challenged. Could they help but wonder how fully they belonged in the United States?" A major irony of American nativism is that the large mass of those who have been feared have had no subversive intentions. On the contrary, the idea and ideals of the United States have had a strong hold on immigrants, and they have looked forward to being part of the country, not changing it. Considering the available evidence for immigrant attitudes in "the second and third quarter of the nineteenth century," Merle Curti concludes that it "points to the loyalty and even enthusiasm of the newcomers for the land of their adoption." The sentiments of Armande Roc, an immigrant from Haiti who was naturalized at a ceremony on Ellis Island in January 1998, are representative of the feelings of two centuries of immigrants: "This country, I am so proud of it. I am so proud of the law of this country. This is something you can fight for. Without the United States, believe me, I don't know what will happen to the world."[45]

The purely civic formality of becoming a citizen of the United States has often been described as a conversion, a deep change in personal identity, that involves much more than a new passport and the right to vote. But then *America* has from its conception been more than a mere country. Many other countries were available to immigrants in the nineteenth and early twentieth centuries, and some did go to other countries in the Americas, in Africa, and in Oceania (all of them, of course, areas with a native population). But no other country could compete with the ideological magnetism of the United States. "The land of opportunity," exclaimed Armande Roc, echoing and summing up the vision of hundreds of thousands before her.

In his analysis of the development of an American ideology, Sacvan Bercovitch has observed that "what our major writers could not conceive, either in their optative or in their tragic ironic moods, was that the United States was neither utopia at best nor dystopia at worst . . . but a certain political system; that *in principle* no less than in practice the American Way was neither providential nor natural but one of many possible forms of society." It may be that most immigrants came here simply because it was a place where they could make a better living than in their country of birth. Many, however, came with a notion of America—maybe not as a utopia but certainly as a land that was more than just another country, more than just "one of many possible forms of society." For them too had been "created in the word 'America' the most compelling cultural symbol of the modern era."[46]

One of the many who embraced this cultural symbol and who joyfully claimed that she had become an entirely new person, an American, was Mary Antin, an immigrant from Russia. She began her best-selling autobiography, *The Promised Land* (1912), with the confession that "I have been made over. . . . I am absolutely other than the person whose story I have to tell." And she concluded her account of becoming an American with the story of a sudden experience of the significance of her new identity, very much in the tradition of religious conversions: "America is the youngest of the nations, and inherits all that went before in history. And I am the youngest of America's children, and into my hands is given all her priceless heritage. . . . Mine is the whole majestic past, and mine is the shining future." The Danish immigrant and journalist Jacob A. Riis also wrote of his sudden awareness of having become an American as a religious conversion experience. On the last page of his autobiography, *The Making of an American* (1901), he tells of his joyful experience of seeing "a ship flying at the top the flag of freedom, blown out on the breeze till every star in it shone bright and clear," while he was lying sick in the home of a friend in Denmark: "I knew then that it was my flag; that my children's home was mine, indeed; that I also had become an American in truth. And I thanked God, and, like unto the man sick of the palsy, arose from my bed and went home, healed."[47]

In 1847 one of the earliest American poems in Norwegian, "Emigrantens Tilbageblik" (The Emigrant Looks Back), does not merely contrast the poverty of the old country with the more just returns for hard labor in the new. It also criticizes Norway for being "governed by the power of the rich / And shackled in bondage" while joyously affirming a new identity as a partner in American liberty that goes beyond mere citizenship:

> I shall take part in the growth
> Of a nation that is great and yet young.
> There the flame of freedom burns
> And freedom of trade has a home.[48]

The sense of having acquired inalienable rights along with a new identity was very much part of the immigrant experience of a woman who refused to open her bag on leaving Yale University's Sterling Memorial Library one fall evening in 1965. The line behind her grew, and she finally gave in and let the embarrassed guard do his duty. As she walked out into the wet and dark New Haven evening, she turned to me and said with a marked accent, "Imagine their doing this to me, an American citizen!" Becoming an American has been a deeply meaningful act for immigrants for two centuries. Although the experience of American reality could not possibly match the promise of the idea, one could still affirm the principle, as Ralph Ellison's unnamed protagonist came to believe his grandfather may have advised.

Anglo-Americans, however, have not always appreciated immigrant pride in becoming an American. Mary Antin laid claim not only to a role in the American future but also to the inheritance of its "majestic past."

In 1917, during the Americanization drive of World War I, with its requirement that immigrants forget their past, their language, and their culture
and become 100 percent American, one of Antin's Boston acquaintances,
the Harvard professor of English Barrett Wendell, told someone in a letter that Antin "has developed an irritating habit of describing herself and
her people as Americans, in distinction from such folks as Edith and me,
who have been here for three hundred years." Such deprecatory responses
to immigrant claims to an American identity were not only expressed in
private. A reviewer of Antin's in the *Atlantic Monthly* wrote ironically
about this Jewish immigrant who called the Pilgrims "kindly, but con-
fusedly . . . our forefathers."[49]

Views and statements that may appear bigoted, even racist, today
were, it must be remembered, in harmony with a view of U.S. history
that was shaped during the mass migrations that wrought such changes
in the American population that Anglo-Americans, culturally and socially
still dominant, were in a minority by the early decades of the twentieth
century.[50] Nina Baym has observed that the the multivolume works of
George Bancroft, Richard Hildreth, and John Gorham Palfrey "anchored"
the history of the United States in New England. Their story of the nation was deliberately designed "to unify the unformed and scattered
American people under the aegis of" that region. At the end of the nineteenth century, this view of history was further refined, she writes, in the
histories of American literature for use in both schools and colleges.
These "histories rather emphasized than played down the English origins
of the American nation, thereby instructing classrooms of children of
non-English ancestry to defer to the Anglo-Saxonism of their new country's heritage. . . . Paradoxically, non-Anglo-Saxons could become American only to the extent of their agreement that only those of Anglo-Saxon
lineage were really Americans." Baym has also pointed to the important
role given to the public schools in thus Americanizing (or perhaps rather anglicizing) the sons and daughters of immigrants who in many areas
made up the majority of the school population: "By no accident, both
Connecticut and Massachusetts established Boards of Education in 1837,
during the decade when substantial numbers of Irish began to settle in
New England."[51]

The ethnic group that most strongly resented the Whig view of
American history was the German Americans. They were also the group
with the greatest confidence to question this history, both because of their
numerical strength and because of their many representatives within
American universities. In his essay, "Research of German-American
History," written during the First World War, the editor of the weekly

Der Zeitgeist (Spirit of the Age), Michael Singer, claimed that, "in American histories up to date we . . . find a falsification of history either by design, or through superficiality regarding German Americans." In support of his critique of U.S. historians he quoted at some length from a 1909 lecture given by Julius Goebel, the University of Illinois professor, at the Twenty-fifth Annual Convention of the American Historical Association. Here Goebel explained the emergence of ethnic historical societies with people's sense

> that our American historical works, even the best, in reality only treated of a part of the nation, which they erroneously . . . conceived to be the whole. They became aware that they were laboring with a fancied type of human being, artificially compounded, which type they falsely called "the American." . . . Certain American historians have decried these observations as untrue, as was to be expected; they even condemned the same as un-American, i.e., unpatriotic. It would have been more advantageous for them as well as for American historians in general, had they meekly asked themselves to what extent such criticism was justified. Or may it be that my children are not like the progenies of Puritans and the Dutch entitled to read in our histories what their German ancestors have done for their country?[52]

At the turn of the nineteenth century, German-American intellectuals in particular had developed a critique of U.S. history that contained many of the central ideas of late twentieth-century multiculturalism. There was, however, as little room for African and Asian Americans in their vision of American history as in the contemporary Anglo-American vision.

Immigrant leaders countered Anglo-Americans' exclusive view of who was at home in the United States with two contrasting strategies. One approach implicitly accepted the dominant racialist ideology that placed Anglo-Saxons at the apex of human development. It argued for the close relationship between a particular nationality and the Anglo-Saxons, because of character and ideology, family ties, or a combination of the two. The other sought justification in history rather than in biological or ideological relationship and aimed at demonstrating that a particular nationality or race had taken part in the making of the nation alongside and on an equal footing with the Anglo-Americans, that this too was a founding nationality. In order to appreciate the rhetoric and the breast-beating nationalism involved in the more popular filiopietistic histories told in immigrant groups as part of their homemaking arguments, it is necessary to keep in mind the nature of the ideology Anglo-Saxons used to keep immigrants at the door. As Baym has pointed out, "Many New England intellectuals at the turn of the [nineteenth] century were certain that Anglo-Saxon behavior could be practiced only by those of Anglo-Saxon descent.".

To illustrate this view Baym quotes from John Gorham Palfrey's introduction to the fifth volume of his history (1876): "It has not yet appeared that the Celtic or the African constitution, or that of the aboriginal red man or of strays from one or another despotism of continental Europe or of the heathen East, is competent to struggles and exploits, or to an acute far-seeing, courageous, and persistent policy, like those by which the later greatness of New England was founded and fashioned by the God-fearing builders of that community."[53] Palfrey here associates immigrants from Ireland as well as from "continental Europe" with the nonwhite races of Africa and Asia and thus questions, if not their legal right, then at least their racial qualifications for citizenship in a nation created by and for Anglo-Saxons. Such was the view of the nation instilled into future public school teachers in academies, normal schools, and colleges, and such was the view they in their turn tried to instill in their immigrant students in large public schools in the growing cities or in small one-room schoolhouses on the western prairies and plains. The problem that so many immigrant leaders saw in the young generation's lack of pride in origin was to no small degree a consequence of the way in which the public schools propagated the Whig view of U.S. history.

The paradox that Baym points to was not the only irony in the way in which the nation welcomed the immigrant. Although the great mission of the public school was to make Americans of the children of foreigners, the implied message in the teaching of American history and literature was that they would always be outsiders. This message could be quite explicit too, as in David Saville Muzzey's *An American History* (1911), which was widely used in schools all over the country. There the children of immigrants confronted this question: "Can we assimilate and mold into citizenship the millions who are coming to our shores, or will they remain an ever-increasing body of aliens, an undigested and indigestible element in our body politic, and a constant menace to our free institutions?"[54] Such ironies and contradictions were also very much evident in the 1915–18 campaign to Americanize the immigrant. The implication of Woodrow Wilson and Theodore Roosevelt's admonitions—that immigrants could not be American *and* something else, that they must cease to speak foreign languages and forget their pasts in order to become 100 percent American—was that if they did submit to this process of elimination, they would actually be accepted as Americans.[55]

Yet the experience of so many immigrants was that their claim to be Americans was what created not only Anglo-American denial but re-sentiment. As immigrants were denied the American recognition of their memories of the old homeland, they were also denied a share in the Anglo-American memory of their new homeland. No wonder, then, that immigrant leaders sought to create American memories for their specific immigrant group. The homemaking myths of the many immigrant groups may, then, be understood as responses to the ways in which immigrants were rebuffed, regardless of whether they claimed a hyphenated American identity or they presented themselves as 100 percent American. In the first instance the message they heard was "Forget who you were and become American"; in the second, "You may believe you are an American, but you are and will remain a foreigner."

Louis Adamic's *A Nation of Nations* is an early paean to a multiethnic America. The preface consists of correspondence between the Slovenian-American author and his Anglo-American friend, Merritt H. Perkins, who once proudly showed him diaries and letters tracing the Perkins family's history in colonial New England. The book is dedicated not only to this friend but to "other Americans of Anglo-Saxon stock" and "to those who—unlike you—occasionally remark, 'Why don't you go back where you came from?'" With Perkins he discusses "two ways of looking at our history":

> One is this: that the United States is an Anglo-Saxon country with a White-Protestant-Anglo-Saxon civilization struggling to preserve itself against infiltration and adulteration by other civilizations brought here by Negroes and hordes of "foreigners."
> The second is this: that the pattern of the United States is not essentially Anglo-Saxon although her language is English. . . . The pattern of America is all of a piece; it is a blend of cultures from many lands, woven of threads from many corners of the world. Diversity itself is the pattern, is the stuff and color of the fabric.[56]

The immigrants developed their homemaking myths in order to highlight the threads from their particular corner of the world in the American pattern. The theory underlying these myths is that, by securing a place of prominence for their group in American history, these immigrants would also secure their position in the nation itself.

This was often a highly competitive affair: for example, Thaddeus Kosciuszko was not a hero Poles and Lithuanians were willing to share. The Finnish-American journalist Akseli Rauanheimo saw the United States as a "field of contest for the nationalities of the world," and Gary London comments that this metaphor suggests a view of "immigrant legitimacy" where "one group gains at the expense of others in competition for the limited resource of national acceptance. In the contest, symbols are an important source of strength, and may provide one contestant with an advantage over others."[57] The aim of Finnish-American leaders, then, was not to argue that immigrants in general had a share in American history but that Finnish Americans had a greater share than other immigrants. Those who took the initiative in 1929 for a Columbus monument in connection with the Chicago World's Fair in 1933 saw it, according to the September 15 edition of *Il Bollettino Sociale* (Social Bulletin), not only as an affirmation of "the triumph of our Italian civilization and the historic importance of the discovery of this continent of America by our glorious fellow-countryman Christopher Columbus" but as "a rebuke to all our adversaries." Symbols are important, and the competition for symbolic recognition could be fierce.

In 1904 a Chicago public school was named for the hero of Italian unification, Giuseppe Garibaldi. The decision was attacked at an Irish-American picnic by a priest who told his listeners that Garibaldi "is as odious [a] man for the Irish people as is Cromwell." To the editors of *La Tribuna Italiana* (Italian Tribune, August 29) this proved their earlier criticism of Irish-American priests: "The Irish people, and particularly some priests, have tried on several occasions to discriminate against Italian patriots." Two days earlier the same newspaper had characterized the editor of the Irish-dominated Catholic newspaper, *New World*, as "a fanatic Irishman." Competition between immigrant groups, however, was not always restricted to verbal exchanges. A story on July 23, 1904, in the Chicago newspaper *L'Italia* was headlined "Quarrel Between Italians and Swedes": "The Italians and Swedes came to blows, last Sunday, between Oak and Sedgwick Sts. A hatred between residents of the two races in that locality had been seething for a long time, but a reason for bringing it to a head did not present itself until then, with the result that the two groups met, armed with knives, guns and sticks."

On June 22, 1916, another Chicago newspaper, the *Svenska Kuriren* (Swedish Courier), advised Swedish Americans to "decline the invitation" to take part in a mass Americanization meeting with Theodore Roosevelt as the main speaker. The editor's negative response was, of course, partly in reaction to Roosevelt's crusade against "hyphenated Americans." But equally unpalatable to the editor was the composition of the local Committee for the Promotion of Loyalty to the United States: "Among the members of the 'Committee' we find: 'Biankini, Czarnecki, Shustek, Palandec, Stepina' and similar Bohemian and Polish names. With these gentlemen, we recognize no solidarity or common ties."[58] Although this editor and other Swedish-American leaders were promoting a self-image of the Swedish Americans as both close relatives of the Anglo-Americans and as one of the founding groups of the United States, they were reluctant to recognize the efforts of more recent immigrant groups for acceptance. In their American story Swedish Americans were inheritors of the seventeenth-century colony of New Sweden in what is now Delaware and were, consequently, as American as Theodore Roosevelt, the descendant of Dutch colonists in neighboring New Amsterdam. Not only were the Biankinis and Czarneckis of more recent origin but their racial credentials were questionable. They could certainly not claim close relationship, as could the Swedes, with the Anglo-Saxons.

Solidarity among different immigrant groups was rare in this period. Indeed, the August 11, 1888, edition of the German-American *Illinois Staats-Zeitung* (Illinois State Journal) argued that Italians should not even be allowed to enter the United States: "There can be no advantage to this country in letting these people come here. At best, they may contribute to bring about a condition of barbarism. If, in addition to this, one takes into consideration that these half-civilized people will have the right to vote a few years hence, and thereby help to decide the destiny of this country, one can not help but shudder as to the future entrusted in such hands." Other editorials in this period argue the same point. Nativist attitudes were not limited to Anglo-Americans. In a period when racialist thinking permeated American society, immigrants were more preoccupied with arguing their own racial credentials than with arguing against the division of society into more and less acceptable races.

In an article called "The Stories Immigrants Tell," Kathleen Neils Conzen finds the negative image of other immigrant groups typical of what she calls "sponsorship tales," that is, stories of how the progress of a particular immigrant is "promoted by the sponsorship of the dominant Yankees." She illustrates her point by describing a cartoon based on *The Last Supper* from a German-American magazine in 1883. Here a noble German American is in the central position, "with Uncle Sam and Lady Liberty toasting him from one end of the table and a scowling, ape-like Irish figure taking the Judas position." The figures representing the Italians, Spanish, French, English, black Americans, and Swedes are not any more flattering, and Conzen observes of this genre that "the favored immigrant basks in the approval of the Yankees and merits the respect or the envy of the others."[59] Rivalries between members of different immigrant groups, particularly in smaller communities, could also find more innocent, even friendly, expression. In Davenport, Iowa, in the last decades of the nineteenth century, many immigrants had come from both sides of the German-Danish border. "The result was a curious ritual, developed over the years, in which the Danes would observe a long-distant victory over the

Germans in Schleswig-Holstein by staging a parade through Davenport which ended in a picnic in the central park. The Germans would line the streets on this occasion and do their best to disrupt the pomp and ceremony with jeers, laughter, and the usual friendly insults. When the Germans staged their parade and picnic celebrating one of Germany's victories over Denmark, however, the roles were naturally reversed."[60]

While derogatory words were often used to characterize the members of other groups, the harshest and most unforgiving language was more often reserved for the many conflicts within immigrant groups. Paradoxically, vicious internal conflicts could be the very cement that bound the various blocks of an immigrant group together in one inward-looking entity. This may be observed in the histories of a wide variety of immigrant groups. Victor Greene's *For God and Country: The Rise of Polish and Lithuanian Ethnic Consciousness in America, 1860–1910* (1975) is very much the history of intense struggles for influence and power within the immigrant communities. And John Bodnar has observed that the campaigns for the celebration of the Polish-American heroes Thaddeus Kosciuszko and Casimir Pulaski may from the outside seem to be expressions of ethnic unity, but they emerged "from a complex struggle for power within the ethnic community itself."[61] Similarly, in the nineteenth century, a varying number of Norwegian-American Lutheran synods were uncompromising in their disputes about the one and only acceptable way of being Lutheran. Small immigrant communities would often have two churches, both more intensely aware of the other than of any other institution outside their immigrant group. Paradoxically, however, such internecine strife could be an expression of the close and inward-looking quality of the immigrant community. Within ethnic groups as within nations, the leaders for various ideological positions may be more frequently engaged in conflict than in proclaiming a family relationship taken for granted.[62] From the 1860s and into the early years of the twentieth century, both Polish and Lithuanian Americans were engaged in an uncompromising battle about the very nature of their nationalism and their Catholicism. Victor Greene explains:

> The disagreement was over the role of their community in America, specifically what qualities constituted membership and how the group should function as a Roman Catholic minority. The interminable, heated debate between the elites occasionally drew the masses into the controversy. It was because the issue touched upon a vital element in peasant-immigrant psychology, control of the parish, that the ordinary group members (parishioners, fraternalists, and readers of the ethnic press) became deeply involved. *It was this experience that forced the immi-*

> *grants to confront the notion of their ethnic identity. It was this inner*
> *ordeal that revealed to all immigrants the parameters of their group.*[63]

A strong inner cohesiveness was a prerequisite for such vicious infighting. At the same time the internal strife prolonged the period in which members of a group would have less interest in the affairs of the society outside their own group.

Although a certain clannishness prevailed and may still be seen to prevail in the activities of many ethnic associations, the extremes of enmity between immigrant groups and the strife within immigrant groups that were so characteristic of the decades around the turn of the nineteenth century have receded as members of these groups have become more and more confident of their rightful place in the American home. By 1934, for instance, the July 1 edition of *Die Sonntagpost* (the Sunday edition of *Die Abendpost,* Evening Post) in Chicago foresaw an America where the "grandchild or great-grandchild" of an immigrant "is just another American without the least vestige of origin. Whether the cradle of his people once stood in England, Ireland, Germany, Russia, Italy, Spain, or elsewhere will eventually make no difference."

This vision of future harmony, however, was held up in order to argue that it "is therefore absurd to speak of America as an Anglo-Saxon nation. In our days, there are just as few Anglo-Saxons as there are Scandinavians, Germans, or Frenchmen. The people were no longer exclusively Anglo-Saxon at the time independence was declared. . . . The 'parent country' of the United States was not England alone, but Europe in general." By the mid-1930s there was less competition for status among immigrant groups in general. German Americans in particular had a history of (selective) generosity in regard to other groups. Nevertheless, German and other European Americans could still strongly resent the dominant position of the Anglo-Americans.

Ten years later, in 1945, solidarity with all immigrant and ethnic groups had become central to the vision of Louis Adamic and to his larger aim of changing the manner in which American history was written so that Americans of all origins could feel equally at home. In his story of America the contributions of all ethnic groups receive equal prominence. His agenda is greater recognition of the immigrant American and the Anglo-American, as well as the African American and the Native American, as Americans of equal standing in a common homeland. Elements in his American story are

> that the Negroes' American tradition of fighting for liberty dates from 1556; that a handful of Polish, German and Armenian workers at

Jamestown, Virginia, in 1619 staged one of the first rebellions in the New World; that John Peter Zenger, a German printer in the 1730s whom the governor of New York jailed for publishing attacks on his regime, fathered the American ideal of freedom of the press; that Philip Mazzei, the Italian friend and neighbor of Thomas Jefferson, influenced the Revolution of 1776; that the Irish were the backbone of the political-military movement that won American independence.

According to Adamic, although these contributions are not sufficiently recognized, America would not be the country we love had it not been for them. He too thinks of the telling of such stories as a process of home-making: "Then all over the country, from the Atlantic to the Pacific, from the Canadian to the Mexican border, Swedish Americans, Russian, German, Italian, Irish, Negro, French, Spanish, Oriental, Czech and double-check Americans will feel the same warmth and pride in their old, yellowing letters and documents which you [an Anglo-American friend from New England] felt in yours. They will feel themselves at home in the history of America."[64]

2 Foundations and Refoundations: We Were Here First

NATIONS HAVE STORIES of how they came about. Because these narratives may relate events that occurred before recorded history and have a teleological bent, they often have the qualities of myth rather than of history. But even in foundation stories, where some of the events themselves may be recorded and documented as history, the stories have often been embellished and become used in ways that are mythical rather than historical. Both the purely mythic Roman foundation story of Romulus and Remus and semidocumented American foundation stories, such as that of the first Thanksgiving or of the "purchase" of Manhattan Island, have mythic qualities and have or have had mythic and symbolic uses. It is, of course, the mythic quality and the mythic uses of the American ethnic stories of foundation that are of interest here and not their "historicity."

The differences between the American voyages of Christopher Columbus and Leif Erikson are significant. Columbus's voyages from Spain, beginning in 1492, had radical historical consequences. The voyages of Erik the Red, his son Leif, and other members of the family setting out from Iceland, Norway, and Greenland around 1000 took place in the early years of the more than five-century history of Norse colonization and settlement of western Greenland; in historical perspective, it was an isolated incident.[1] As Franco D'Amico concluded in his account of reactions to the proclamation of October 9, 1936, as "Leif Erickson Day" in Chicago and Illinois: "Conceding hypothetically that Leif Erickson at the end of the tenth century, his nutshell buffeted by a tempest, scrambled for life upon the coast of America, what did the world gain by his accidental discovery if there was any? None whatsoever! It took Christopher Columbus to triumphantly reveal the existence of a new continent to the people of the earth and the existence of a [sic] said continent has been known only since 1492, and never before."[2] Yet regardless of their different historical influence, Columbus and Erikson have played similar and central roles in foundation myths created by American ethnic groups. In 1936 D'Amico was not so much engaged in historiographical criticism as in defending one particular foundation story and the right it gave members of his group to a home in the United States.

In the second half of the nineteenth century, immigrants in the United States did not always distinguish between the adjectives used for the country and for the country's language. Both "American" and "English" were used indiscriminately to characterize the Anglo-American population and their institutions. Immigrants would refer to their native-born neighbors as either English or American and to public schools as "English schools" to distinguish them from parochial schools, which were often conducted in a language other than English.[3] Not many outside his group could say with the equanimity of a German immigrant in Iowa in 1884, "How sad . . . that many think that this country is English." Indeed, in the late nineteenth century, German-American leaders were exceptional in often insisting on German as an American language with the same status and rights as the English language.[4]

But there was little doubt in most immigrants' minds that the American language was English, nor was there any doubt that the Republic was founded by the English ancestors of the Anglo-Americans. This gave members of the founding English group a privileged position as the country moved westward, even in new settlements in areas where non-British immigrants and their children comprised a majority of the population. Johannes B. Wist, an Iowa editor and novelist in the early decades of the twentieth century, observed:

> The prairie had no tradition for the settler and the tradition of the country was not his, for in nine out of ten instances he was an immigrant and had his roots in another tradition and another culture. This is what has given the Yankee his great advantage over the others in the making of those traits that are characteristic of the American West. This has made

it possible for his kind above all others to become an upper class in the many-hued society that has been created in this part of the country. The Yankee brought the country's own tradition to the settlement.[5]

In the parlance of the turn of the nineteenth century, Anglo-Americans were native Americans. All immigrant groups other than the British have in their time been looked at askance as "foreigners."

Although the foundation stories of European immigrant groups certainly were in competition with those of other groups, only German Americans felt confident enough to challenge the basic belief in the Anglo-American foundation of the United States. The German immigrant in Iowa who deplored the notion that the United States was an English country may not have been thinking primarily of language but of the foundation and cultural heritage of the country.

Many years later, in 1917, when German-American leaders were facing their greatest challenge, *Der Zeitgeist*—"a weekly," to translate the subtitle, "for politics, art, literature, social economics and society"—began publication in Chicago. The nature of the challenge was precisely formulated in the editor's opening statement on the aims of the journal: "Also German America has brought difficult sacrifices to this war; perhaps the most difficult, since it concerns a conflict between the homeland of free choice and the land of birth. And it causes fury when people in the land of birth evidently cannot understand that the only duties of an American citizen are to his American homeland and when people in America will not understand that a patriotism characterized by the joy of sacrifice does not exclude the love of an inherited language and traditions." In a supplement in English, a regular feature of the journal, the headline on a piece by Thomas J. Diven, an Irish American, asked, "Is This an English Country?" Diven argued for a view of the United States as made up of "the American race, a conglomerate in which the English is a minor element." Indeed, he claimed to "have shown beyond question that at least half of the population of the country at the time of the revolution was composed of German and Irish blood, the former predominating."[6]

Other immigrant groups were more accepting of the founding role and status of the Anglo-Americans. An important aim of their homemaking arguments was to be recognized by Anglo-Americans as another and coequal founding group. Their homemaking stories would typically try to demonstrate that members or even a single member of a particular group had arrived before or as early as the ancestors of the Anglo-Americans, or that they too could look back to participation in American colonial history. Members of an ethnic group with American roots at least as long and as deep as those of the Anglo-Americans could not, the implied argument of these stories went, be considered foreigners. One irony in the construction of we-were-here-first stories is that only one story in the genre was unbeatable, and it did not give descendants of the land's original inhabitants a particularly high social status in the eyes of the nation.[7] Nor did it privilege their culture. Until recently, this irony evaded those who have insisted that a Norwegian ("we," they would say) rather than an Italian ("we," they too would say) *discovered* America.[8] One pre-Columbian founding myth is that of Aztlán, the long-claimed homeland in the American Southwest of the Aztecs. When the Mexican-American myth of Aztlán was revived in 1969, however, it was more as a symbol for contemporary political action than as a homemaking myth that it captured the Mexican-American imagination.[9]

So powerful has the hold of the Anglo-American myth of foundation been that the strategy of some immigrant stories was to claim a share in this myth rather than to compete with it. One way this was done was through stories of kinship, either direct or indirect, with the Anglo-Saxons in general or with specific American heroes such as Washington and Lincoln. In his account of Greek-American responses to Americanization and naturalization in the early decades of the twentieth century, the historian Theodore Saloutos tells of "one superpatriot [who] even emphasized the Hellenic origins of the Anglo-Saxons. The Anglo-Saxons, he claimed, came closer to the ancient Greek ideal than the representatives of any other living group; and all patriotic Greeks knew, he added, that the history of ancient and modern Greece was long and unbroken." Thus the Anglo-American qualities of "true Americanism" were actually Greek.[10]

Similar accounts may be found in other groups. In an introductory note to his *The Armenians in America*, M. Vartan Malcom observed in 1919 that "those who are competent to judge and speak of the Armenians have described them as 'The Anglo-Saxons of the East'"; in the preface to Malcom's book, Leon Dominian compared the Armenians to "the Puritans of old" and added that they had "many similar traits of character, they came bringing the same earnestness of religious conviction, the same willingness to endure hardships of pioneer life and the same belief ingrained in their minds that they were traveling to a free land." Immigrants from northern Europe made much of their racial and cultural relationship with the Anglo-Americans. William Widgery Thomas, former U.S. minister to Stockholm and a great admirer of all things Swedish, gave the main speech at the 1888 Minneapolis celebration of the 250th anniversary of the founding of the colony of New Sweden. Thomas was, H. Arnold Barton suggests, inspired by the Swedish-American journalist Johan Enander when he flattered his audience by expressing his belief that "no immigrants of today, in both faith and works, so closely resemble the sturdy pilgrim fathers of New England as the Swedes."[11]

German Americans may not have insisted so much on participation in Columbian or pre-Columbian arrivals in America—as have, for instance, Greeks, Jews, Croatians, Swedes, and Poles—but they made much of their relationship with the Anglo-Saxons. Indeed, one speaker at a German-American celebration in New York in 1912 claimed that the Germans had created the basis for the later Anglo-Saxon conquest of North America as far back as A.D. 9 when German tribes vanquished the Romans in the Battle of the Teutoburg Forest. They had thus paved the way for the Anglo-Saxons, the speaker said, and, it was implied, for the United States. Indeed, the German influence on the founding of the United States was also more immediate and more direct than this, according to the same speaker. He noted that without Luther there would have been "no Pilgrim Fathers, no Puritans, no New England." Indeed a German had also paved the way for 1492: "Without Copernicus no Christopher Columbus."[12] In Chicago's *Die Abendpost* for March 9, 1930, Karl A. Schultz argued for a still earlier German foundation of not merely the United States but of the English-speaking world when he argued for the "legitimate position" of the German language "in the national life. The German language, Gothic, is the mother of the English language, and possesses a birthright, wherever the English language is spoken." With such pre-Columbian stories of foundation and relationship with the Anglo-Saxons, Germans were practicing a kind of one-upmanship with the Italians, who by this time had won recognition for Columbus as their particular American hero.[13]

More than one side could play the game of who is related to whom, however. John Higham has shown how, after the United States entered World War I, "leading race-thinkers strove . . . to bring their theories into harmony with the spirit of the hour." In a revised edition of *The Passing of the Great Race* in 1918, Madison Grant eliminated "references to early American settlers as Teutonic" and present-day Germans were declared "Alpines rather than Nordics." According to another scientist of race, "the modern German population was actually descended from Asiatic barbarians."[14] The logic of this view would be that Germans were not qualified for citizenship because they could be defined as a non-European race and, consequently, nonwhite.

Norwegian Americans developed an elaborate set of interlocking myths that are discussed in greater detail in Chapter 5. One of their stories was of the close blood relationship between the Norwegians and the English who established the New England colonies. This relationship was partly due to the density of medieval Norse settlements in the eastern parts of England and partly forged by the Normans, who were descendants of Norwegian Vikings. Some found evidence that George Washington was a Scandinavian in a strange volume by Albert Welles, president of the American College for Genealogical Registry and Heraldry, *The Pedigree and History of the Washington Family Derived from Odin, the Founder of Scandinavia, B.C. 70, Involving a Period of Eighteen Centuries and Including Fifty-Five Generations Down to General George Washington, First President of the United States* (1879).[15] Even though the claim that Washington was a Scandinavian seems to have struck most immigrant leaders as too preposterous to function as a credible homemaking myth, several used it in the decades before and after the turn of the last century. It surfaces, for instance, with great insistence in the pages of *Northern Review: Cultural Magazine for Northwest,* a journal created at the beginning of World War I in Europe and edited in Minneapolis by J. N. Lenker as a pro-German voice for U.S. neutrality. It was directed at Americans of Scandinavian and German descent in the Midwest, and most of the January 1918 issue is devoted to articles on "Great Men of the North"—the first is titled "Washington a Scandinavian" and gives a summary of the book by Albert Welles.[16]

Italian Americans have also laid claim to Washington, but while the story used by Norwegian Americans has him born a Norwegian (or a Scandinavian when that suited the purpose better), the Italian-American story has him die an Italian. Where proponents of the Norwegian Washington story resorted to the hard "facts" of genetic descent, Angelo Flavio Guidi, in a 1933 article called "Washington and the Italians," made use of a rhetoric of sensibility to argue the emotional truth of his story. Indeed, he began his essay by acknowledging that historical records provide little evidence of a close relationship between Washington and the Italians. Nevertheless, Guidi tells us, whetting our appetites, he is now able to "show something truly remarkable." In part his story is about Italian participation in the Revolutionary War, but his "remarkable" contribution is that he can present evidence of the close ties between Washington and Italy. Among the elements of this story are the general's admiration for Cincinnatus, the books in his library "on Rome and Italy," that the first and "fatidical" name of the place that became the nation's capital was Rome, and "the fact that Washington was the first to greet Filippo Mazzei upon his arrival in Virginia in 1773." "Even the pictures hanging on the walls of his home were reminders of that far-away land, whose infinite spell he felt, and the importance of whose moral influence, exerted over mankind throughout millennial periods of history, he understood." All this builds up to a "mantelpiece, of Italian marble" at Mount Vernon, "surely the work of some Siennese sculptor":

> By that fireplace, wherein burned the logs from Virginia woods, Washington was wont to sit while conversing with his family or with the soldiers and statesmen that called on him. By that hearth he lingered for the last time that evening when, wet and covered with sleet, he returned home and retired, never to rise again. His last glance was for that mantelpiece. His eyes rested on the carved forms he so much loved, envisaging their beauty with an Italian sentiment, full of fondness—then he saw no more. His last caress was for that marble of Siena, warm from the fire that burned in the grate. Perhaps Washington mused that his glory had missed the vision of one of those fields the carvings on the mantel depicted, missed the warmth of the sunshine of Italy, the smile of the Neapolitan sky, a view of Rome from the height of the Capitol. All this he had loved, without ever having seen it.

That this story of Washington's becoming Italian at the moment of his death had the ability to move those for whom it was primarily written and that it functioned as a homemaking story is evident in the way Michael Musmanno, still rankling from his childhood experience, uses it with piety in *The Story of the Italians in America* in 1965 as part of his argument that he was not a foreigner in the United States, the country of his birth.[17] Claiming a special relationship with the father of the country is one version of the more general theme of claiming relationship with the founding Anglo-American group.[18]

In insisting on their close ties to the Anglo-Saxons, both Greeks and Armenians may have been responding to contemporary racial theory as much as to the all-dominant national foundation story. Both the racial theory and the foundation story privileged Americans of English origin. Greeks, however, were among the European immigrant groups whose white status was not entirely secure. Thus the view popularized by Charles Dudley Warner in 1877 and later sanctioned by the Dillingham Commission was that modern Greeks were "mongrelized" and not closely related to the much admired citizens of ancient Greece. Armenians were even more marginalized in that they could not, strictly speaking, be defined as European. The right of an Armenian to be considered white and, consequently, qualified for citizenship according to the Naturalization Act of 1790, was contested in 1909. The question was settled in the favor of Armenian inclusion by a Massachusetts court that granted Armenians what Matthew Frye Jacobson has called "borderline whiteness."[19]

The first European immigrant group to be exposed to systematic exclusion on the basis of race was the Irish. Given the Irish history of suppression by England, a homemaking argument based on a claim to relationship with the English or the Anglo-Saxons was not likely to be developed by leaders of Irish immigrants in the United States. David Roediger has reminded us that "the evil 'race' that plagued the Irish Catholic imagination was white and British, not Black and African." As Jacobson has observed, their history made many Irish Americans agree with the idea of a racial difference between Celts and Anglo-Saxons, although they "rejected the argument of Celtic inferiority." To claim whiteness, however, became essential because the Irish-American leaders were faced with nativist propaganda that denied them white skins and, consequently, their humanity. Indeed, Jacobson has demonstrated how public opinion in the aftermath of the 1863 draft riots in New York City turned against the Irish, who were not only characterized as "brutish," "animal," "savage," and "inhuman ruffians" but were as a race often placed below the Negro. Comparing the two races, a commentator in the *Atlantic Monthly* observed that "the emancipated Negro is at least as industrious and thrifty as the Celt, takes more pride in self-support, is far more eager for education, and has fewer vices. It is impossible to name any standard of requisites for the full rights of citizenship which will give the vote to the Celt and exclude the Negro." Irish Americans, however, found that African Americans were the only other group they could attack with impunity, as was brought out, for example, when Irish-American dock workers unsuccessfully tried "to expel *German* longshoremen from jobs under the banner of campaigning for an 'all-white waterfront.'" Consequently, in making their homemaking argument for whiteness, many Irish-American leaders singled out African Americans as their main adversaries.[20]

Some African-American leaders, on the other hand, sought to reverse the immigrant argument for acceptance on the basis of whiteness by placing the immigrant in the position of the Other. In the 1890s, as we saw earlier, Booker T. Washington and Paul Lawrence Dunbar presented narratives that contrast blacks and whites, both native to the United States, with foreigners. In Atlanta in 1895 Booker T. Washington pointed to the long and shared history of the Anglo-American and African-American races where "we have proved our loyalty to you" and promised the white South that "in our humble way, we shall stand by you with a devotion that no foreigner can approach, ready to lay down our lives, if need be, in defense of yours, interlacing our industrial, commercial, civil, and religious life with yours in a way that shall make the interests of both races one." A few years later Dunbar made the same argument in his short story

"At Shaft 11," in which loyal and reliable black strikebreakers are pitted against devious, unreliable, and violent Irish strikers and win the respect and patronage of the Anglo-American mine owners.[21]

Kinship, even in the most shallow form of a shared skin color, however, has proved to be a more efficacious argument for inclusion in the American home than service. Successive groups of immigrants that have claimed relationship with or affinity to the founding Anglo-Saxons have thus adapted to and augmented a racism that appears endemic in many cultures, not merely in the United States. At times, expressions of claims to a shared "whiteness" could be ugly and offensive, as when the *Narod Polski* (Polish Nation) raised, in an editorial of August 6, 1919, the question of why there were pogroms against Jews in Europe and "pogroms of negroes [sic] . . . recently in St. Louis, Washington and Chicago" and answered that it was "because they have earned it"—the Jews for "materializing the world" and living "in wealth while the Christians died of hunger," and the Negroes for "attacking white women and girls" and wrenching "work from white hands." In the special pleading implicit in homemaking stories there is always the suggestion, happily not always so blatant as in the *Narod Polski,* that somehow the group spoken for is superior to some other group. Not all could, with the equanimity of Rabbi Emil G. Hirsch in 1891, speak warmly for a patriotism based on "that broader sentiment and inspiration that recognized the fatherhood of God and the brotherhood of humanity" and for a "True Americanism" that is not "all of native growth, but . . . the assimilation of all patriotic impulses."[22]

In the so-called antihyphen and 100 percent American campaigns of the First World War period, Woodrow Wilson, Theodore Roosevelt, and others insisted that true Americans could not have the divided loyalties suggested by the then-hyphenated phrases such as Italian-American or German-American. To be a 100 percent American meant not only to cease to call yourself a Swedish-American, that is, cease to parade a hyphenated identity, but to conform 100 percent with the cultural norms associated with true Americans. An apparently implied corollary of their message was that as soon as immigrants became unhyphenated, that is, ceased to speak a "foreign" language and ceased to think of themselves as Americans "and something else," they would be fully accepted as Americans and be the equals of "native" Americans.

Although immigrants who went through this "American process of elimination"—as Jane Addams characterized the demand that immigrants forget the past—never seem to have impressed the Anglo-American elite as worthy of inclusion, disclaiming the country of origin became one variation of the we-are-the-real-Americans story. It was, for instance, used by the Yiddish *Daily Jewish Courier* as a response to the discussion in "Chicago's English newspapers" of the anti-Semitism propagated by Henry Ford's *Dearborn Independent*. The Yiddish newspaper noted that the *Chicago Tribune* had declared "that the best means to keep America free from anti-Semitism is for the American Jew to reject any form of hyphenism and be Americans only." "If there are any hyphens in America," responded the *Courier* on December 6, 1920, "they certainly are not the American Jews. Every naturalized American Jew, without exception, has full-heartedly disclaimed the country of his birth, where he was treated as a stepchild. He no longer has any interest in that country, except thoughts of his suffering relations who remained there."[23] While this negative claim to a home in America based on repudiation may be rare in immigrant publications and in the speeches of immigrant leaders outside the Jewish-American group, it nevertheless reflects a common Americanization process for many individuals in all immigrant groups. A common denominator, however, in all immigrant accounts of who was the most American is the belief that America was not founded one time for all but that the story of America is a story of constant refoundation wherein successive groups lay claim to their special status as "American."

Scandinavian Americans, then, were among the groups that forcefully claimed a special and close relationship with the Anglo-Americans. A main shaper of the Swedish-American story was the journalist and educator Johan Enander, whom H. Arnold Barton has characterized as "unquestionably the most influential Swedish-American opinionmaker."[24] Enander was in turn influenced by Rasmus B. Anderson, a second-generation Norwegian American and professor at the University of Wisconsin, who in 1874 initiated his lifelong campaign to have Norwegians recognized as the true discoverers of America with a slim volume with the bombastic title *America Not Discovered by Columbus*. Anderson was not alone, however, as an early champion of the cause of Leif Erikson as discoverer of America. The Norwegian violin virtuoso Ole Bull, who lived in Cambridge, Massachusetts, in the late 1870s and was a regular visitor in the Longfellow home, spoke often and enthusiastically of the Viking discoverer and sought recognition for Erikson. Many prominent late nineteenth-century New Englanders were convinced that they lived in the land Leif Erikson had named Vinland.[25] But Columbus nevertheless had a firm place in the American imagination, and no one seems to have been ready to rename the capital city the District of Leif.

Who, then, was this navigator who believed he had come to Asia in 1492? Italian and Hispanic Americans have not been the only contenders for the right to use Columbus to say "we" discovered America. Although Jewish Americans have yet to launch their own Columbus Day parades, the authors of popular filiopietistic Jewish-American histories often speculate on the probability of the Jewish origin of Christopher Columbus. Scholars with varying credentials have argued that he was Spanish and that his parents were converted Jews, or Marranos. Typically, however, Anita Libman Lebeson, in her *Jewish Pioneers in America, 1492–1848* (1931), merely referred to some of the evidence put forward by scholars and left the question open in order to present a less controversial Jewish foundation story: "Whether Columbus was a Jew is uncertain," she wrote. "But there is no doubt of the fact that he was materially assisted in his venture by a number of influential Jews." Moreover, she added, Jewish participation in his first voyage, which coincided with the general expulsion of Jews from Spain, is undisputed. A possibly Jewish Columbus character rarely appears in Jewish-American foundation stories, but much is made of both those Jews who helped him and those who went with him on his first voyage: "For it was a Jew that gave to Columbus the means to come to this country; and there were five Jews—a number entirely out of proportion to the Jewish population of Spain—that accompanied him on his voyages of discovery." Peter Wiernik called the first chapter of his *History of the Jews in America* "The Participation of Jews in the Discovery of the New World." A special place in Jewish-American foundation stories is given to Luis de Torres, Columbus's interpreter, who was one of the two "first known white men to land in America," as Wiernik put it.

The story of discovery is given truly mythic proportions when it is seen as part of God's plan for his Chosen People: "Sad, indeed, was the plight of the Jews that year [1492], and yet in the same year came the discovery of America. Is it not true that God had again shown Israel, in its hour of need, the Promised Land?" This view of the New World as especially provided for the Jewish people was presented in 1930 and seems to have been traditional. In 1906 it was expressed at the celebration of the 250th anniversary of Jewish settlement in the United States: "Doubt it, ye of little faith! As for me, I see as clearly the hand of compelling fate in Isabella's signing the order for Columbus's voyage of discovery on the very day she signed the expulsion edict of the Jew, as I see the hand of Providence manifest in the afflictions that, in our days, have come upon the house of the Romanoffs and upon the Russians for the afflictions they have brought upon the house of Israel."[26] The New England Puritans were not alone in seeing their migration to the New World as ordained by Providence. The right of Jews to a home in America was not only the right of the first to arrive but a right by the intervention of God.

Other groups also linked their stories of foundation to the voyages of Columbus. Indeed, in a book mostly written in Greek and thus aimed at a Greek immigrant audience, Seraphim G. Canoutas, a lawyer and author of handbooks for immigrants, suggested that the Greeks may have come to America before 1492. It is, he wrote, a "still undecided question whether America was known to ancient peoples and particularly the Greeks, and whether Greeks had been in America before its discovery by Columbus." He also claimed that it is "not . . . improbable at all" that Columbus "visited the Greek island Scio, or Chios, in 1474, and took his abode at a certain Captain Andreas who afterwards, with three other Chiote Sailors, accompanied him in his long voyage." Indeed, he argued, wandering Greeks "must have sought the occasion to go aboard the vessels sailing for the New World," and he explained that it was the prejudice against Greeks and the tendency to change names in America that has kept them from view in the New World. Canoutas continued to study the role of Greeks in the discovery of the New World, and by 1943, when he published his findings at his own expense, he had become convinced that Columbus was a Greek nobleman.[27] Canoutas sent his book to Louis Adamic, who "found it almost as fascinating" as a book he had read presenting much "circumstantial evidence" that Columbus was a Jew.[28] Indeed, one of the remarkable aspects of Adamic's *Nation of Nations* is that he seems equally enthusiastic about the foundation stories of all immigrant groups.

Polish Americans too were among the several immigrant groups that claimed to have arrived before Columbus—by sixteen years, to be precise. Their explorer representative was a Jan z Kolna, or John of Colno, the pilot of an expedition supposedly sent by the king of Denmark and Norway to search for the Norse settlements in Greenland in 1476. The expedition is said to have visited Labrador and sailed down the American coast as far as Delaware. No matter that the expedition was Danish and its two leaders German, its story opens the chapter called "Poland and the Discovery of America" in Miecislaus Haiman's 1939 book, *Polish Past in America, 1608–1865*. Even Adamic did not place much faith in this particular story. He seems to have read Haiman, however, and dutifully, if somewhat facetiously, entered the "legend" of this early seafarer who "bumped into Labrador" in his *Nation of Nations*. Polish-American leaders, who tended to focus on the bravery of Thaddeus Kosciuszko and Casimir Pulaski in their homemaking arguments, did not make much use of Jan z Kolna, even though he does get mentioned in filiopietistic listings of Poles in the United States.[29] German Americans have not used the story of this alleged expedition led by two Hanseatic seafarers to claim pre-Columbian "discovery."

The Croats too were a seafaring people, and a Croatian historian has expressed the belief "that among the crew on Columbus' caravels were sailors from the Yugoslav Dalmatian littoral, although facts to prove the claim are wanting." Ready to accept the foundation stories of all immigrant groups, Adamic was convinced of the truth of the Yugoslavian one: "Little doubt exists that on Columbus' ships were cosmopolitan Croatians from the famous Dalmatian city-republic of Ragusa (now Dubrovnik on Yugoslav maps). . . . In the fifteenth and sixteenth centuries its members sailed on ships of all seafaring nations, especially, it seems, on those engaged in the India spice trade. It is very unlikely that some of them did not get in on the great Adventure of 1492."[30] That there may have been considerable conjecture in the discovery stories of Greek, Polish, and Yugoslav immigrants is beside the point, which is that Greek Americans, Polish Americans, and Croatian Americans are Americans and rightfully at home in the land of their choice.

Stories of discovery, early explorations, and early settlements are all elements in this kind of mythologizing. Stories of discovery, however, have been the most valued and controversial. Above all other such stories, the one featuring Columbus has had the greatest appeal. Despite some competition, the Italian Americans have been most successful in appropriating Columbus as their special ethnic hero, and they have had the greatest popular influence with their central myth of foundation: the Italian discovery of America. But regardless of his genetic makeup or his place of birth, Columbus was certainly not Italian in our sense of the word in 1492. Italy, like several other European nation-states, was a creation of the late nineteenth century. In 1892, when Americans celebrated the four-hundredth anniversary of his first voyage, Columbus was still mainly an American national symbol. One hundred years later, in 1992, the notion of discovery had become so ambiguous, to say the least, that there was little celebration compared to the 1892 outpourings of nationalism in cities like New York and Chicago. But Columbus had become an Italian-American mythological hero.[31] The ethnicization of Columbus, however, has weakened his attraction as a national—which traditionally has meant Anglo-American—symbolic character. How, then, did Christopher Columbus become an Italian American?

When the federal capital was named the District of Columbia, this was neither to honor an Italian navigator nor the few Americans of Italian descent. Nor did Columbus, Ohio, have any ethnic connotations for those who gave the city its name in 1812. In the early years of the Republic, Christopher Columbus was an American national symbol, in particular favored by those of a Federalist persuasion. This national symbol was often named and figured as Columbia, a mother figure rather than a father. The undisputed father was George Washington. When David Humphreys addressed his patriotic *A Poem on Industry* to "Citizens of the United States of America" (1794), his favored name for his country was Columbia, and its citizens were variously called Columbians and Sons of Columbia, and its poets were "Columbian Bards."[32]

In Joel Barlow's *Vision of Columbus* (1787), as well as in the revised and expanded version of 1807, *The Columbiad*, the epic hero is indeed Christopher Columbus, but the center of the long poem is his vision of the future greatness not only of the United States but of all mankind, as shown to him by Hesper, the guardian angel of the New World. In his preface Barlow distinguished between "the fictitious object of the action and the real object of the poem." The purpose of his vision "is to soothe and satisfy the desponding mind of Columbus; to show him that his labors, tho ill rewarded by his cotemporaries [*sic*], had not been performed in vain; that he had opened the way to the most extensive career of civilization and public happiness; and that he would one day be recognised as the author of the greatest benefits to the human race." When, in the concluding "Book the Tenth," "the legates of all empires" meet "in general congress . . . to hear and give the counsels of mankind," this takes place neither in the United States nor in Europe but on the banks of the Nile, "the place / Where man first sought to socialize his race." The vision Barlow created for Columbus takes him far beyond any concern for what we call ethnicity and little concern for nation. Even the later role assigned to Columbus as defender of the Christian or Roman Catholic faith is too limiting for the far grander role given him by Barlow. For Barlow, the glorious future can only begin after all that divides the race of man lies "trampled in the dust":

> Each envoy here unloads his wearied hand
> Of some old idol from his native land;
> One flings a pagod on the mingled heap,
> One lays a crescent, *one a cross to sleep*;
> Swords, sceptres, mitres, crowns and globes and stars,
> Codes of false fame and stimulants to wars
> Sink in the settling mass; since guile began,
> These are the agents of the woes of man.[33]

In the early years of the United States, then, Columbus was not associated with Italy, his place of birth, nor with the Spanish empire, on whose mission he sailed, nor, indeed, with the Catholic faith but rather with the spirit of the young Republic and its democratic ideals.

As late as 1882, when Irish Americans founded the Catholic fraternal order of the Knights of Columbus in New Haven, Connecticut (which became a very Italian-American city), the Knights had no Italian connotations. Columbus was uniquely suited for their purposes. As Timothy Meagher put it in a 1985 article in the *New England Quarterly*, "Columbus seemed an apt choice to serve as the patron of the new American Catholic group, for as the first Catholic in America, he was the symbolic ancestor of all American Catholics, whatever their ethnic background."[34] This view of the symbolic homemaking importance of Columbus for Catholics was expressed in 1892 by a Boston journal, the *Sacred Heart Review*, the main sponsor of a Columbus monument in Santo Domingo on the site of the first Catholic church in the New World. "By this public act of commemoration we hope to direct public attention to this modest birthplace of our Mother Church, which stands to-day deserted and unhonored like a pauper's grave." Although the birthplace may have been modest, the *Sacred Heart Review* was not at all modest in explaining why its church was the true American church:

> One hundred and twenty-six years before the Congregationalist church landed on Plymouth Rock, 110 years before the Anglican church came to Jamestown, and thirty-five years before the word Protestant was invented, this church was erected, and the gospel announced to the New World by zealous missionaries of the Catholic faith. No other denomination of Christians in America can claim priority or even equal duration with us in point of time. No other can show through all the centuries of history such venerous self-sacrifice and heroic missionary efforts.

Columbus is the ideal Catholic hero because his religion "seems to pervade everything he touches." But at the same time, Columbus was ideally suited as a Catholic homemaking symbol because he was, after all, also a national symbol: "Protestants no less than Catholics share in the fruit of his work, and, we are glad to say, vie with Catholics in proclaiming and honoring his exalted character, his courage, fortitude, and the beneficent work he accomplished for mankind."[35] The *Sacred Heart Review* did not mention his nationality.

The first public secular celebration of a centenary of the 1492 voyage seems to have been in New York in 1792 at the initiative of the recently organized Society of St. Tammany, also known as the Columbian Order. Little attention was paid to this tercentennial, however, and the private erection of a Columbus monument that same year in Baltimore by a wealthy Frenchman, a former representative of France to the colonies, seems not to have gained much notice. A hundred years later an estimated two million New Yorkers turned out on the last of three days of celebration of the quadricentennial. One reason for this change in attention may have been the growth of the Republic and along with it the growth of the self-confidence and national awareness of its citizens. Another may have been, as suggested by a reporter for *Harper's Weekly,* the changed composition of the American people, or at least the population of New York City, which was no longer

> American in the sense in which the rest of the country is. It may have had local patriotic traditions once, but they were long since lost in the flood of foreign sentiment that has poured into the life of the city. The names of Washington, Lincoln, Grant, mean nothing to the great majority of foreign-born or foreign-parented New-Yorkers. The name of Columbus, remote and mythical as Columbus is, means to that majority liberation from conditions approaching, in the case of the Irish, German, Italian, Bohemian, Hungarian, and Russian population of New York, slavery. . . . Columbus's discovery meant a place to make a living to these people—the majority of us. They had all heard his name before they came here.[36]

It may be that the story of how Europeans "discovered" America had a greater appeal to immigrants from Europe than the "local patriotic" story of how Washington became father of the nation, as this journalist believed. He demonstrated little understanding, however, when he saw the participation of immigrants in the 1892 celebration merely as an expression of "foreign sentiment." Surely they were all celebrating being Americans together in a manner that a century later seems more "American" than the exclusive and ethnically narrow nationalism of the journalist. What may, however, strike a later observer as noteworthy about the 1892 New York celebration, as described by *Harper's Weekly,* is the degree to which it was controlled and dominated by an Anglo-American minority despite the many immigrants who turned out for the event.

Some signs of change in the iconic meaning of Columbus were evident even before the spectacular increase in immigration in the 1880s gave Italian Americans both a need to bolster their ethnic pride and the confidence in numbers to begin to lay claim to Columbus as their special ethnic hero. As early as 1849 the Italian-American merchants of Boston had presented a statue of the navigator to the city. In 1876 "the combined Italian societies of Philadelphia" gave a Columbus statue to the Centennial Exposition, and in 1892 the "Italian citizens resident in Baltimore" gave yet another statue to that city. Before the quadricentennial, however, most monuments do not seem to have been the initiatives of Italian Americans.[37] The 1892 celebrations in New York and Chicago and the 1893 Columbian Exposition were primarily tributes to American national grandeur and were fully in the hands of a wealthy elite, inspired, the *Harper's* reporter implied, by a national rather than a "foreign" sentiment. Ellen M. Litwicky says of the 1893 "Procession of the Centuries" in Chicago that it "interpreted American culture in narrow political and patriotic terms that essentially froze it at some date prior to the current waves of immigration." There was no recognition of any particular Italian contribution to the discovery, nor were any Italian Americans among the forty-five members of the board of directors. Indeed, "the Chicago business class which financed, planned, and directed the Columbian celebration sought to propagate [a tradition] that positioned them firmly at the top of a cultural hierarchy that defined itself in terms of both the American Revolution and the progress of the Anglo-Saxon race in America." There was, however, also a civic parade that "purposefully celebrated the ethnic and racial diversity of the city." Here not only members of many immigrant groups paraded in costumes of the old homeland but also a group of buffalo soldiers from the black Ninth Battalion and three hundred Native American schoolboys.[38]

Baltimore was not the only place where a growing Italian-American elite had made its presence felt in matters pertaining to the 1492 voyage of Christopher Columbus. Indeed, since the 1860s Italian Americans had been organizing some celebration of October 12, mostly in New York but also in other cities. In Chicago in the 1880s and 1890s Italian-American organizations sponsored annual celebrations of Columbus on October 12. But judging from extracts from the Italian-American press in the *Chicago Foreign Language Press Survey*, Columbus was merely one of several Italian-American heroes to receive such attention; understandably, as much attention was given to the celebration of Garibaldi as to the discoverer of America. Moreover, Columbus Day celebrations were usually closed social functions for members of the Italian immigrant society, as in 1887, when a dance "commemorating the discovery of America" was given at Turner Hall.[39]

In 1892 the Christopher Columbus Patriotic Club took the initiative for a Columbus Day parade, but the following year the initiative was in the hands of the organizers of the exposition. *L'Italia* noted that "Thursday October 12th is the day dedicated by the Columbian Exposition Committee of Chicago to the Italians of America so that they may celebrate officially the memory of Christopher Columbus." Hoping that "this event will be a success," the editor expressed his gratitude: "We must say that it was very kind of the committee to offer the Italian colony this day of remembrance to the glory of civilization." At the time of the quadricentennial, then, Columbus was still primarily a national rather than an ethnic symbolic figure. Although there had been attempts to appropriate him as a symbol for the Catholic cause as well as for the promotion of Italian ethnic pride, Columbus was not yet perceived as either Italian or Catholic but American. Columbus Day may have been celebrated by Italian Americans, but it had clearly not yet been appropriated by Italian Americans. When members of the German-Jewish elite in St. Louis established a "social club to promote community relations" in 1892, they called themselves the Columbian Club, thereby signaling that they were Americans first.[40]

Although Italian Americans seem to have had little involvement in the planning and organizing of the quadricentennial in New York beyond participation in the civic parade along with other groups, Italian-American leaders had nevertheless made a major and lasting, yet uninvited, contribution to the way in which New Yorkers experienced the event. The journalist for *Harper's Weekly* postured as a bemused observer of the waning influence of the Anglo-American elite, who "will find themselves a small and not very popular 'cult' in the course of a very few generations." "In proof of this perhaps unpalatable prophecy," he wrote, "may be instanced the fact that never before in the history of celebrations in this country has there been one before that grew out of the hands of its original contrivers as this one did." He described the immigrant contributions to the celebrations as the irritating interference of aliens in the work of the appointed officials of the city:

> In the case of the Columbian celebration, it will be remembered that a few foreign-born gentlemen met at a dinner party in the city just a year ago, and agreed to send a professional costumer to Spain in order to arrange an allegorical pageant in commemoration of the discovery. Contemporaneously, the editor of an Italian newspaper opened a subscription-list for a monument. When the success of the subscription was assured the promoters of the plan asked the Park Commission for the best site in the city whereon to place their monument. The Commission demurred. The Grand Circle of Central Park was not only the finest site in the city, but of the New World, and ultimately would be of both worlds. They thought that in a few years the place would be wanted for a monument to the soldiers and sailors of New York who perished in the Rebellion. But . . . they found that in the city of New York less and less "stock" was "taken" yearly in the soldiers and sailors of the Rebellion. . . . So the Park Commission gave the site to Columbus, and there he stands today.

The success of Columbus Circle and the monument marked the beginning of concerted efforts by Italian Americans all over the country not only to create memorials for Columbus but to have October 12 recognized as an official day of commemoration and celebration.

Most of the many Columbus monuments since 1892 have been the initiative of Italian Americans. Italian Americans had the support of the Knights of Columbus in their campaign to have October 12 officially recognized as a day of celebration. The first presidential proclamation designating October 12 as Columbus Day was made by Herbert Hoover in 1932. In 1968 Congress designated the second Monday in October as Columbus Day and made it a federal holiday. Rep. Peter Rodino, a sponsor of the bill, noted that "the observance of Columbus Day is an appropriate means of recognizing the United States as a 'nation of immigrants.'"[41] Such general recognition of Columbus Day, however, was the result of the efforts and vigilance of many decades.

Two obstacles that confronted Italian-Americans in their efforts to appropriate Columbus were in different ways both related to Columbus's status as a Catholic hero. On the one hand they faced the prejudice of the dominant Protestants. Ironically, Scandinavian Americans appealed to such prejudice in their campaigns for the recognition of Leif Erikson as the discoverer of America. Surely, the Christianity, such as it was, of this Icelandic or Greenlander navigator was as Roman Catholic as that of the one from Genoa. Yet in 1893 the Swedish-American journalist Johan Enander claimed that the lack of recognition of Leif Erikson as the discoverer of America was due to "the strong influence of the Italians in the U.S. and to the Pope," who had made the inspired discovery of Columbus an article of faith.[42]

On the other hand they faced other Catholic ethnic groups, such as the Irish Americans, who wanted their piece of the action. In Worcester, Massachusetts, a city in which Irish Americans were the largest ethnic group in the second half of the nineteenth century, the Irish-dominated Knights of Columbus organized Columbus Day parades from 1910 to 1913. For some time in the late nineteenth century, the several Irish associations in the city had been able to cooperate in the celebration of St. Patrick's Day, but by 1895 the joint preparatory conventions of the secular Ancient Order of Hibernians and the Catholic Very Reverend Father Mathew Benevolent Total Abstinence Society, the city's largest ethnic social organization, ceased to function, and the tradition of annual St. Patrick's Day parades came to an end in 1911. Although the Irish Americans could not agree about their traditional ethnic celebration, the Columbus Day parades were quite successful and "dwarfed the earlier St. Patrick's Day processions." When the Knights nevertheless abandoned the Columbus Day parades after only three years, this was primarily because ethnicity proved a stronger element in people's identity than religious faith, according to historian Timothy J. Meagher. While some ethnic groups were skeptical about celebrating an Italian, the Italian Americans "seemed nettled that the Knights had upstaged their own celebrations of the famed Italian sailor and complained about the Knights' attempt to depict Columbus as an exclusively Catholic figure rather than as a hero for all Americans."[43] In Chicago, with its larger Italian population, Columbus Day had by this time definitely become recognized as an Italian-American event. Even though Columbus's usefulness as an ethnic hero depended on his status as a national one, there were no initiatives to have the celebrations taken over by municipal institutions or civic nonethnic (i.e., Anglo-American) groups. Columbus was mainly the concern of Italian Americans and they guarded him jealously.[44] The honor of Columbus was the honor of all Italian Americans. In October 1930 the journal *Vita Nuova*, under the heading "The Whole World Glorified Columbus," reported that a "perfidy" committed to "satisfy the fanaticism and jealousy" of "the Swedish people" had been "canceled with a noble and historic telegram" by Herbert Hoover, president of the United States. The occasion for this outburst was a bust

> erected by this cosmopolitan metropolis [New York] to the famous "Leif Erickson" pretended explorer of these lands. . . . It was a perfidious act; and perfidious were all those who groping in the dark, search for other discoverers of this great nation or else dispute the Italian origin of the bold Italian navigator. Books of historical facts, manuscripts, public and private acts, photographs, authentic documents, accumulated with diligent care and research by our government and by valiant writers prove without a doubt that Columbus belongs to the glory of Italy.

Hoover was neither the first nor the last public official who discovered the need for a balancing act in such cases, in order to support the aspirations of the leadership of one ethnic group while taking care not to appear to be dishonoring those of any other. The president's "noble and historic telegram" to Chevalier Confessa, president of the Sezione Columbiana of New York, in fact makes no ethnic references but expresses admiration for Columbus as an example to all: "The story of the discovery of America by Christopher Columbus will never lose the fascination that it has for us, not because it relates to us events which made possible the actual existence of this nation but because the example of his enterprising life, the energy, patience, resourcefulness and courage has been very influential in keeping present those qualities before the eyes of our children as traditions that should be followed."

It may be that such experiences with Italian-American proprietary attitudes toward Columbus made Hoover's advisers change their view of Columbus as a national symbol. When Hoover issued his proclamation about Columbus Day in 1932, it was expressly designated as a day for "his compatriots," that is, for Americans of Italian descent rather than for all Americans. After serving as an American national symbol since the turn of the eighteenth century, Columbus became an Italian-American symbol by presidential proclamation in 1932. But by then he had been an Italian American for some time. "Italians Feel at Home Here," announced Dr. Camillo Violini, a member of the White Hand Society, in a polemic leveled at the *Chicago Tribune* in 1908. While other peoples too "may have derived benefits from [Columbus's] work, long before the Italians did . . . [this] does not conceal the truth, that we ought to feel at home here, at least as much as all the rest of the people who sailed from Europe a few generations ahead of us." That Columbus, in this instance with the assistance of Amerigo Vespucci, served to make America a legitimate home for Italians was also made clear in 1935 by a John De Grazia, when he spoke of "our claim by right of discovery and of the name given to this country" as well as of "our contribution to its development" and concluded that "we Italians are not guests but masters of the house."[45] The story of the Italian discovery of America had become one of the many American homemaking myths, that is, a story to demonstrate the special right of a particular immigrant group to a home in the United States.

The appropriation of the Columbus story as an Italian-American story rather than as one of Anglo-American nationalism, as in Joel Barlow's *Columbiad*, was not without its price. For as Columbus became an ethnic hero, his importance for others diminished. In her 1920 book, *Immigration and the Future*, Frances Kellor discussed the "apparent unwillingness or inability of the Americans to connect in their own minds the immigrant with his heritage" and observed that "it scarcely occurs to us that there is reason for a joint celebration on Columbus Day by native Americans and foreign born Italians. . . . By such lack of appreciation we have failed to convey to the members of almost every race [i.e., nationality] whatever concept we may have had of their racial accomplishments." Her observation would hardly have made sense to those Ohio citizens who, 108 years earlier, as a patriotic gesture, had proudly named their city Columbus. So successful was the campaign to make Columbus an ethnic hero, however, that Kellor and her contemporaries recognized him as a symbol of the "racial accomplishments" of Italian Americans. The dominant narrow view of an American history limited to

Anglo-American contributions and traditions barred even recognition of the contributions and traditions of other ethnic segments of society.[46]

Consequently, the Italian-American promotion of Columbus required constant vigilance as he ceased to have symbolic power for the still dominant Anglo-American elite. In 1912 J. Albertelli, a Chicago businessman, discovered that none of the three Columbus monuments created in 1892–93 remained. The one on the exposition grounds had been destroyed, the one on the lakefront had been stored in the attic of a public school to make room for a statue of William McKinley, and the one in front of the city hall had been moved to a less prominent location. All this was, he declared, "an insult to our colony. The Americans have taken away from the public eye the thing which gives the Italians most honor." He pledged $200 for a new "memorial to our patriot, Christopher Columbus." To this Chicago businessman at the beginning of the twentieth century, Columbus was "our patriot," that is, an Italian American.[47]

He remains an Italian American, and his celebration is largely regarded as an ethnic affair as we enter the twenty-first century. The ethnicity of Columbus was, for instance, noted by the *New Haven Register* in its observance of Columbus Day in 1998: "In Italian-American communities, he's honored as the Italian who opened the door to Europe, who discovered the land to which tens of thousands of Italians emigrated centuries later." The newspaper further underscored this ethnicity when it characterized Columbus Day as "the traditional final ethnic celebration of the year in a city where ethnic pride is cherished." This does not mean that his ethnicity is undisputed. As the prologue discussed, Hispanics also celebrate Columbus Day. In the controversy about the site for a gigantic Columbus statue in Cataño, Puerto Rico, in 1998 the question of whether he was an Italian was certainly not an issue in this Hispanic community. That Columbus had become ethnic was nevertheless evident. Alternative sites were in south Florida, not in the District of Columbia.[48]

Despite some later competition from Hispanic Americans, there can be little question that by the early decades of the twentieth century Italian Americans had succeeded in making the dominant American story of discovery their own and that it has served as the centerpiece of their homemaking argument. Consequently, the homemaking arguments of many other ethnic groups have been based on stories of early arrival rather than discovery. We too are a founding group is the burden of such stories, and we too took part in the foundation of the Republic. Although some have been able to point to a well-documented colonial presence, others have made much of conjecture.

An article called "Yugoslavs in the United States: Their Contribution to American Culture and Civilization," in the program book for the "First All-Slavic Singing Festival," organized by the United Slavic Choral Societies in Chicago in December 1934, considered the evidence pointing to Croatian involvement in New World settlement before 1590. This was the year John White returned to Roanoke Island and found no traces of the colonists who had been left behind, and, we are told, discovered a tree on which had been carved the single word "CROATAN." So, the author continued, "it can be conjectured that a Croatian ship . . . left its imprint on the tree, or even salvaged the entire settlement from the destruction that was taking place and hurriedly left only the name of their ship, the Croatan[,] on the tree." "This constitutes," he concludes, "the first recorded history linking America with Yugoslavs, or their Croatian branch."[49] Louis Adamic seems to have had a strong need to believe in stories that placed people from Yugoslavia in North America before or at the same time as the first English colonists. To him there was as "little doubt that Ragusan ships . . . sailed to America during the half century immediately following the Discovery" as there was that Croats had sailed with Columbus in 1492.

> It is almost certain that in 1540, or thereabouts, a fleet of ships left Ragusa [i.e., Dubrovnik] for America, hoping to find a region suitable for refugees streaming into the Ragusan republic from the Turkish rule oppressing the Balkan interior. And it seems that one or more of these ships were wrecked off what is now the coast of North Carolina; that a number of sailors rescued themselves on one of the islands, probably Roanoke . . . and that they then mixed with the inhabitants, who have since been known as the Croatan Indians.

Adamic acknowledges that this story was not generally accepted by "scholars," but he concludes that "it seems entirely plausible."[50]

The establishment of links to early American history were important in homemaking arguments, but the quality of the link was also important, not only for the persuasiveness of the story in the homemaking argument but for the emotional impact of the story on the members of the group itself. It was as important to develop a group identity as Americans of a special quality as it was to persuade the dominant Anglo-American elite of an immigrant group's right to a special status in the American ethnic hierarchy. While immigrant homemaking stories in general have done little to persuade Anglo-Americans, the available evidence suggests that the stories about Croatians on the North Carolina coast have not even had a significant impact on the American identity of immigrants from what then was Yugoslavia.

Although Anglo-Americans may never have taken seriously any suggestions by the original inhabitants of the continent—those who today are known as Native Americans—that Anglo-Americans themselves were foreigners in the land, they too have foundation stories with mythic qualities similar to the homemaking stories of other ethnic groups. The *Mayflower* story has had a powerful influence and has served as one of the central all-American foundation myths, both because of its great emotional appeal and because it has proved so flexible in serving shifting demands and requirements. "The Mayflower Compact of 1620 was originally designed to ensure Pilgrim control of the new colony," David Lowenthal reminds us. "Later heritage promoters recycled the Compact into an emblem of Revolutionary freedom, a fin-de-siècle symbol of Anglo-Saxon democracy and social cohesion, a WASP genealogical bona fide, and, most recently, a hallmark of community self-help."[51]

Little wonder, then, that other groups have also tried to promote their *"Mayflower"* stories. One such is the Jewish-American story of the *St. Catarina*, which arrived in New Amsterdam in 1655. This story has elements similar to those that have made the *Mayflower* story serve so well as a national foundation myth: persecution, exile in another country, and the subsequent search for freedom of expression and religious practice in what was to become the United States. As the Jewish story was used and embellished at the 250th anniversary in 1905, the Jews had been unique in coming to South America "in search of home and liberty." But in the Spanish and Portuguese colonies of the New World, they continued for a century to endure the same persecutions as in the Old World, "until it almost seemed as if the curse of the old world would ultimately whelm the Jews in the new." But then, "in the northern part of this same new world there was about to loom into sight a new era in the history of man, the brightest the world had yet witnessed; there was about to dawn a new conception of right and liberty, the best the world had yet enjoyed." A few years after the Dutch landing in New York in 1614 and that of the Pilgrims at Plymouth Rock in 1620, the Jews who arrived on the *St. Catarina* in 1655 to seek liberty "helped to lay the foundation of the greatest nation on the face of the earth." In another address at the celebration of the 250th anniversary of this event, Judge Julian W. Mack made explicit the homemaking argument implied in this and other stories by proclaiming (the word is his) that Jews were "American citizens by our own birthright. . . . The settlement in New York two hundred and fifty years ago makes the Jew the equal of the Pilgrim, the Puritans of Massachusetts, and the Cavaliers of Maryland and Virginia, in claiming this country as their own."[52]

Typically, the Dutch were not included in this list of worthy equals. The American process of homemaking has included few demonstrations of hospitality toward others. Dutch immigrants themselves do not seem to have felt a great need to trumpet their own colonial presence. In 1921 a Chicago weekly newspaper, *Onze Toekomst* (Our Future), for instance, declared that "the largest contribution to America by the Dutch emigrants, is the true religion planted here, especially the Christian Reformed Church." The report mentioned other, more worldly contributions but nothing of the voyages of Henry Hudson or of New Netherland. In fact, Dutch immigrants in the Midwest at the turn of the century expressed a sense of distance between themselves and the New York elite's descendants of the colonial Dutch; the midwesterners even referred to the New Yorkers as "effete, degenerate sons of sturdy, noble Dutch sires." The dominant group of nineteenth-century immigrants from the Netherlands was seceders from the established Reformed Church. At first, their church leaders organized their congregations within the New York–based Reformed Church in America, but the cultural and theological differences were such that the new immigrants seceded again in 1857. This deliberate break with the descendants of the colonists of New Netherland may explain why later Dutch immigrants made so little use of colonial foundation myths. There was, of course, an awareness of early Dutch history in the New World but little sense of its potential importance for the status of contemporary Dutch Americans. On April 24, 1908, the upcoming celebration in New York of the tercentennial of Hudson's 1609 exploration of the river later named for him was given a brief notice in *Onze Toekomst*, which quoted the New York newspaper the *Amsterdam Standard*. As with the Columbus quadricentennial some years earlier, the celebration was not planned as an ethnic affair, and the *Amsterdam Standard* seems to have had no significant objections to being on the sidelines. "Our desire at this time is to have the Netherlands, as well as the Holland Society of New York participate in this jubilee. We are glad that a group of men have taken the initiative and are contacting interested people to see what can be done." A year later a letter to *Onze Toekomst* asked what the Dutch in Chicago were doing to commemorate the Hudson voyage, and the editor's reply was, "As far as we know nothing is being done."[53] The matter had been considered, but apparently no one was sufficiently motivated to organize a celebration. Judging from the little book published by the Netherland Chamber of Commerce in America (in New York) for the tercentennial, *1609–1909: The Dutch in New Netherland and the United States*, a homemaking argument based on a Dutch story of foundation was not a prominent part of the celebration in New

York, either. The solidly entrenched elite descendants of the settlers of New Netherland clearly did not feel any need to argue that they belonged in a country that had had a Van Buren and a Roosevelt as presidents.

The New Sweden colony, however, in the area bordering the Delaware River from present-day Trenton, New Jersey, to Wilmington, Delaware, has played prominent roles in the homemaking stories of both Swedish and Finnish Americans (the Finns were then under the Swedish crown and constituted a majority of the New Sweden colonists). The Swedish historian Dag Blanck has shown how a Swedish-American leadership "created a new historical tradition, which we can call a Swedish-American history," at the turn of the nineteenth century and that New Sweden was an important element in this narrative. Although links between the early seventeenth-century colonists and the late nineteenth-century immigrants "were virtually non-existent," Swedish-American leaders portrayed these colonists as the "forerunners" of contemporary Swedish Americans. As the prominent early Swedish immigrant Hans Mattson affirmed in his autobiography, "Yes, it is verily true that the Scandinavian immigrants, from the early colonists of 1638 to the present time, have furnished strong hands, clear heads and loyal hearts to the republic." While it was natural that the colony of New Sweden should figure prominently in any Swedish account of American history, all Swedish-American (amateur) historians did not necessarily make use of it as a homemaking myth. One prominent journalist and man of letters, C. F. Peterson, for instance, wrote a popular survey of U.S. history; the chapter on New Sweden is indeed a few pages longer than the one on New Netherland, but he does not idealize the colonists or suggest any link between them and later immigrants.[54] For Johan Enander, another journalist and author of a five-volume history of the United States (1874–80) that H. Arnold Barton has suggested was probably more widely distributed than any other Swedish-American book, Swedish-American history was all of a piece, from the arrival of Vikings around 1000 to the most recent immigrant. Indeed, in Enander's account Vikings lived and thrived in Vinland for several hundred years, eventually succumbing to "the Black Death in the mid-fourteenth century." According to Barton, "Here Enander tread on uncertain ground, for he had not only to confront the Italians . . . but also . . . the Norwegians, who understandably regarded Leif Erikson and his companions as uniquely their own. To Enander, they were 'Northmen' from Greenland, 'descended from Sweden, Norway, and Denmark.'" And this gave later Swedish immigrants a right to "regain that part of Vinland the Good that was once their fathers' 'possession.'"[55] The story of medieval discovery and settlement, however, did not figure as prominently in the Swedish-American homemaking mythology as did New Sweden, nor did it have quite the same appeal to the imagination of Swedish immigrants as it did to that of those from Norway.[56]

As Blanck has demonstrated, the elaboration of parallels between the seventeenth-century colonists and the later immigrants was central to the making of a New Sweden story that could function as part of the larger story of Swedish America. This strategy is clearly seen in a story in a Swedish-language reader published in 1917 for use in the schools of the Lutheran Augustana Synod. The story is set in 1691, long after the Swedish colony became part of a British colony, and the descendants of the colonists of New Sweden were rapidly becoming anglicized. It presents an idealized image of these early Swedish Americans, in particular in their relations with Native Americans. Not only does the story show that the seventeenth-century settlers, like the later immigrants, "had struggled against harsh conditions but succeeded in building a prosperous community" but it has them "concerned about the same issues that were confronting the Swedish-American community in general and the Augustana synod in particular around the turn of the century, namely how to maintain the language and religion of their Swedish ancestors."

Another central element in the New Sweden story is the account of how, through the resolute behavior of a descendant of the colonists, the colony led directly to the Declaration of Independence and the founding of the United States of America. In Enander's colorful version, it was "the respectable Swedish-American John Morton," a delegate from Pennsylvania, who cast the deciding vote in Philadelphia in 1776, thus "determining the future of the fatherland."[57] John Morton has been celebrated in fiction and verse, as in the 1896 poem "Ett fosterländskt minne" (A Patriotic Memory) by the Swedish-American poet Ludvig Holmes. In Blanck's paraphrase "Holmes conjures up the scene of the final vote on the Declaration, which was tied when John Morton cast the deciding vote . . . causing Holmes to comment that 'John Morton was Swedish, and the vote he gave was Swedish, because it put an end to the oppression.' The poem ends with a small Swedish boy running to ask his Swedish father to ring the bell when the vote is final. In the last stanza . . . the boy tells his father in 'pure Swedish': 'Now ring Father! Now Ring Father! It is done! America has taken leave from England!'"

Many of the homemaking stories about John Morton, however, have been Finnish rather than Swedish American, and although there seems to be agreement among historians that John Morton probably descended from one of the settlers in New Sweden, opinion is divided on whether this settler was a Swede by the name of Mårten Mårtensson, who arrived in 1654, or a Finn by the name of Martti Marttinen (both last names are patronymics), who came in 1641. While the genealogy of John Morton may have to remain undecided, it seems that the genealogy of the story itself may be decided in favor of the Finns: It was first told in 1863 by Yrjö Koskinen, a Finnish politician.[58] The two John Morton stories differ in two essentials: in the one the very basis for his courage and integrity is Swedish and he is one reason Swedish Americans have a special right to a home in America; in the other story these same qualities are Finnish, and he is one reason Finnish Americans have a special right to a home in America. With reference to Salomon Ilmonen, a clergyman and the author of *Amerikan ensimmälset suomalaiset* (The First Finns in America, 1916), Gary London explains that "Morton as the quintessent Finn, is the means by which all Americans of Finnish descent can vicariously share 'in the important early events of America.'" As Ilmonen put it, "Through this signer of the Declaration of Independence we, too, Americans of Finnish descent, are made to share in the important early historical events of America. Morton leaves his nationality, as it were, a precious certificate of nobility." An idealized Morton is the protagonist of several Finnish-American novels; drama is added to the event in Philadelphia, and he takes part in adventures that are not documented in the life of the historical Morton. Common to all stories about him and the Finnish colonial settlement in Delaware (not New Sweden in this narrative) is the contention that "the position of the Finns in colonial America was superior, or at least similar, to that of other national groups." Indeed, to one author of a filiopietistic history the early Finnish settlement was "the foundation of American civilization."[59]

Finnish and Swedish Americans were not alone in competing for a role as founders of the nation, although immigrants from countries without a history as colonial powers in North America may have been somewhat more modest in their various claims and made less of them in their homemaking arguments. Polish Americans could and did point to the presence of Poles in the Jamestown colony in 1608 and to Poles in British, Dutch, and Swedish colonies later in the century. In 1930 a Chicago Lithuanian-American newspaper, *Sandara* (Unity), promoted the idea of a celebration of the 250th anniversary of "the founding of the first Lithuanian colony in America" in 1688. These "Lithuanian Pilgrims" first settled on Guadeloupe Island near Cuba and then moved on to New York. The newspaper used their story as part of an argument against "a flood of un-American propaganda from the British who seek to give the United States an 'English character.'" "All American citizens, irrespective of national origin," the newspaper insisted, thus making a story of seventeenth-century immigrants part of a twentieth-century homemaking argument, "are guaranteed equal rights and opportunities by the Constitution." Similar stories, frequently based on well-documented evidence, abound in many other immigrant groups. A thick book was published in Minneapolis in 1916 about Norwegians in New Netherland. Correspondingly filiopietistic histories by Italian Americans have stories of the American deeds of Italians in the eighteenth century. Although the writer for a Romanian-American newspaper in 1942 had no evidence of many Romanian immigrants before the late 1890s, he made up for this by observing that "the first link between Romania and America was forged by Captain John Smith. Before going to Virginia, this gallant adventurer fought with the Romanians against the Turks."[60]

In the late nineteenth century the *Illinois Staats-Zeitung* saw no reason to compete with Americans of French, Swedish, or Norwegian origin when it frequently responded to the perceived nativism of another Chicago daily, the *Times*. On the contrary *Staats-Zeitung* could be magnanimous in its support of the rights of such groups to use their languages in the United States. As a newspaper representing the largest non-British immigrant group, it recognized only the Anglo-Americans as competitors for the status of German Americans as founders of the nation. On July 21, 1871, the issue was a recurrent one: a proposal to stop the teaching of German in the public schools. "We simply deny that English is the language of the country," the editor wrote, arguing not only with numbers ("For more than a million of American citizens German is the native language") but with the rights of German Americans as founders: "Their co-nationals have populated Pennsylvania and the Mohawk Valley possibly before the ancestors of Wilier F. Story [the *Times*'s editor] had emigrated from England."[61]

German-American leaders often spoke with a confidence that was seldom matched by those of other groups. In his speech at the celebration of the Vereinigten Deutschen Gesellschaften der Stadt New York (the United German Associations of New York City) in 1912, Julius Goebel, the University of Illinois professor, explained why the vision in "the Zionist leader" Israel Zangwill's play *The Melting Pot* was "unhistorical" so far as the Germans were concerned: "For we did not come to the American nation as an outcast or persecuted race seeking shelter and help but rather as a part of this nation with equal rights as members of a noble race that found its second home here more than two hundred years ago and has founded and built this society in cooperation with the Anglo-Saxon race." Another speaker, Albert J. W. Kern, used the image of two pillars—one pillar represented German history and the other German-

American history. The history of the United States rested firmly on the former and could be traced to the decisive Germanic victory over the Romans in A.D. 9. And American history was no less dependent on the latter, as Kern suggested in a series of rhetorical questions:

> Should not our American children, and in particular those of New York, learn that it was a German, Christiansen von Kleve, who built the first cabin on Manhattan Island in 1613, seven years before the arrival of the Pilgrim Fathers, that Minnewit, the first governor of the Dutch company, came from Wesel am Rhin, and that he was the one who purchased Manhattan Island from the Indians in 1626 for 60 guilder? Should not . . . Jacob Leisler from Frankfurt am Main be recognized as the first popularly elected governor of the Colony of New York? In American history he is branded as a traitor and yet he was a martyr for liberty. And Pastorius, Herchheimer, Mühlenberg, Steuben, and the other great men of our tribe, should not the rising generation learn what America owes to these pioneers? Should American history remain merely the history of the Anglo Saxons?

The homemaking argument of these German-American stories of foundation may not be different from those made in the stories of other ethnic groups. But the rhetoric of Kern's conclusion, while representative of the attitude of some German-Americans leaders, is rarely heard, even in their more celebratory moods, from leaders of other groups with more modest goals of acceptance: "We can change this and much else if we will. We have the right and the power on our side. If we agree! If we act together. If we learn how to do battle from Arminius of the Cherusci, from Luther, from Bismarck—if we speak German as Bismarck did with his enemies—and we will win."[62]

The right to a home in America is always the message, implied or explicit, in the foundation stories of immigrant groups. And foundation is not seen as something merely accomplished in the distant past but something that is achieved repeatedly as immigrants and the descendants of immigrants take part in the development and expansion of the land. Although immigrant groups have not always been given their due in the traditional "Old Settlers" celebrations of the rural and urban American West and Midwest, they have tried to make their voices heard. And their motivation has been the same as that expressed by H. L. Metes in his account of the contributions of Jewish Americans to the founding of Chicago and Illinois, "Illinois 100 Years Ago," which was published in the *Sunday Jewish Courier* for April 21, 1918: "The Jew is always and everywhere looked upon as a foreigner, as a guest. If there were a possibility—and there is one now—to show the world, even ourselves and our children, that we Jews have contributed much, very much to the remarkable growth and development of the State of Illinois, to neglect that opportunity would be a crime against ourselves and the future generations." In rural areas and cities, in counties and states all over the United States, central to the agenda of immigrant leaders has been to make people aware of the important contribution of their particular group to the "remarkable growth and development" of their country.

The stories used to demonstrate such contributions are too many even to enumerate. Many focus on enterprising and successful men in business, technology, and politics who on a local or national level contributed to the foundation of national success and prosperity. It may also be difficult to distinguish between stories of the kind considered in this chapter and those that are the subject of the chapter on stories of sacrifice. Many focus on how a member (a representative, in the mythic use of the stories) of an immigrant group has, like the Finnish or Swedish John Morton, saved or helped the nation in a time of crisis and thus secured the right to an American home for his mythic descendants. One such story, which will have to represent the many others, was central to Swedish Americans' celebrations of themselves and their right to an American home in the early decades of the twentieth century. Ironically, the hero of this story, John Ericsson, made little of his Swedish origin himself. For Swedish Americans of a later generation, however, he had, to borrow a term used by Willi Paul Adams, the status of a central "culture hero" in their homemaking mythology.[63]

Ericsson was an engineer who began his career as a topographical surveyor in the Swedish army and then went to England in 1829, where he, among other projects, constructed a steam locomotive for the competition won by George Stephenson's *Rocket*. Ericsson then turned to naval engineering and patented a screw propeller. For the U.S. Navy he fitted a small iron vessel, the *Princeton*, with engines and screw, and he immigrated soon after, in 1839. He became a citizen in 1848. During the Civil War his design for a steam-powered, screw-driven warship with a revolving armored turret was accepted by the navy, and on March 9, 1862, the *Monitor* successfully fought the Confederate *Virginia* at the Battle of Hampton Roads and prevented the destruction of other Union vessels. This success led to the building of more ships of the same type, which were important for the naval blockade of the Confederacy. There is little to connect the New York engineer Ericsson with the mass of Swedish immigrants to the Midwest and even less with the seventeenth-century Delaware River colony.

Nevertheless, beginning in 1888, the year before his death, when the

250th anniversary of the founding of New Sweden was celebrated in Minneapolis, Ericsson became a central character in Swedish-American mythology, along with the New Sweden colonists, at Swedish-American celebrations. In the main oration by William Widgery Thomas, a former minister to Sweden, Ericsson was the last in a long line of Swedish heroes and heroines from "Nordic antiquity" to the present. Hans Mattson, who had chaired the committee that organized the celebration, wrote in his memoirs a few years later about how a Swede, John Morton, had secured passage of "the sacred document" of American independence in 1776 and how, "nearly a century later," three other Swedes had contributed to the saving of the Union: Gen. Robert Anderson at Fort Sumter, Adm. J. A. B. Dahlgren, who designed artillery, and John Ericsson, "who by his inventive genius, saved the navy and the great seaports of the United States."[64]

Dag Blanck has shown how the Swedish-American Augustana Synod played a prominent role in making Ericsson a symbol of the great contribution of the Swedish-American people to the Republic, an effort that to some extent was crowned by the erection of a commemorative statue of the engineer near the Lincoln Memorial, with funds largely raised by the synod. In 1926, a year after he had in a similar manner praised the Norwegian Americans in St. Paul, President Calvin Coolidge spoke at the unveiling of the statue "in highly congratulatory terms of both Ericsson and Swedish Americans in general."

Ericsson was made to serve political purposes, for example, when a Swedish-American Republican League was formed in Illinois in the 1890s, but his most important use was as a cultural symbol. In the Augustana Synod's cultural periodical, *Prärieblomman* (Prairie Blossom), as well as in its journal for young people, *Ungdomsvännen* (Friend of Youth), he was featured in several articles and presented as "a typical Swedish American." A speech by the Reverend C. A. Blomberg, published in 1893, gave Ericsson truly heroic proportions as a crucial figure in "the defense of the American union and the abolition of slavery." Indeed, Blomberg drew a parallel between the late nineteenth-century engineer and the early seventeenth-century Swedish king, Gustavus Adolphus, and his chancellor, Axel Oxenstierna. Blomberg observed that "a son of Svea" emerged to save the United States "like Gustavus Adolphus and Oxenstierna came forth and saved Europe," and Blomberg concluded that "in the Pantheon of America . . . his [Ericsson's] picture will be placed among the foremost, and the jubilations of the people will be mixed with the waves of the Atlantic and the Pacific in a song of praise of the greatest Swede in the new World." And there was never any doubt that the great contribution of John Ericsson reflected favorably on all Swedish Americans, who vicariously could figure as saviors of the Republic. It is "appropriate for us Swedes to honor a man whose life lends credit to Swedes wherever they live and work," the church journal *Augustana* observed in 1912 on the fiftieth anniversary of the Battle of Hampton Roads.[65]

Presidents, governors, mayors, and other office holders turned up at all kinds of immigrant celebrations to make rather standard remarks about the greatness and the contributions of whatever group they were visiting. Rank-and-file immigrants as well as leaders were gratified by this attention. As we have seen, however, politicians found it difficult to honor one group without appearing to neglect or even denigrate another. While men in political office, locally as well as nationally, necessarily were acquainted with the foundation stories of the many immigrant groups that made up their constituencies, one may with good reason doubt whether they were so impressed that they began to regard these foreign-born potential voters as "real" Americans and the equals of Anglo-Americans in status and importance in history, culture, and social life.

Evaluating the effect of the writing of Finnish-American "nationalists," Gary London concludes that "there is little evidence that their efforts to elevate the level of public consciousness regarding the significance of the Delaware Finns and the Finnish ancestry of John Morton had much effect on the improving position of Finnish immigrants." Rather, he observes, "legitimacy for Finnish-Americans came largely as a result of environmental change and improvement in their education, occupations, and income. With an increase in their standard of living, Finns broke the barriers of identification with the lower class and advanced into middle-class respectability."[66] The same point could probably be made about all the European immigrant groups discussed in this chapter. But, as London suggests, the repeated telling of such stories and the insistence that they were evidence of a right to a home in America may have hastened "the Americanization of the Finns" and other immigrant groups. The telling of the stories was of course an expression of a desire to be—and to be regarded as—Americans. Faith in the mythic meaning of these stories may well have helped individual immigrants to relate to an American history that otherwise tended not to mention them, except as problematic immigrants, members of the foreign huddled masses who should be grateful for being allowed to camp on the grounds of the Anglo-American home. Whatever function these foundation stories may have had in the past, they are mostly either forgotten today or exist merely as ritualistic elements in a largely symbolic ethnicity.[67]

3 Sacrifice: We Have Given Our Blood

THE HORROR THAT IS WAR has in recorded history been given a coating made up of all manly virtues and even some sweetness and decorum. This dressing-up of ugliness in pretty garments is not only a political exercise but also a traditional academic one. This is, perhaps, exemplified in one of the John Singer Sargent murals in Harvard University's Widener Memorial Library, in which, at the moment of death, a World War I soldier embraces two female figures, one representing Victory, the other Death, over the legend: "Happy those who with a glowing faith in one embrace clasped death and victory." In time, pain, death, and unimaginable horror may become both dulce and decora in the context of patriotism rather than of the battlefield. The ethnic celebration of war and the heroes of war are no different than national celebrations in this respect. In this chapter what may appear as meaningless suffering and death to the jaundiced eye is always noble and full of purpose. The suffering is made especially noble because it is not only for the glory of the patria but on behalf of the ethnic group. Its purpose is to demonstrate "our" right to a home in America. Typically, one filiopietistic ethnic history is dedicated "to the memory of the Polish pioneers of America, who always worked loyally and bravely died for the cause of the United States."[1] In this, it is implied, they also worked and died for the recognition of Polish Americans.

Such attitudes are in no way peculiar to American immigrants nor to the United States. "Willingness to die for a collective cause is the supreme seal of national faith," David Lowenthal has observed, and immigrant leaders who pointed to evidence of such willingness among the members of their group were acting in accordance with views as powerful in the countries they had left as in the one they had chosen. "The Fatherland is the land of our fathers, the soil cleared and defended by them," the French right-wing nationalist Jean-Marie Le Pen put it in 1984; "the foreigner . . . can be integrated into the Fatherland only by a sacrificial act: the spilling of his blood."[2]

It is not always possible to make a clear distinction between some of the stories that Chapter 2 discusses as myths of foundation and those considered here as myths of sacrifice. Although his place was at the drawing board and in the workshop rather than on the battlefield, John Ericsson "saved" the Union in a naval battle in one of the central Swedish-American homemaking stories.[3] Indeed, John Morton played not only a crucial role in the creation of the United States by casting the deciding vote in 1776 on behalf of either the Swedish or the Finnish Americans, depending on who was telling the story; in at least one Finnish-American novel he is also a hero on the battlefields of the Revolutionary War as the leader of brave Finnish-American volunteers.[4] Although heroes who have actually died for the United States figure prominently in homemaking arguments, those who have merely demonstrated their willingness to do so through their bravery in America's wars are equally present. Wars are not only won on the battlefield, moreover, and narratives of other kinds of loyal support of their country in times of crisis also enter into the homemaking arguments of American immigrant groups.

In many foundation stories the history of the United States begins with the first arrival in the western hemisphere of a German, a Scandinavian, a Greek, a Jew, or the "representative" of some other nineteenth-century immigrant group, depending on the occasion and on who is telling the story. In stories of sacrifice the history of the United States begins with the crucial role played by one or several Poles, Lithuanians, Italians, Germans, or others, again depending on the occasion and on who is telling the story, in the War of Independence. In immigrant foundation stories the country is founded and refounded by successive groups. Similarly, in stories of sacrifice the Republic is not saved once and for all but saved again and again in a series of crises. All wars between the United States and other nations, however, do not have equal status in these stories. There are few stories where participation in massacres of Indians form part of a homemaking argument. Nor is much made of the war with Britain in 1812 or of the conquest of large areas of Mexico in 1848. The battlefields on which immigrants have demonstrated their right to a home in America have mainly been those of the Revolutionary War, the Civil War, the war with Spain in 1898, and World War I.

By the time of the Second World War the need to argue for the right to a home in America was no longer so strongly felt in most European immigrant groups. German-American associations have not celebrated Eisenhower as evidence of their loyalty and contribution to America. He was simply (and in his own view) an American. Ethnic organizations based on immigration from allied European countries did engage in relief and information work for their countries of origin during World War II, but this was usually done on the basis of being confidently American.[5] To a great extent the American home by this time was comfortable for most European immigrant groups, and little of the excessive insistence on immigrant American loyalty, so typical of the homefront during the First World War, was in evidence. The experience of Japanese immigrants, still denied the citizenship that the Naturalization Act of 1790 limited to "free white persons," was tragically different.[6] Although European immigrants were no longer exposed to the racism of the early decades of the century, once again immigrants from some European countries experienced a need to affirm their American loyalty during the Second World War.

One such immigrant group was the Romanian Americans, whose country of origin was allied with the Axis. Beginning in 1942, the journal *New Pioneer* was "published periodically by the Cultural Association for Americans of Romanian Descent, with national headquarters in Cleveland, Ohio." In the first issue the editors typically promised to "publish anything and everything about the war activities of our youth in the American armed forces" and had a letter of loyalty addressed to the president on the front page. Also typically, the letter was careful to distinguish between "aliens" from Romania and "the German, Italian and Japanese aliens." As we have noted, homemaking arguments often argue for an exclusive right. Typical as well is the intention to speak not only to members of the group but to the "thousands who until now had no way of being informed about us." The main article in this World War II journal, however, concerns another and much earlier war: "Two Romanians in the Civil War." The implied point is that although we may have been few, "we" have fought bravely for our country in time of need and will do so again.[7] The scholarly bibliography by Vladimir Wertsman, *The Romanians in America and Canada: A Guide to Information Sources,* may not in itself be a contribution to the homemaking branch of history, but much of the historical writing it surveys is of a filiopietistic nature. The very themes by which the history part of the bibliography is organized reflects the homemaking intentions of most of the publications listed. The headings are "Colonial Period" (one entry), "Civil War" (seven entries focusing on the two Romanians referred to earlier), "Spanish-American War" (one entry), "World War I" (four entries), "World War II" (six entries) and "Post–World War II" with one entry that is also concerned with military service. In writing about their history in the United States, then, Romanian Americans have, apart from the one article on an early colonial presence, largely been concerned with presenting stories of sacrifice.[8]

This exclusive focus on participation in wars is an extreme instance of a kind of filiopietistic history writing found in most immigrant groups. Of the five main sections in Miecislaus Haiman's *Polish Past in America, 1608–1865* (1939), two concern discovery and a colonial presence, and two are devoted to the American Revolution and the Civil War. The sacrifice made by Italians on behalf of all Italian Americans is an important part of Michael Musmanno's homemaking argument: "Italians have fought for the United States in every war in which she has pitted her might, honor, and destiny against those who would destroy her. Italian fighters for American freedom have been lowered into graves in nearly every one of the states, but those graves were not always marked nor 'long remembered.'"[9]

It should not be difficult to appreciate the need and motivation behind so much of immigrant filiopietistic writing about participation in American wars. Immigrants have tended to be invisible in both scholarly and popular war histories. In part, this may be because their diaries, letters, and memoirs in languages other than English have not been accessible to most U.S. scholars. This kind of material has rarely been systematically collected by historical societies, except for those organized by immigrants and their descendants. Even when immigrant source material may be physically available, it has nevertheless not been so for linguistic reasons.

An equally important reason for the lack of attention paid to the large numbers of immigrants fighting for the United States, however, is that they have been regarded as foreigners, not as real Americans.[10] Although it is true that a so-called foreign-language newspaper would primarily write about American wars with a focus on the activities of members of the immigrant group for which it was published, the English-language newspapers would in a similar fashion focus on Anglo-Americans, making immigrants virtually invisible. With a few notable exceptions such as Lafayette, main characters who speak languages other than English have been absent from Anglo-American accounts of America's wars. In a similar manner they have been excluded from histories and popular fictions of the

West.[11] Little wonder, then, that immigrant leaders saw an obligation to make the loyalty and sacrifice of immigrants visible and in doing so to promote the view of immigrants as Americans, not foreigners.

Immigrant leaders were not entirely without assistance in their endeavors. Beginning with George Washington, presidents have on occasion spoken or written in praise of their foreign-born constituents. In part such praise may well have been prompted by genuine admiration. In part it has also surely been an expression of political expedience. Whatever the motives behind public proclamations or more personal statements may have been, they have always been taken to heart by the immigrant groups involved and made use of by their leaders. In homemaking stories and arguments no praise has been coveted as much as that from the mouth of Washington. Whether his praise is historically documented or pure fiction is less important here than its mythic use.

A main architect of the Swedish-American homemaking mythology was Johan Enander, and in a speech he made in 1890 at an "Our Forefathers' Day" celebration in Chicago he wove together the many strands of his story. Fittingly, his vision of Swedish-American history, which began with the arrival of Vikings around 1000, is entitled "En Dröm" (A Dream). He placed "Swedish-American troops," that is, descendants of the colonists who had come to the Delaware River area almost 150 years earlier, at the front lines of the Battle of Trenton and had George Washington reflecting, "If only all my troops were such heroes as these descendants of Swedes, to whom no undertaking is too difficult, no obstacle insurmountable or no duty too heavy."[12]

Writing about Washington's death, Angelo Guidi had him not only aware of the many Italians who had "fallen by his side, fighting for a country they did not consider foreign" but becoming one with them: "In the silence of the tomb, Glory united the Leader of the Victorious Army of America and the First President of the United States with the dauntless Italian heroes, forgotten or unknown, who had fallen fighting for America, asking for naught."[13] One implied argument here, as in all stories of sacrifice, is that because those who gave their lives did not consider America a "foreign" country, their "descendants" should not be considered foreign in the country of their choice. More specifically, the stories involving George Washington have the implied message that those who have been welcomed as Americans by the father of the nation cannot be foreigners.

It has been important for members of many immigrant groups to be able to say that "they" took part in the Revolutionary War. Some groups have singled out specific heroes for celebration. Such heroes were evidently so often talked about and their exploits so well known to the members of a particular group that the mere mention of a name was considered sufficient to evoke an appropriate response from an audience. Such a hero for Italian Americans was Francesco Vigo (1740–1836), whose exploits in the West during the war earned him the title "Savior of the Midwest" in one filiopietistic account. In 1936 George J. Spatuzza proposed to the Illinois chapter of the Order of the Sons of Italy in America that an annual banquet be held for all young men and women of Italian descent residing in Illinois who had been awarded a university diploma. Spatuzza, an officer in the organization, explained that he intended "by this noble gesture inspired by a disinterested principle of brotherhood, to confer deserved value on that conspicuous contribution of Latin intelligence and initiative, that the offspring of the immigrant is ready to offer to this land so dear to us, *because it is the land of* Columbus, Vespucci, Verrazzano, Toriti, Vigo, Meucci, and many others, who are too numerous to be mentioned." Not only was the homemaking function of these heroes made explicit; it is also evident that they were assumed to be well known to the intended audience. In similar manner Albert J. W. Kern could simply list names in his speech of welcome at the banquet for the tenth anniversary of the Vereinigten Deutschen Gesellschaften der Stadt New York (United German Associations of New York City): "Pastorius, Herchheimer, Mühlenberg, Steuben and the other great men of our tribe."[14] Apart from Pastorius—the founder of Germantown, Pennsylvania, in 1683—these were officers in the Continental Army: Niklas Herkimer, who commanded militia in the Mohawk Valley; John Peter Gabriel Muhlenberg, son of the organizer of the first Lutheran synod in America and the commander of infantry at the Battle of Yorktown; and Frederick William von Steuben, the Prussian officer who did much to train the Continental Army. Their names have a prominent place in the German-American homemaking story. They were so prominent that Kern was confident that the mere mention of the names would be enough to evoke the stories behind them in his listeners' minds.[15]

When the 250th anniversary of the "Settlement of the Jews in the United States" was celebrated in New York in 1905, the address that focused on early history, "The Jewish Pilgrim Fathers" by Dr. Joseph Krauskopf, noted that "scarcely had he [i.e., the Jew] settled at New Amsterdam, when he voluntarily asked to be permitted to render military service alongside the other burghers."

> Well may our heart swell with pride as we follow the record of the Jew in the War of Independence. . . . Read the names of those who shed their

heart's blood on the battlefields fighting for *their country's liberty,* and you read the names of scores of Jews. Read the names of those who poured forth their treasures and their all to enable the colonies to carry on their war for independence, and among the most generous and most self-sacrificing, stand the names of scores of Jewish patriots. Read the name of the lieutenant of Benedict Arnold, and note that while the general is found guilty of foul treason, the lieutenant is entrusted with special dispatches to Franklin at the court of France—and that lieutenant is a Jew. Read the names of the patriots who made possible the proud monument of Bunker Hill, and you find one of the two givers of princely sums a Jew.[16]

Even then, as the country was in the making, it was *their* country and the war they fought to make this country was *their* war. How, it is implied, could this country not be the country of the descendants of nineteenth-century Jewish immigrants? In homemaking myths descent is by association, that is, imagined.

In an address in Salem, Massachusetts, some years later—*The Contribution of the Chosen Race to Civic Progress in America*—Max Goldberg spends much time on the Jewish contribution to America's wars, and in particular to the War of Independence, noting both the relatively large number of active participants and instances of particular heroism as well as the significant financial contributions of Haym Salomon.[17] But the Jews were not alone in securing the independence of their country. In the stories of so many groups their particular representative heroes are singled out in the sense that it may appear that each group is unique in its heroic sacrifice. Thus Dr. Thomas Baxevanis, in a 1931 speech entitled "Enlightening the Americans About Grecian Contributions," reminded his listeners that "during the American Revolution a grandfather of the Greek patriot, Ypsilanti, served under Washington, with a number of Greek volunteers who distinguished themselves in several battles."[18] These Italian, German, Jewish, and Greek speakers were all arguing that the imagined descendants of those who fought in the War of Independence could not be considered outsiders in America.

Although many groups in this manner made much of "their" participation in the American Revolution, few made it the very cornerstone of their homemaking argument, as did the Polish Americans in their celebration of their two heroes, Casimir Pulaski and Thaddeus Kosciuszko, especially the latter.[19] On January 23, 1907, the *Dziennik Chicagoski* (Chicago Daily) had an article on the many significant Polish contributions "to American life," indeed to humanity as a whole, listing names of scientists, musicians, and writers such as Copernicus, Marie Curie, Ignacy Paderewski, Henryk Sienkiewicz, and Joseph Conrad. "But no Pole is so secure of a predominant, a living place, in American history, as Kosciuszko. No American can hear the name of Kosciuszko without remembering with the deepest gratitude his valuable service to his country."

The names of the two Polish heroes of the Revolutionary War were religiously brought up in all manner of contexts in which attention was called to Polish contributions to U.S. society. The editorial by the *Dziennik Zwiazkowy* (Alliance Daily) for Decoration Day, May 29, 1911, naturally drew attention to the Civil War, noting that there "were not very many Poles at that time in America, but those who happened to be there contributed also their share of blood and hardship," as did, for example, General Wladimir Krzyzanowski. Polish Americans, the editor wrote, were aware that the war was fought "for the purpose of preserving the Union of this great Republic." But the central concern of the editorial is to confirm the Polish memory of Kosciuszko and Pulaski. In 1914 the editorial in the *Dziennik Zwiazkowy* for the next day's "Fourth of July, Greatest American Holiday," again reminds its readers of the two heroes: "Pulaski sacrificed his life at Savannah, in the state of Georgia. Kosciuszko was the spirit of the entire colonial war, giving inestimable services to the new nation as engineer, building entrenchments and forts which exist until to-day (West Point) and which give testimony to the genius of our national hero and his commander in chief." Washington was not the only president whose name was linked with that of Kosciuszko. On February 12, 1915, the *Dziennik Zwiazkowy* reminded its readers that it was the birthday of two great men: Abraham Lincoln, "the emancipator of the slaves," and Thaddeus Kosciuszko, "the hero of two hemispheres." "These two, although not contemporaries, were beautifully alike in spirit," the editorial concluded, echoing the notion of Washington's becoming Italian in his dying moment.

Columbus monuments were a priority for many Italian-American organizations. Monuments to honor the two Polish-American heroes had a similar place in the homemaking work of Polish Americans. Kosciuszko was especially suited for Polish-American hero worship because he had fought for American as well as for Polish liberty and independence.[20] With one gesture Polish Americans could both point to a convincing homemaking argument and express support for the independence of the old homeland. Despite this, however, it was no simple matter to create the kind of concerted action necessary to raise the money and pull the political strings necessary for a large public monument. When Polish organizations finally were able to unite in a successful celebration of the designated Polish Day on October 7, 1893, in connection with the World's Columbian Exposition in Chicago, it seemed that it would also be possible to get support from all factions for a Kosciuszko monument. But Greene notes that several years later, in 1896, the monument fund was still so small that critics suggested it be "used for some other purpose." For Greene this is an illustration of how warring factions within the Polish-American community made concerted action difficult. However, it should also be appreciated that working-class immigrants did not have much money to spare and that their parishes would have given a higher priority to their charities than to monuments.[21]

Moreover, Kosciuszko did not have the same all-American symbolic appeal as Columbus. Nor could he possibly have had the same monumental importance for Polish Americans as Columbus had and to some extent still has for Italian Americans. Lack of concord among Polish Americans does not mean that their hero ceased to function as an important ethnic symbol. That same year there was an appeal in the *Dziennik Chicagoski* to "all Polish businessmen, grocers, butchers, etc." to close their doors on the Fourth of July in honor of "the great Kosciuszko Festival" to be held in a city park. As noted by Jon Gjerde, national celebrations could, as in this instance, successfully accommodate immigrants' need to signal "multiple loyalties."[22] On the Fourth of July Polish Americans could affirm their allegiance to the United States, celebrate their own participation in the War of Independence, and demonstrate solidarity with the cause for Polish independence.

The Thaddeus Kosciuszko monument was eventually completed. The unveiling ceremony in Chicago's Humboldt Park in 1904 has, along with the ordination of the first Polish-American bishop in 1908 and Polish Day at the Columbian Exposition in 1893, been characterized as "a landmark in the history of Polish America."[23] The *Narod Polski* noted one indication of how Kosciuszko had opened doors for the acceptance of Polish Americans in the American home: "Information of the great celebration was appraised properly by the local press, not only the Polish but all others, not excluding the German newspapers." But the main proof that the "lone fact of the unveiling of the monument is an incident of great importance to us" was the "message of the President of the Republic and the telegrams sent to us from Lwow, Cracow, Warsaw and Poznan."

Surely, readers did not miss the suggestion that their loyalties could be multiple yet undivided nor the reminder that as Americans they could be greeted by the president of an undivided nation but that the telegrams from the old homeland were from the three different sections of a divided nation. That the Polish-American committee member who presented the monument to the state park commissioners was the city attorney and that the park commissioner who accepted the monument on behalf of the state also was a Polish American had a similar signal effect. The monument "draped with Polish and American flags" must have been a spectacular sight to the fifty thousand participants in the parade with seven hundred floats. More important, it also symbolized their acceptance not simply as Americans but as Americans of Polish descent. When "the telegram from President Theodore Roosevelt, congratulating the Poles on their great accomplishment" was read to the crowd estimated at 100,000, it was "received by a thunder of applause and joyful cheer."[24] Of course, this event did not give any real solutions to the many social and economic problems confronting most Polish Americans. Nor did the even greater symbolic event in Washington, D.C., in 1910 when national monuments to both Polish-American heroes were unveiled. The importance of such events for identity building and homemaking should nevertheless not be undervalued.

Thaddeus Kosciuszko was certainly a Polish-American hero, but the question of whether he was Polish or Lithuanian was complicated by the changing borders and sovereignties in so much of Europe. Twentieth-century concepts of nationhood cannot be comfortably applied to the eighteenth century. According to one authority, the Lithuanian-American Chicago newspaper *Sandara*, in 1930, "Tad Koscinsko [was] the great Lithuanian hero of the American Revolution." In the 1890s, despite a growing Lithuanian nationalism, some members of both immigrant groups were still trying to get them to work together for a Kosciuszko monument. The *Lietuva* (Lithuanian) appealed to its readers to "take example from the Poles one way or the other, [and] help to raise money for this great cause." "While Kosciuszko was a Lithuanian," the editor explained, "we Lithuanians must help the Poles. It is our duty to remember our great man of the past." The relationship soured, however, because one of the ways in which Lithuanian-American leaders tried to gain recognition for their group and develop immigrant pride in a distinct Lithuanian heritage was to distance themselves from the Poles. Polish-American newspapers do not mention Lithuanian participation in the 1904 unveiling ceremony in Humboldt Park in Chicago. Some years later, on April 23, 1909, a headline in the *Lietuva* declared, "The Poles Are Eternal Enemies of Lithuanians." Cooperation between the two peoples was now impossible, even though the newspaper acknowledged that there was reason to be proud that Kosciuszko, "a son of Lithuania[,] is recognized as a hero and a pillar of liberty." Three weeks earlier the newspaper had urged a Lithuanian boycott of the celebrations in Washington set for the following year.[25]

Fewer in number than their neighbors, Lithuanian Americans were not as successful as Polish Americans in gaining recognition for Kosciuszko as their particular American hero. Indeed, the recognition of Kosciuszko as Lithuanian was secondary to the primary and very basic aim of Lithuanian-American leaders of gaining recognition for themselves as Lithuanian Americans. Not until 1910 did the U.S. Bureau of the Census cease to register Lithuanians as either Russian or Polish and recognize them as a distinct group. Although the contexts may be different, this conflict between two ethnic groups over one and the same hero is quite similar to the Finnish-American and Swedish-American dispute regarding the true identity of John Morton.

At the turn of the nineteenth century, the Civil War was far more present in people's minds than the distant War of Independence. On Decoration Day, in areas with large numbers of European immigrants (which would be in Union states rather than in those of the former Confederacy), veterans marched, speeches were held at monuments, and children in public schools were reminded of the virtues of patriotism and sacrifice. Little was said on such occasions by representatives of the Anglo-American cultural and social elite about the special contributions made by immigrants in saving the Union. It is nevertheless a fact that many regiments were largely made up of members of a specific immigrant group and that the language of command in such regiments would often be a language other than English, such as German.[26] Consequently, ethnic veterans' organizations were also common and played important roles in the group's efforts to be recognized as more American than other groups.

After the meeting of a Swedish soldiers' convention in 1878, the *Svenska Tribunen* (Swedish Tribune) reminded its readers of the time when "it was requested of every man to offer [i.e., sacrifice] himself on the country's altar" and that among those who responded "were thousands and thousands who called this country their adopted land. Their offer [i.e., sacrifice] was the greatest, their love the purest. Among them were the Swedes. With unusual willingness did they obey the call issued by Lincoln, and they fought bravely on the battlefields."[27] In one Swedish-American story about Civil War participation, the Union was saved on an engineer's drawing board; in another (from 1895), the abolition of slavery was decided in midwestern voting booths in 1860 and 1864. As the *Svenska Tribunen* of February 27, 1895, explained,

> It is a fact that Abraham Lincoln never could have been elected president of the Republic had it not been for the Scandinavians in the West, who so unanimously voted for him. . . . Had he failed to be elected president—well, nobody knows how it might have gone with the Union. It

is quite possible . . . that there would have been a compromise between the North and the South, and that the latter would have kept their beloved institution, slavery. That would have been a tremendous blow for the growth of the world for human victory over darkness and force. A few thousand Swedish-American votes cast as one in the political issue weighed the balance.

Swedish Americans were not alone in telling such stories. The readers of the *Illinois Staats-Zeitung* for January 29, 1901, were reminded that the Union had actually been saved on that same day in 1854 by "Chicago's Germans" who "fashioned our national history." The reason for "this memorable event" was German resentment of Stephen Douglas's Kansas-Nebraska bill. "Incendiary resolutions were passed, denouncing the growth of slavery." Although the bill allowing federal territories to decide whether to enter as free or slave states eventually became law, a majority of Germans changed their allegiance from the Democratic to the new Republican Party, and "the great gathering of Germans on January 29, 1854, represents the first intense manifestation of an irate public's opinion about" the bill. The switch to the Republicans was not without its problems, however, because of the nativist element in the party. Again, on February 22, Germans saved the Union, this time by proposing a resolution against nativism at the founding party convention in Decatur, Illinois.

As in so many homemaking stories, representatives of various ethnic groups stood by the federal government when independent nationhood was in the balance, so here in Decatur in 1854 the German George Schneider and Abraham Lincoln together carried the day: "Gentlemen!" said Lincoln, "Mr. Schneider's resolution is nothing new. It is contained in the Declaration of Independence. And you cannot form a new party based on principles of persecution and proscriptive laws!" Not only had German Americans stood up for their country in a time of crisis but they had done so by honoring American principles embedded in the Declaration of Independence and with the support of Abraham Lincoln. And the newspaper is careful to note that those Germans who remained with the Democratic Party stood, with Douglas, for the Union. They were all inspired by the same patriotism that "prompted the German Democrats, in common with German Republicans, to fight for the tenets of the Union."[28]

More common than stories of special technological or political contributions to safeguarding the Union are the stories of actual blood sacrifice. Not only did "official" accounts of the war seldom pay much attention to the multiethnic composition of the Union army but some immigrant groups found themselves being attacked for not standing up for their country. The December 1891 issue of *North American Review* had a brief article by J. M. Rogers, who insisted that in the course of eighteen months of service in the Civil War, he could not "recall meeting one Jew in uniform or hearing of any Jewish soldier." Nor had he in the years after the war "found any who remembered serving with Jews . . . except in General Sherman's department, and he promptly ordered them out of it for speculating in cotton and conveying information to the Confederates."[29] This overtly anti-Semitic accusation became the occasion of several attempts to set the record straight, among them an article by Simon Wolf in the *Washington Post* (December 10, 1891) and one by Frederik Mayer in the *Reform Advocate* (January 2, 1892). These articles list the names of some Jewish officers and their exploits and give accounts of Jewish companies in demonstration of the readiness of Jews to sacrifice themselves for their country of choice.[30]

Some years later, in 1905, Emil G. Hirsch explicitly used Jewish participation in the Civil War as a symbol of America as the rightful home of Jews. Arguing against Zionism, he explained that "we need not return to Palestine. We need no special flag. We have a flag of our own, the flag for which 6,000 Jews, twenty per cent of the Jewish population at that time, offered up their lives in the great combat against slavery." Through sacrifice in war, Jews had made the American flag their own. They should therefore not be considered hyphenated Americans with "a foreign prefix to the glorious title of simple American." In this they are the equal partners of the Anglo-Americans, or, as Hirsch put it, "Our people alone have stood shoulder to shoulder with that sturdy type of citizenship which created and has maintained the public schools of this country."[31] As is so often the case when ethnic group leaders are developing homemaking arguments, the claim is an exclusive one: "our people alone."

As late as 1930, the *Reform Advocate* was drawing attention to Jewish sacrifice in the Civil War. Now, however, the story of the company of Jewish volunteers in the Eighty-second Illinois Volunteers is retold more to create ethnic pride in general and pride in the B'nai B'rith in particular than as part of a homemaking argument:

> At the outbreak of the Civil War, under the auspices of the Ramah Lodge, a mass meeting of Chicago Jews was called for the purpose of raising money to recruit a company of Jewish volunteers to form a part of the 82nd Regiment of Illinois Volunteers commanded by Colonel Frederick Hecker and Lieutenant Colonel Edward S. Solomon. . . . With one exception, all of the officers of the company were Jews and they achieved a splendid record in the war. Shortly after the enlistment, brothers Henry Greenebaum, Abraham Hart and Joseph Frank went to Camp Butler near

Springfield to deliver a regimental flag which had been made by Jewish women whose husbands and brothers were affiliated with Ramah Lodge. The flag was entrusted to the Jewish company, Company C[,] and the same flag was carried throughout the war by a Jewish soldier named Levi. A committee of Ramah Lodge was very active all through the war in seeing to it that the families of the married men in the company were properly taken care of and also carried on a recruiting office to secure recruits. On June 17th, 1865, the 82nd regiment returned to Chicago. The flag was riddled with bullets and out of the thousand members of the regiment, only two hundred and fifty returned.[32]

One element that distinguishes this story from most similar ethnic stories of Civil War sacrifice is the inclusion of families left behind and of what later became known as the homefront.

All immigrant groups had voices that spoke loudly of blood sacrifice and of serving the nation in the Civil War. As seen in the example of Romanian parading of Civil War heroes during World War II, the period and the manner in which this was done would depend on the period of main immigration and the degree of integration. Thus Russians, who in 1934 regarded themselves as belonging to "the most recent national groups of immigrants in this country," would point to one of their own who had served the Union as a general and who had been personally recognized by Lincoln.[33] By this time Swedish Americans had little need to distinguish themselves in this manner, but their nineteenth-century leaders, such as Hans Mattson, had done so frequently and insistently some decades earlier: "When . . . the great rebellion burst upon the land, a gallant descendant of the Swedes, Gen. Robert Anderson, met its first shock at Fort Sumter, and, during the bitter struggle of four years which followed, the Scandinavian-Americans were as true and loyal to their adopted country as their native-born neighbors, giving their unanimous support to the cause of the Union and fighting valiantly for it."[34]

In evaluating this kind of ethnic glorification of blood sacrifice, which is obviously related to a rather primitive breast-beating nationalism, keep in mind that both the context and the aim of this kind of ethnic fervor distinguish it from the extreme nationalism known as chauvinism. It is best understood as a knocking on the door of a home that will not accept you as a full member of the family. And the loudness and insistence of the knocking is more a response to being closed out than it is a glorification of ethnic excellence. Moreover, the collective experience of the door's either not being opened or, if opened, all too often being slammed shut again, led to an internalized acceptance of the point of view of the door-keepers and a negative self-image that, as perceived by immigrant leaders, was in sore need of uplift. To confuse the stories of how Americans of Swedish, German, or Jewish descent had been the saviors of the nation with expressions of chauvinism in nation-states would be a serious misreading of the homemaking arguments of American immigrants.

Czechs, or Bohemians as they were known at the turn of the nineteenth century, were one of many groups with the additional problem of not having an easily identifiable national identity before the creation of Czechoslovakia and other nation-states after World War I. When Louis Pregler wrote to the *Chicago Tribune* on July 31, 1879, to complain of the newspaper's confusion of Bohemians with Germans, his way of trying to make Bohemians visible as an American ethnic group was to point to the sacrifices of his people: "I think myself justified in recalling to memory our last Civil War. . . . Then we can see how many Bohemians carried arms in the service of the United States, and see how many Bohemians died on the battlefield; also how many widow[s] and orphans are crying for their husband[s] and fathers. Our most respectable and honorable men have been in the service of the United States." This particular writer had recently served in the U.S. Army in the West under a General Miles, and his letter to the editor, which also points to Bohemians as "amongst the massacred ones" with Custer, is the only instance I have seen of using participation in the wars against the Native Americans as part of the homemaking argument. Pregler's was not a lone voice among Bohemians, however, in calling attention to his people's sacrifice during the Civil War.

As in other immigrant groups, Decoration Day was an important day for ethnic celebration and ethnic memory among Czech Americans. In 1915 a large gathering in Chicago commemorated "what the Bohemians did for their new country during the great Civil War." On the same occasion two years earlier a speaker had noted, "Today the American nation observes a great holiday, the next greatest after Independence Day. . . . But we who are assembled here are not Americans, only. Our hearts burn with ardent love for two countries, and thus we think with pride of those Bohemians who, in going to the war, followed their patriotism as Americans, their American conviction." That such celebrations were central to an immigrant group's homemaking argument is made clear in the important lesson to be drawn from the proud history of Bohemians as warriors, in Europe as well as in the United States: "Let America learn that she has taken into her great family members of an honorable nation—a nation whose sons are always ready to seal with blood their pledge of love and devotion to the land of their choice and to its liberty."[35]

As might be expected, such occasions marked an increase in the intensity of expressions of nationalism among Czechs and other immigrant groups that originated in regions within the Austrian-Hungarian Empire in the period before and during World War I. But the use of Decoration Day to promote ethnic pride was by no means limited to this period of national awakening at the prospect of independence. On May 30, 1892, the Chicago newspaper *Svornost* (Unity) reported on the "Unveiling Ceremonies at the Bohemian National Cemetery" as a "Grand Bohemi-an-American Manifestation." The editor explained: "It proved that Bo-hemians do not come to this land merely to enjoy its freedom,—but that whenever the occasion requires it, they are willing to defend this free-dom with their lives. . . . Even if we are not as strong numerically as other nationalities, still the American people must realize that the Bohemian element is one of the strongest pillars in the foundation of this republic."

Jon Gjerde's concept of a "complementary identity" helps us under-stand how, after the new country of Czechoslovakia was created at the end of World War I, the Czechoslovak Independence Day could in the United States be used to celebrate American nationalism and to com-memorate Czech-American sacrifices for the land of their choice. In its reminder of the Independence Day celebrations in Chicago on October 28, 1922, *Denní Hlasatel* reported three days earlier that there would be a ceremony in memory of the Czechs who "during the memorable years of 1861–1865, under the presidency of Abraham Lincoln, stood embat-tled under The Star-Spangled Banner to shed their blood for the equality and the rights of humanity." Now, however, a more recent war loomed larger in people's minds. While only a "mere handful of aged [Czech] veterans of the Civil War" would be present, the newspaper noted that far more and younger "American veterans in full uniform" from the world war would be taking part in the ceremony. Although the occasion was the celebration of the independence of a European country, the message was that Czech Americans had sacrificed their blood for their own coun-try, for the United States.

The various ethnic Civil War stories largely follow a common pattern. Although they of course differ in that they highlight the quite special ef-forts of particular groups, they all tend to focus on service to the Union. Although in these stories the members of each group are inspired by the quite special and inherent national (or racial) qualities of the group in ques-tion, they are always motivated by the same love and loyalty to their cho-sen country and its great ideals. The ethnic accounts of World War I sac-rifices, however, are not only more competitive than those about the Civil War, they are also often implicitly or explicitly motivated by the wartime status of the European homeland. Although German Americans had to

argue for their loyalty and their sacrifices for a skeptical audience that identified them with the enemy, members of groups whose countries stood
to benefit from an Allied victory and thus had a common cause with the
United States could bask in the warmth of public sympathy.

Such special pleading for the common cause of ethnic group and
nation, however, was not limited to the World War I or to contemporary
events. A special Jewish version of the war with Spain in 1898 was that
Jews had more to remember and revenge than the *Maine* and that they
therefore were inspired by a greater national fervor than most other
Americans:

> When war was declared in the Congress of the United States against
> Spain, the Jews of this country were instantly aroused. The reasons as-
> cribed for their interest were two-fold, to demonstrate their patriotism
> and loyalty to the country which had given them a home and a place of
> refuge; and they would take part in a war to help two oppressed nations,
> Cuba and Porto Rico [*sic*] in their struggle for liberty and independence,
> against the yoke of Spain. But back of the two obvious reasons there was
> a third one which was not openly admitted by the Jew, even to himself;
> namely a secret desire to avenge the thousands of Jewish martyrs who
> perished during the days of the Inquisition. These three reasons, each of
> which was sufficient to stir the heart of every Jew, who was able to bear
> arms, and give his life in a conflict for his beloved United States and
> against his old foe, Spain. It kindled a flame in the hearts of American
> Jewry which broke out into a conflagration. Three violent passions of the
> human heart were now at play in the soul of the American Jew: Patrio-
> tism, love of liberty, and revenge.

The article, published in the *Reform Advocate* on May 31, 1930, reflects
on "the great change wrought in the soul of the Jew" by immigration: "In
the land of the Czars he made every effort to escape military service; in
the new land he made every effort to give his very life in return for the
privileges which he received." So while the Jew had a centuries-old common cause with the United States in the war with Spain, it was as an
American, as a new man in a new land, that he had not only the opportunity but the patriotic spirit "to give his very life" for a cause that was
at once both American and Jewish. The article also speaks of neglect and
lack of recognition in a manner similar to that of so many other ethnic
stories of sacrifice. It notes that though many of those who volunteered
were turned away because relatively few soldiers were needed at the front,
the names of those Jews who served with distinction were generally
omitted in accounts of the war.

The promotion of a unique common cause in World War I was a common feature of the homemaking arguments of those immigrant groups that regarded their old homelands as victims of enemies of the United States. Their hopes that their former homelands would achieve independence because of the war were largely fulfilled at Versailles; this too had an effect on the nature of their American nationalism and, consequently, on their homemaking arguments. Before the United States entered the war, Polish-American and Bohemian-American newspapers became increasingly nationalistic, not so much on behalf of the United States, which after all was neutral, but on behalf of their former and not-yet-independent homelands. It was not always clear where their primary allegiance lay when, for instance, they called for volunteers for the war in Europe. Given the sympathies of Anglo-Americans for the British cause, however, some immigrant loyalties could be divided without being perceived to be in conflict.

The wartime activities of Czech Americans may illustrate how easily some groups could adapt their rhetoric to American entry in the war. Czech Americans began to organize on behalf of an independent Bohemia in September 1914 with the New York American Committee for the Liberation of the Czech People. A national organization, the Bohemian National Alliance, was formed at a meeting in Chicago some months later. No sooner had the United States declared war in 1917, however, than "the Alliance promptly readjusted its programme to meet the new conditions. . . . Heretofore the Alliance had labored for Čechoslovak freedom. From that time on its branches became the sentinels of wholesome, loyal Americanism, efficient agencies for the sale of Liberty Bonds, rallying points for volunteering and for war activities in general."[36] On April 17, 1917, the editor of *Denní Hlasatel* insisted that Czech-American participation in the approaching war was simply a continuation of the earlier participation of Czech Americans in wars fought for American freedom:

> Fifty years ago, it was the Bohemian Slavonic Rifle Company in the State of Illinois which first offered its services to President Lincoln to help keep the Union intact and abolish slavery. Today, again, our brave Sokols are rallying behind the Star Spangled Banner to prove that they are in the front of all others. We may have faults and deficiencies just as have all other nationalities in the large complex of the United States. There is, however, one trait to which we may always point with pride. It is the sincerity and earnestness with which we regard the oath that binds us to the vital interests of this great republic, with its destiny, and better future.

From such groups as the Czechs came the warmest support for American intervention in the war.

For the leaders of groups such as the German Americans, whose former homeland was at war with Britain and France and their allies, or such as the Scandinavian Americans, whose former homelands remained neutral in the conflict, professions of loyalty "to the vital interests of this great republic" were far more problematic than they were for the leaders of groups whose new and former homelands were on the same side. The Minnesota periodical *Northern Review* openly supported the German side and advocated U.S. neutrality before the United States declared war. "Did any good come from the American Revolutionary and Civil Wars?" asked the editor in the opening sentence of a 1916 article, "The World After the War." "Yes," he answered, "a freer and more united American people." And he then suggested that Germany was fighting a war for Europe with the same goals in mind that the United States had achieved in its earlier wars: "May not some like good come to the world from the present world war? Will we be surprised if the result be a freer and more united Europe?"[37] Thus immigrant groups with loyalties on both sides of the conflict tried to lay claim to a common cause with the United States, albeit not with equal ease. But regardless of Old World alliances and origins, once war was declared, leaders of all groups spoke of their loyalty to the new rather than the old homeland, and competition for the greater sacrifices to prove this loyalty began.[38]

The competition was made all the more poignant when it was between immigrant groups whose former European homelands were on opposite sides in the war. In 1915, while the United States was still neutral, the editor of *Denní Hlasatel* insisted that "the much abused hyphen is not a sign of cleavage, but a sign of unity." He also made clear that differences between immigrant groups were important: "With the exception of some half-crazy Germans and Irish, the millions of naturalized citizens are not only the staunchest followers of the slogan 'America First,' but also the most sincere admirers of Mr. Wilson and his policies." In 1918, as the war was coming to a close, the editor again spoke out against nativism, and again it was obvious that some immigrant groups were better than others: "We Czechs need not defend ourselves in this respect. Even before war was declared against Germany and Austria, our boys hastened to enlist in the United States army and navy. We may fairly claim that there are fewer draft dodgers of our nationality than of any other." A few weeks later an editorial in *Denní Hlasatel* suggested that the war in Europe was also a war between ethnic groups in the United States and that one way of demonstrating your loyalty and your Americanism was to attack German Americans. The editorial approved of the removal of a bust of Bismarck, the renaming of streets with German names, and the dismissal of a teacher who "flaunts his pro-Germanism." "In brief, Chicago, as well as other American cities, has arrived at the conclusion that German influence will have to be broken radically, at last, and that everything tainted with the provocative Hun hue must unconditionally give way to Americanism."[39] Seldom did one marginalized immigrant group come to the support of another in time of need. The competition for entry into the American home could be vicious.

Polish Americans too had a strong interest in the outcome of the war. Indeed, unlike the leaders of most immigrant groups, Polish-American leaders had tended to promote an exile Polish identity rather than the hyphenated American identity more typical of the rhetoric of other groups. Karen Majewski has demonstrated how Polish-American fiction at the turn of the nineteenth century "has as its moral touchstone the reestablishment of Polish sovereignty and the affirmation of Polish identity." "The authors of these narratives," she concludes, "reconstructed the immigrant journey in order to provide readers with moral and ideological maps by which to trace the paths that had led them from Europe, to position themselves in American Polonia, and, ultimately, to find a way back to Poland." When the opportunity came to return to an independent Poland after the war, however, there was no mass exodus of immigrants from the United States, and the existence of an independent Poland marked a shift in Polish-American priorities toward an American identity.[40]

After Polish independence, sacrifice in the World War I for the United States became an important element in the Polish-American homemaking argument: "Polish-American Veterans the Proof of Loyalty." Under this heading, the *Dziennik Zjednoczenia* (Polish Roman Catholic Union Daily) of September 3, 1927, used the veterans as an irrefutable argument against Anglo-American nativism:

> It has been a rule of life, that one who cannot defend himself against attacks must perish. Very fortunately there are, among us, those who have found an excellent method by which we can defend ourselves against similar attacks, by those who represent themselves as true Americans, and this method is the organization of Poles, who, not by mere words, but *by deeds filled with sacrifice, proved their status as Americans,* by loyalty to the Star Spangled Banner at a time when this country was put to the supreme sacrifice of its citizens, and likewise, those who have not as yet become citizens but who are endowed with a sense of loyalty to their adopted country which has provided food, shelter, and freedom through the medium of the Declaration of Independence.
>
> We know that in the ranks of the United States Army, during the war, several hundred thousand soldiers of Polish descent served the country bravely and the lions [sic] share of these were volunteers. Records of the

War Department indicate that the Polish people had the largest percentage of enlistment, in proportion to the population. Let us then ask, is this display of loyalty not a *proof of good citizenship*? We say yes, it exceeds the loyalty of those 100% Americans who stood on the side lines and let the parade go by.

In order to properly "display" the loyalty of Polish Americans it was necessary to have all Polish-American veterans become members of the Polish Veterans Alliance. The editor was careful to explain that no criticism of the American Legion, which plays an "important role . . . in civic life," was intended but that a separate Polish organization was necessary "to protect and sustain *the rights of citizens who are most unjustly referred to as foreigners*. In forming this organization, we are serving notice to these enemies of the foreign element, that there is such a unit as the Polish American Veterans Alliance, thus checking in the bud, the promiscuous use of the word, foreigner."[41] Although the homemaking argument was not always made so explicitly as here, it was always the burden of immigrants' stories of sacrifice.

German Americans had enjoyed a far more secure position in American society than groups that arrived later, such as the Poles. German-American confidence, however, received a severe blow with the dominant anti-German sentiments during the war. Once regarded as an asset, a German name suddenly became a reason to have your loyalty questioned. John Higham, who gives several illustrations of the high esteem German Americans enjoyed before the outbreak of the war in Europe, calls the change that took place "the most spectacular reversal of judgment in the history of American nativism."[42] The shame and low self-esteem addressed by leaders in so many other immigrant groups now became a matter of concern among German Americans too. Their spokesmen too spoke of sacrifice as a reason for pride and a proof of loyalty.

"Change of Name?—Unnecessary!" was the headline on a September 1 editorial in 1918 in *Die Sonntagpost*, the Sunday edition of *Die Abendpost*. With the *Chicago Tribune* as their source, the editors related the words of Chris Nehmer of Ontonagon, Michigan, to a group of German prisoners of war: "Folks at home advised me to change my name, but my fighting here proves that that isn't necessary, because it makes my Americanism clearly evident." They also reported the explanation given by an officer when asked why the American forces were so active on a particular sector of the front: "Forty-one percent of this division is of German descent. All are volunteers. Now draw your own conclusions." In case the conclusions should not be entirely self-evident, the editors spelled out the "two *special* objectives which are peculiar to" American soldiers of German descent: "to give the lie to the foolish gossip that Americans of German blood should not and would not fight against the Germans—their blood relatives—and to prove by their *actions* that German blood is also keeping faith with America and is willing to do its duty." By fighting so valiantly and "carrying the Stars and Stripes—the flag of righteous democracy—forward to victory," the German-American soldiers were not only giving their full support to America's declared war aims but were also supporting the people of Germany against a "military autocracy": "Their earnest desire is to expose any expression of doubt as to the loyalty of Americans of German origin as an infamous slander, to secure for the German people a speedy liberation from an unworthy rule, and to secure for all progressive nations the right of self-determination." Thus the homemaking argument of fighting for a common cause could be made even by German-American leaders when the United States and Germany were at war with each other. Here the complementarity of loyalties is insisted upon even when they might be seen to be in conflict: to stand up for America in its time of need was also in the best interest of the old homeland—even when it was defined as the enemy of the United States.

Some days later, on October 13, a headline in *Die Abendpost* reads: "One out of Four Is German: Better American Soldiers Are Not to Be Found." Again, the appearance of objectivity is ensured by using an English-language newspaper, this time the *New York Times*, as a source, and again the large numbers—25 percent of the fighting force is the cited figure—and the exceptional bravery of soldiers of German descent are at the center of the story. Even though the newspaper, perhaps wisely given the circumstances, made no critical comment, the praise by the *New York Times* for the American soldiers of German descent was somewhat backhanded or, at best, ambiguous. The *Times* correspondent did not feel they should be called "'German-Americans'; why, I could not even find a trace of *Kultur* in them. If they had ever been inoculated with it, they certainly have gotten rid of it." So his praise is also for the ability of "our political and social system" to integrate "the relatively new elements in our national body as completely as those whose forebears lived [here] during the period of the War of Independence." On two counts this went against the basic political aims of German-American leaders: their story was of a culturally and racially well-defined group of Americans who had been central to the creation and development of the country since the seventeenth century and of an American homeland with a culture that was as much German as it was English. But in 1918 stories of sacrifice were given precedence over all other homemaking stories.

The leaders of immigrant groups whose old homelands stood to win independence with American victory did not need to step as carefully as did Americans of German descent. Although the latter had to distance themselves politically from Germany, for example, by seeing the defeat of the German regime as a victory for the German people, the former could celebrate their Old World ties without restraint. As they were announced and described in the Czech-American newspapers of Chicago, Czech ethnic festivals and pageants during the war and in the years immediately following had as their central theme pride in Czech history and culture.

In contrast with German Americans, who of course did not have many celebrations during the war, there seems to have been very little interest in a specifically American ethnic tradition among Czech Americans at this point. Because they could harmonize their support for the American war effort with their emotional as well as political ties to their former homelands, they could celebrate their Old World nationality without jeopardizing their recognition as loyal Americans. To fight for the United States and to fight for the liberation of Czechs and Slovaks from Austrian and German dominance were identical causes. Even in their celebrations of a U.S. national holiday like Decoration Day, leaders of Czech Americans could seem as interested in highlighting Old World issues and Old World exploits as in making arguments for their home in the new one. It goes without saying, of course, that on such a day due tribute was paid to those Czech Americans who had sacrificed their lives for the United States. So confident were Czech leaders of the privileged position given them by their common cause, however, that they could afford to argue against the excesses of the Americanization movement and for the importance of Czech-language maintenance: their 100 percent support of the war effort was never in doubt. So while German Americans had to conduct the difficult balancing act of celebrating their homemaking stories of sacrifice as well as of foundation and ideological contributions, Czechs could unabashedly celebrate and promote their Old World nationalism without contradicting their homemaking arguments.

While German Americans had a special need to prove their loyalty during the world war, the need for Jewish Americans to do so had little to do with the particular politics and alliances of the war. As had been the case during the Civil War, Jewish-American leaders were faced with ancient prejudices that had little basis in fact but were all the more difficult to dispel. Therefore it was of particular importance for them to broadcast statistics to prove "their share of sacrifices on the altar of true patriotism." Consequently, the Bureau of Jewish War Records was established in New York to "gather as much material as possible pertaining to Jewish patriotism in America both military and civil. They rightly . foresaw," wrote the *Daily Jewish Courier* of May 19, 1919, "that information of such a character would be of great value to the Jewish people." By the end of 1918 the bureau could present figures showing that while Jews made up 3 percent of the U.S. population, their proportion in the armed forces was between 4 and 5 percent. The director of the bureau concluded his report by remarking that the statistics "have proven the quality of Jewish loyalty."[43]

That statistics of blood sacrifice were evidence of the right to be American was also clear to the leaders of the Swedish Historical Society of America. Their appeal for information on all of Swedish descent who had served in the world war was supported by the *Svenska Kuriren* in an editorial of April 25, 1918, reminding its readers of "the two outstanding virtues of the Swedish national character": trustworthiness and respect for law and order. "Every page of Swedish-American history reflects the good character of the Swedes." The editor traced these good qualities from the colony of New Sweden through the War of Rebellion and the Civil War: "American citizens of Swedish descent, have offered many sacrifices on the altar of their adopted country."

However, this proud history was not sufficiently well known, for instance, the "well known fact that in Illinois every fifth Swede and in four states every sixth Swede fought in the Union Army during the [Civil] War. The loyal Swedes have not been given full honor or credit for their services and sacrifices during that time of need." So it was therefore necessary to see that this did not happen again and that "a complete account" of the "thousands of young men of Swedish descent [who] serve in the army and the navy" should be made. The society invited "all Swedish and Swedish-American societies to cooperate" in providing "the names of all persons, who serve their country in one way or another." To the editor this "resolution speaks for itself." That may be, and what it now speaks of to the historian is the deep-felt need in every European immigrant group to have its sacrifices for its country counted and recorded so that it should not be said again that they were foreigners in their own land.

Leaders of most groups express a similar compulsion to count soldiers of their particular ethnic group, as did the Czech-American Chicago newspaper *Denní Hlasatel* for March 21, 1922. Its editorial, "Dulce et Decorum Est pro Patria Mori," reported that "The County Board of Commissioners will, in the next few days, publish a list of soldiers who laid down their lives for America in the Civil, Spanish-American, and World Wars. As this list will supposedly be a complete one, we advise our countrymen, who are relatives or parents of these, our heroes, to see to it that all Czechoslovak names be actually included in it."[44]

Percentages and numbers were important for the tellers of stories of sacrifice, but they could also use the single, outstanding patriotic sacrifice as a forceful homemaking argument. Few sacrifices were exploited to the degree that Greek Americans made use of the death of Private George Dilboy of Massachusetts. It should be noted that the First World War was not of equal importance for all groups. Those who had cherished stories of sacrifice from the two founding wars of the United States, the Revolutionary War and the Civil War, continued to call attention to their contribution in the creation and saving of the Union. For groups such as the Greek Americans, with a more recent history in the United States, the world war became the most important opportunity to demonstrate that they too had sacrificed their blood for their land of choice. The celebration of the blood sacrifice of George Dilboy was for many years a Greek-American homemaking ritual.

George Dilboy was a World War I Audie Murphy with the important difference that he did not survive his heroics. According to the official account issued by the War Department in connection with his reburial in Arlington National Cemetery in 1923, he had, after volunteering to take care of the problem, singlehandedly wiped out a machine-gun nest that was holding up his unit. He had continued his advance on the enemy position after several wounds, one of them mortal: "Lying on one side and raising his right hand, he gave his squadron the signal to advance and died with a smile on his face."[45]

The account in the *Boston Post*, as excerpted in the souvenir program for the twelfth annual ball of the Hellenic Association of Boston in 1919, added even more color to the story and told of his father's admonition before he left for France: "Remember the motto of our country, of Greece, 'Return with your shield of honor.' Come home with victory—or die with honor." About half of this pamphlet consists of commercial advertisements; there are also some portraits of prominent Greeks and Greek Americans, but the sacrifice of the Greek doughboy receives more space than any other topic, with a full page on his heroism and two with photos: a portrait, the Congressional Medal of Honor, and a general pinning the medal on the shoulder of the hero's father. When the Greek Americans of Boston came together in Paul Revere Hall for their annual ball on May 2 of that year, there could be no question that they felt that the glory bestowed on George Dilboy to no small extent reflected on them and that it was evidence of their right to a home in America.[46]

Although George Dilboy may no longer be a household name, even for Americans of Greek descent, he was used as a symbol of Greek-American patriotism for many years. One Greek-American association took his name. The George Dilboy Society, with at least thirteen chapters by 1931, had as one of its functions the assistance of veterans of Greek descent. There was a George Dilboy chapter of the American Legion, and Dilboy's name continued to be celebrated with balls for many years.[47] As the Polish Americans had their statues of Kosciuszko and Pulaski, so Greek Americans eventually got their statue of George Dilboy in Somerville, Massachusetts, in 1930. A speech given by Dr. Thomas Baxevanis and reported in the *Greek Press* on January 29, 1931, as "Enlightening the Americans About Grecian Contributions," began with an historical survey of Greek greatness and importance from ancient times and continued with examples of Greek contributions to the United States in peace and war. It all, however, was a mere preamble to a eulogy for the great hero of the world war, "one of the ten great heroes," according to General George Pershing, who had "died in the battlefield of France with super-human heroism and valor." Not only Greek Americans could bask in the glory of George Dilboy. At the unveiling of his statue in 1930, both President Calvin Coolidge and Senator David Walsh of Massachusetts "paid a glowing tribute to immigrants in general who fought for their adopted country."

The intimate relation between individual sacrifice and the recognition of members of the ethnic group as loyal Americans was the theme of Sotirios Nicholson's oration on behalf of the American Hellenic Progressive Association, and "also in the name of 65,000 men of Greek origin who served in the American Military . . . during the World War," at the Tomb of the Unknown Soldier on Decoration Day of 1931. Here he addressed the "unknown" as "possibly one of our very own brothers." The address expanded and explained his conceit: "We . . . somehow wish to feel that as an American citizen of Greek origin you sprang to the defense of your adopted country because, like those of us who here honor you on this Memorial Day, you sought to be a living manifestation of loyalty to the United States, of allegiance to its flag, of support for its Constitution, of obedience to its laws, and of reverence for its history and traditions."[48]

When members of the Greek community in Chicago met at Hull House on August 7, 1917, to exhort all Greek Americans to support the war effort, the themes struck in their public statement and four-point resolution were representative of similar exhortations by leaders of other immigrant groups as the United States entered the war in Europe. They were also representative when they insisted that there could be no conflict of loyalty: by supporting their country they would also be supporting their old homeland. "When the congress of peace takes place, the American Greeks must have valid ground to request America to speak in behalf of Greece. And that valid ground will be our response to the needs of America." But the call to arms was for the new homeland: "America is at war. Clothe yourself with the grandest emblcm in the world, the United States flag. Fight under it and you will be honored." Implicit in this promised honor was that they would be honored as Americans. That America was the home of Greek Americans was made explicit in the explanation that the resolution was born of "the inherent impulse of Greeks to serve their country that is the United States, in which they live, breathe, and function." The resolution not only exhorted young men "proudly to appear . . . before the constituted authorities and place themselves at the disposal of the United States flag" but also reminded those who could not enlist that there were other ways of demonstrating loyalty: "It further exhorts its members to buy more and more Liberty Bonds and also to contribute to the American Red Cross to their utmost ability."[49]

For the intense period of American participation in the war, the four Liberty bond drives took on the symbolic meaning of a demonstration of true Americanism for all immigrants. When the editor of *Syrian World* asked, in June 1932, many years after the war was over, "Are Syrians Unpatriotic?" his evidence for the patriotism of Syrian Americans was not only the large number of young men who had served the United States during the world war (13,965) but the significant contribution of Syrian Americans in their purchase of war bonds: the sum of $1,207,900 in New York alone.[50]

The intense wartime Americanization propaganda had a lasting effect on immigrant cultures out of proportion to the brief period it was carried on at full strength. Faced with an anti-immigrant chauvinism of often hysterical proportions, immigrant leaders realized that this was no longer a time for stories of past exploits alone. The desperate counting of soldiers overseas, the macabre holding up of the maimed and dead— all as proof of loyalty to the country on which immigrants had already staked not only their own lives but those of their descendants—went far beyond the telling of the traditional homemaking myths that were as much aimed at their own collective moral uplift as at society at large. Nothing shows both the desperation of the immigrants and the basic hostility of the native born so well as the scramble for acceptance caused by the four Liberty Loan drives of 1917–18. The purpose of these drives, which were authorized by the Liberty Loan Act, was to raise money for wartime loans to Allied countries.

Although there is a world of difference between fluid myth and hard cash, the need to tell the world that a particular immigrant group had demonstrated its loyalty by purchasing more Liberty bonds than its neighbors was born of the same insecurity that gave rise to the many homemaking stories. The major irony of the Americanization drive, however, was that while most immigrants were eager to be accepted as Americans, they remained foreign to the native born who were demanding that the immigrants Americanize themselves.[51] In the immigrants' need for faith in the homemaking efficacy of their support of the Liberty Loan drives and in the rhetoric they used to express this faith, the immigrant stories of financial sacrifice for the war effort take on mythic qualities.

In its propaganda for the Liberty Loans, the War Loan Organization of the U.S. Treasury Department made direct appeals to the various immigrant groups, issuing pamphlets addressed to each group, even relatively small groups such as the Russians. The first page of the fourth Liberty Loan pamphlet addressed to this group was of the same general nature as those aimed at other immigrants and had appeals from the president and from the director of publicity of the War Loan Organization. It also included, however, an appeal specifically addressed to Russian Americans, reminding them of how Germany was endangering "the rights to which Russians in this country are accustomed" and that "money is needed to defeat the Kaiser." But a threat is explicit in the appeal: "If the Russians do not buy they are not 100 per cent Americans." The intense competition between the immigrant groups caused by the Liberty Loan campaigns was a result of the Americanization movement and the deliberate policy of the U.S. Treasury to threaten immigrant groups with the stigma of disloyalty should they not meet the quotas set. Carl Chrislock has observed that the "cooperation of both public and private agencies invested the campaigns . . . with the aura of a religious crusade."[52]

The intensity of the Americanization propaganda, the widespread fears of disloyalty among the "foreign element," the quotas set for each ethnic group, and the traditional role of immigrant leaders in arguing for the right of their group to a home in America all made for a situation in which contributions to the Liberty bond drives became highly competitive. The issue of these drives was as much the demonstration of patriotism and loyalty as the actual need for extra funding for the war effort. The different immigrant groups made competing claims to the highest level of contributions, while the national and state organizers of the drives made good use of the situation, establishing Liberty bond drive committees for the various ethnic groups. Anglo-Americans, who did not need to prove that they were American, were not part of this competition. Nor was the same pressure to dig deep in their purses brought to bear on them.[53] All others were expected to prove that they were as loyal and patriotic as the Anglo-Americans were assumed to be as a matter of course. Hardly an immigrant group was free from this pressure. The only special point about the Syrian-American use of its response to the Liberty bond drives as evidence of its loyalty may be that it was made several years after the pressure was gone and the competition about who would give the most money to demonstrate their patriotism was no longer on people's minds.

When an editorial in the *Saloniki* for May 11, 1918, began with the rather disparaging reflection that "the results of the Third Liberty Loan did not measure up to the expectations of the Greek people," it should be noted that the editor's measuring stick was what the Greeks should expect of themselves. Moreover, even then the result was poor only "when compared to the proceeds of the Second Liberty Loan which exceeded the two-million-dollar mark in Chicago alone." As for the third one, "the totals, compared with those of other nationalities, were sufficiently satisfactory and reflect honor and prestige on our nationality." Indeed, it turned out that the Greeks had done very well in this third drive:

> By our enthusiasm and promptness in purchasing the newly issued bonds, we over-subscribed our share of the loan in Chicago, surpassing every other nationality. The Greeks of Chicago contributed $167 per capita, thus ranking the highest in average individual contributions in proportion to the numbers of other foreign-language minorities of Chicago. The second highest contribution was $128 per capita. The Italian subscription averaged $28 dollars [sic]; the Germans came next with $11 per capita. It is thus conclusively proven and reaffirmed that the Greek people have a superior and higher conception of patriotism, that material things are considered of far lesser significance than sentiment and moral duty.

There seems no limit to all the noble characteristics that were proved by this achievement, which was seen as a consequence of "our rich and inexhaustible historic and intellectual background [which] is the foundation of modern languages, science, and art." Not only were the purchase of bonds in the present and the glory of the past linked in the minds of the editor, the dollars paid were proof of the truth of the stories of the past. It may also be noted that the runner-up in this competition was not identified by the Greek-American editor, whereas competing immigrant groups that had done poorly got special mention.

These impressive results did not just happen. Greek Americans, like other groups, had their own Liberty Loan committee, and one of the methods used by the Greek-American committee was to award honorary prizes for those individuals who had done most for the campaign. In the *Saloniki* for August 10, 1918, the winners of the prizes for committee workers in the third drive were praised, and others were exhorted to "offer their services" for the fourth drive. When the time came for the last of the Liberty Loans in 1919, "the final test of our patriotism," the *Saloniki* (May 10) again urged all to contribute so that "Greek-Americans will again distinguish themselves among all citizens of foreign descent by their subscription. . . . Let us, then, show our gratitude to America by oversubscribing our quota to the Victory Liberty Loan."

The editors of the *Denní Hlasatel* also seem obsessed with the necessity to demonstrate loyalty through the Liberty Loan drives of 1917 and 1918. Had the Czech wards of Chicago met their quotas? This question was a constant theme in the newspaper. The editorial for October 16, 1917, was one of many urging Czech Americans to "Buy Liberty Bonds!" And the primary motivation is clearly that of making America their home: "Let us Czechs endeavor to render America's judgment of our behavior a most favorable one. We shall then be in a position to point proudly to this record when the time comes to repulse the attacks by the know-nothings, of whom there is no dearth at any time." Again and again the editors reminded their readers that the purchase of bonds was not merely to support the war effort but to ensure that Czech Americans would be welcomed in the American home: "Our campaign is to be conducted in such a manner that every bond bought by our people should be credited to our own nationality. Do not let us forget that this concerns our national honor! Do not allow yourself to be persuaded into buying a bond in your place of employment when you can obtain the same bond from people of your own nationality" (September 25, 1918). When the editors on October 24, 1917, could report that "Chicago Czechs" had met the $1 million quota for the second Liberty Loan, as they had for the first, they concluded, "These two million dollars demonstrate that the Czechs stand in first place among other nationalities of Chicago."

The same concern that payments be credited to the immigrant group was expressed by the *Svenska Kuriren* in 1918: "The Swedes in Chicago have subscribed to over $2,500,000 for the Third Liberty Loan. For the reason that many Swedes bought Bonds without having their purchases accredited to any particular group, it is almost impossible to estimate the exact amount they have purchased." To make clear just who was doing their duty, the editor published the figures achieved by various fraternal lodges and other organizations.[54]

We may imagine the pressure on the individual to pay up in each drive. The large sums collected were as much the result of considerable arm twisting as of selfless patriotism. The pressure was all the greater because it came from within the group and was executed by neighbors in rural communities or urban wards. "In many places," writes Frederick Luebke, "committees designated specific amounts for individual citizens to subscribe. Extraordinary social pressure was often applied which literally forced persons to supply the required sums." In many communities the names of "slackers" were published. The homes of those who had not bought bonds were often "marked with large yellow signs" and in "several midwestern communities, caravans of superpatriots, accompanied by photographers and stenographers, coerced allegedly disloyal citizens to buy."[55] German Americans in particular were exposed to what can only be described as terror. That members of other ethnic groups also could be under intense pressure is illustrated in Rølvaag's novel *Pure Gold* (1930), in which the home of a miserly farmer couple is burned down. In this case, as so often happened, they are coerced by members of their own group.[56] A more common form of coercion was the application of yellow paint by vigilantes, both on the outside and inside of homes of "slackers."[57]

On May 19, 1919, the *Daily Jewish Courier* proudly reminded its readers that "the success of the sale of the Liberty Bonds among the workers of the garment industries and the numerous subscriptions from Jewish businessmen is very well known and needs no special mention." One may speculate on the degree of coercion involved in the sale of Liberty bonds to members of all ethnic groups without thereby questioning the loyalty of even the most reluctant buyer of bonds. At the time, no one questioned the loyalty of Anglo-Americans, of whom no proof was required.

The frenzy, the chauvinism, and the sometimes extreme expressions of suspicion of all foreign elements may make the world war situation seem special. Seen in the long tradition of assurances of loyalty and expressions of eagerness to sacrifice made by the leaders of all immigrant groups, however, the importance they gave to their contributions to the Liberty Loan drives appears less a special aberration of the period of the First World War than yet another instance in a long history of immigrant endeavors to give evidence that America was their home. All these endeavors had a dual purpose: to make the immigrants feel at home in America without surrendering their ethnicity and to convince Anglo-Americans that other Americans too were at home in America. Of these two aims the second was the more difficult to achieve. So deep were the suspicions of the basic disloyalty of the so-called foreign element in the dominant Anglo-American culture, and so intense was the fervor of the Americanization crusade of the First World War period, that it mattered little what members of some immigrant groups said or did to prove their loyalty to the United States. "It did little good when patriotic German-Americans urged their fellows to buy bonds and to show their loyalty to America in every possible way," Merle Curti has observed, "including 'fighting in the front ranks for freedom.'" Nor were their stories of past sacrifices and loyalty of much help. Indeed, Curti sees the driving of "a deeper wedge between the 'hyphenated Americans' and other groups making up the nation" as the main result of the Americanization crusade.[58]

Another reason it was difficult for immigrant leaders to make a convincing homemaking argument to people outside their group was the more practical one that Anglo-Americans were rare in ethnic audiences and thus never got the message. On June 23, 1904, Chicago's *Die Abend-post*, in taking note of a celebration of the Civil War general Peter J. Osterhaus, reported that there had been "Roaring Applause" but that those who should have heard the message were absent: "The contents of all the short but substantially enthusiastic speeches dealt not only with honoring the merits of General Osterhaus and of our adopted fatherland in particular, but more with the honoring of the Germans in general. It is only regrettable, that certain elements could not hear how men like Generals Grant and Leake and Colonel Foster feel and think about the German element and its sacrifices of life and property for the preservation of the Union."

Although this book is about European immigrant responses to the closed doors of their chosen homeland, it is worth remembering that in this period immigrants from other parts of the world could not attain even the basic legal acceptance marked by citizenship. With citizenship denied, the Japanese immigrant could hardly even think of the United States as a homeland, chosen or not. In a Japanese-American comic book by Henry Kiyama, first published in an American-flavored Japanese in San Francisco in 1931, one of the strips, "The Great War in Europe," satirizes the belief that service in the First World War would open the door to a home in America for a Japanese immigrant. In the first panel the character Charlie has heard that "you can get *citizenship* by serving, so I'm gonna join up," and in the next one he tells his friend: "Some people say Americans won't recognize us til we have 10,000 *tombstones* in our San Mateo cemetery. But I think I oughta join up, get citizenship, and then run for *president*." Charlie enlists, and several panels show him mock-heroically cutting down German soldiers with a samurai sword. After armistice he returns home, goes to city hall in full uniform, and, giving a military salute, requests his citizenship, only to be rebuffed with, "Not for Orientals yet." No wonder Charlie, in the last panel and still in his uniform, exclaims, "After that I feel like a real idiot."[59]

It may be, however, that Charlie had little more reason to feel like an idiot than had the many European immigrant leaders who had urged their flocks that their sacrifices, whether bloody or pecuniary, would gain them recognition and a right to a bright room in the American home. True, in the first ten to fifteen years after the First World War, Americans seemed to become more and more ready to accept European immigrants as fellow Americans, and this change in attitude took away much of the immigrants' need to make homemaking arguments. But the change was caused less by stories of immigrant sacrifices in the First World War and other American wars than by the drastic reduction of immigration itself, first temporarily because of the war and then, with what seemed like finality, because of the immigration restriction acts of 1921 and 1924.

Less spectacular than myths of foundation and myths of sacrifice, myths of a close ideological relationship between the immigrants' nationality—often explicitly referred to as their race—and the United States and its people, nevertheless seem to have run deeper than the other two genres of myths used in homemaking arguments.

4 Ideology: We Were American to Begin With

NOT ALL FOUNDATION MYTHS have met with success. Some have appeared more credible than others. Few outside the city of Alexandria in western Minnesota now believe that Vikings wandered around in that state in the fourteenth century, thus giving nineteenth-century Scandinavian settlers in Minnesota a tradition of medieval migrations and medieval roots in the Midwest.[1] By contrast, most Americans know that Columbus "discovered" America and that he was an Italian. *It All Started with Columbus* was the title of a humorous and "improbable account of American history" by Richard Armour in 1953. Even though the Columbus story may have lost much of its value and prestige, because indigenous peoples have become more visible and vocal than they were in the period studied here, and even though the question of Columbus's American ethnicity has not been uncontested, Italian Americans clearly have been successful in making the Columbus story their particular homemaking myth.

Myths of sacrifice are for good reason less exclusive than are myths of foundation. As new immigrant groups have continued to come to the United States, their new country has provided them with wars in which they have been expected to prove their loyalty—and for which relatively recently arrived immigrants have volunteered, whether to prove anything or not. While scarcely an immigrant group exists that cannot claim the sacrifice of a liberal amount of blood for the nation, the loyalty proved by such sacrifice has often been claimed to be a natural—indeed, a constitutional—characteristic of a particular nationality. The claim is that "we" were really "American" even before immigration: we were American to begin with. Given such a constitutional slant, stories of sacrifice may take on some of the exclusive qualities of the stories of foundation. The exclusiveness, however, is a quality of each individual claim. As a genre, stories that claim a particular ideological relationship between an immigrant group and the United States have been common to a wide range of immigrant groups and are no more exclusive than are the other kinds of narratives that are the subject of this book.

In some stories of sacrifice we have seen that the leaders of some immigrant groups have argued that their particular group had more reason to go to battle for the United States than had others. Going to war was not merely a question of immigrants' simple loyalty to their new country: the members of a particular group could have a special historical reason to feel strongly about a particular war or a particular enemy and thus had an ethnically defined cause to fight for in addition to the national one. Many narratives of a common cause, however, were situational and were not in themselves claims for a deeper kind of spiritual or ideological relationship between a specific immigrant group and the new homeland, which was often imagined as an Anglo America. When, during World War I, Polish and Czech Americans argued that by supporting the war effort they were also supporting the cause of independence of their former home countries, they were claiming a common cause in a specific historical and political situation. Similarly, the Jewish story of revenge for the evils of the Spanish inquisition was a special ethnic motivation for sacrifice in the 1898 war with Spain.

The third genre of homemaking myths, which is the subject of this chapter, speaks of a deep spiritual and ideological relationship between the immigrant group and the American nation. A myth of ideological relationship is of course also a story of a common cause, but it is essentially timeless and not related to a specific conflict; it is indeed mythic in its claim for the immanent and always noble characteristics of a particular nation. These characteristics are invariably also American. On March 5, 1918, the Chicago newspaper *Denní Hlasatel* proudly announced that Czech Americans "fulfill their duty and intend to do so until the end of the war" by continuing to purchase Liberty bonds. The reason the editor was so confident of the exemplary behavior of his particular immigrant group was that "Czech newspapers, schools, and Czech organizations have taught our people to perform the work in true Czech spirit, *which is at the same time American.* Both spell democracy, justice, and humanitarianism" (emphasis added). The only remarkable thing about the manner in which this claim for a shared Americanism—a common "spirit"—was made was that the editor, perhaps moved by a wartime sense of solidarity, actually did not insist that this spiritual relationship between the immigrant and the United States was exclusive for the Czechs. "The same spirit prevails among immigrants of other nationalities," he wrote, "particularly the Slavs, who have given conclusive proof of their loyalty to America." The editor headlined this editorial as "Americanization of Immigrants" and was arguing that immigrants whose "true Czech spirit" was by nature American had no need of the efforts of the Americanization movement of World War I.

The largest mass of immigrants began arriving during the last three decades of the nineteenth century; in this period the leaders of most immigrant groups developed ways of countering American rejection. But the Irish, who arrived in large numbers in the first half of the century, bore the brunt of nativism alone for many years and, consequently, developed their responses to it at a far earlier date than most other immigrant groups. A common cause had a central place in the Irish-American homemaking argument: they too had a history of struggle against the British for their freedom and independence. Matthew Jacobson has observed that "Anglophobia . . . was a convenient idiom in which the Irish could lay claim to American citizenship. Far from being 'bad' Americans, as the nativists charged, the Irish could claim the strongest attachment of all to America's historic ideals." From Catherine Conway's novel, *Lalor's Maples,* Jacobson quotes a piece of dialogue in which one character (who seems to have internalized nativist rejection) wonders whether the Irish were not foreigners in the United States, and another responds, "Not they, Miss Mildred. They belong everywhere, but especially in America." Jacobson observes, "Defined by a past of 'political agitation' and tragedy, and now having found wonderful asylum in America, the Irish were *especially* American for being ineradicably Irish."[2]

The shared experience of the Irish and the United States went beyond merely having had a common enemy. The strongest bond between them was their common ideological cause: freedom and independence. Several historians have noted that narratives of common cause were frequent in the homemaking arguments of Irish Americans and that central to their self-image was the view that being Irish was being American. In his important book, *American Immigrant Leaders,* Victor Greene has shown that Irish-American leaders took up the theme of the ideological bonds between the Irish and the Americans from the early years of the Republic. St. Patrick was, for instance, celebrated as one who had given "his people a religious identity separate from that of the English and thereby welded together the Irish and American national struggles." As Thomas O'Connor, editor of the *Shamrock and Hibernian Chronicle* from 1814, pointed out, his readers, "as refugees from the Irish struggle . . . were in fact already Americans." In his view, "the Irishman differed from the native only in place of birth; in terms of political purpose, they were alike." Some decades later Patrick Donahoe, editor of the *Pilot* in Boston, also pointed to the shared political ideals of the Irish and the United States and insisted "that Irish immigrants were *by nature* good Americans" and that they had a "natural love for this sheltering democracy." Greene concludes his discussion of Irish immigrant leaders by adopting the views of Michael Funchion (*Chicago's Irish Nationalists, 1881–90* [1978]), in having the Irish regard themselves as "intrinsically even more 'American . . . than most other immigrants.' As one Irish Chicagoan wrote after his arrival, 'There are none of the foreigners [here] for their hearts and loves were in America' and were devoted to what the nation stands for 'long before they thought of sailing' to the New World."[3] As used by many Irish Americans, their story of a common cause went far deeper than a shared history of a specific political and national struggle with the British. The Irish were American by nature and were therefore naturally at home in the United States.

The Irish may have been first, but they had many followers who also promoted a narrative of themselves that made the United States the natural home of a particular immigrant group for historical and ideological reasons. One of the more unpleasant characteristics of nationalism is that it is at its most fervent in times of war. At the beginning of the Spanish-American War, the Holland Society of Chicago passed a resolution proclaiming the shared ideals of the Dutch and the Americans: both peoples loved liberty and had a history of fighting despotism. Implied was a claim to a deep underlying relationship between the two peoples, a relationship that gave Dutch immigrants a special right to a home in America. The immediate inspiration for the jingoism of the resolution may have been the yellow press, but the member of the society who proposed the resolution began by appealing to the history of the heroic Dutch. "Our ancestors in little Holland resisted for eighty years the efforts of Spain to conquer them. By force of arms they pursued that resistance, backed by indomitable Dutch courage and perseverance. It is fitting for us assembled here tonight, as descendants of those Dutchmen, to suitably express in this public manner our sympathy for a people who, today, that same Spain is endeavoring to destroy." The preamble of the resolution first drew attention to Spanish "treachery," the "imperishable memories" of the "descendants of the Netherlands," and the "savagery of Spain's treatment of Cubans, followed by the destruction of the battle-ship Maine, and its noble crew," which had placed Spain "outside the pale of civilized apology or immunity." It concluded that "we, the descendants of the Holland heroes of eighty years' war, hereby approve the course of the government of the United States in declaring that Cuba must be free and that Spanish tyranny and savagery must depart from the Western hemisphere."[4]

In World War I, even though the enemy was no longer Spain, similar sentiments were expressed in demonstration of the natural Dutch-American support of the war effort in an editorial in *Onze Toekomst* for April 4, 1919. Here it was the "born love of freedom" of the Dutch and "their unconquerable wish to make their own way and be ruled by those whom he himself elects, and his deep rooted respect for law and order" that was the reason both for their decision to make their home "in the United States of America with *people whose ideals are so much like their own*" and to rally to the support of their new country "when the call came to defend that country against force in the Great War."[5]

Unlike the leaders of some other immigrant groups, Dutch Americans may not have insisted that U.S. institutions and the American love of liberty actually were of Dutch origin, but they certainly found the question worth close consideration. As in the 1898 resolution, they did insist on a *shared* democratic tradition going back to the colonial period. This comes out clearly in a little book, *1609–1909: The Dutch in New Netherland and the United States*, published in connection with the Hudson-Fulton Celebration in New York in 1909. While the author modestly acknowledged that "representative government of the people in the western hemisphere, is not of Dutch origin," he nevertheless suggested that the Dutch came quite close to introducing democracy in the New World. In his filiopietistic account of life and institutions in New Amsterdam, he explained that if the burghers' desire for free institutions had not been tempered by their need for protection against the English and the "savages" on the one hand and their respect for the law on the other, they would have had "local government" before any of the English colonies.

From "home" they had brought with them the "ideals of political and religious freedom . . . which they transplanted to American soil." Indeed, when it came to "the fundamental principles of our great republic, the Dutch were far ahead of their English neighbors." New Amsterdam had, we are told, more religious freedom, better public education (for boys *and* girls), and a "greater freedom of speech and the written word." Actually, it would seem that the foundation of twentieth-century America was more solidly placed among the "democratic Dutch" than among the less informed and certainly less liberal Puritans to the north: "Such occurrences as burning of witches would have been impossible in New Netherland, as the people were too well read and too enlightened to make such things possible."[6] The implication was, then, that it might be wiser to look to the enlightened Dutch colony in the later New York than to the Puritans of New England for a true genealogy of American values.

A more midwestern and also a more recent perspective was applied by the young man who responded to and won a competition sponsored by Edward Bok, editor of the *Ladies' Home Journal,* for the same quadricentennial with his essay, "What the Dutch Have Done in the West of the United States." Writing about the Calvinist secessionist emigration in the midnineteenth century, the young man, George Ford Huizinga, was more interested in the parallels between the founding of Dutch Calvinist communities in the Midwest and the founding of a Calvinist New England than in an imagined descent from the Dutch colonists in New Netherland. He concluded, "And while to our fellow Americans the old Dutch who have so long lived in their midst may seem a quaint and lowly people, to us, the children of the [nineteenth century] emigration, they are in a peculiar sense fathers and mothers in Israel—the Puritan heroes of a faith that would not wane. We owe them our glory as American citizens. They owe much to America, and the United States owes more than a little to them."[7] His "old Dutch" were the midnineteenth-century immigrants. They, rather than the colonial Dutch, brought American ideals with them to the United States.

Swedes and Finns also laid claim to a tradition going back to the seventeenth century in North America. Representatives of both groups created stories in which Swedes or Finns, depending on who is telling the story, introduce "American" values as well as log cabins to the New World. "The early Swedish colonists in Delaware, Pennsylvania and New Jersey worked as hard for liberty and independence as the English did in New England and in the South," wrote Hans Mattson in 1891. Summing up some of the great contributions of Swedish Americans, he concluded, "Surely love of freedom, valor, genius, patriotism and religious fervor was [sic] not planted in America by the seeds brought over in the Mayflower alone." His botanical metaphor had been used with similar intent by Johan Enander in 1876, and both were, as the next chapter will show, influenced by the imagery as well as the historical vision of the Norwegian-American Rasmus Bjørn Anderson in a speech he gave and published in Chicago in 1875. But while Anderson spoke of all that was good and valuable in the United States as coming out of medieval Nor-

way, for Enander and Mattson the source was Sweden. As H. Arnold
Barton puts it, in a speech Enander gave in Philadelphia on the centennial of the Declaration of Independence, he declared that "'the seeds of
that freedom and independence which ripened under the sun of America by the 4th of July 1776 . . . had centuries earlier . . . been planted in a
land beneath the North Star, poor in silver and gold but rich in honor and
faith.' From 'freedom's home on earth'—as Sweden was traditionally
described—some Northmen had gone to England, bringing with them the
ideal of liberty. In time, some Englishmen, seeking greater freedom, had
moved to America." And those who had come from Sweden to America
had brought not only these ideals but also the will to defend them, as
Enander declared eleven years later: "Whenever the freedom of the American, which traces its earliest roots to the freeborn peoples of the Scandinavian North, has been seriously threatened, Swedish steel has always
flashed in the thick of battle in its defense." Moreover, as Barton observes,
Enander actually claimed that Swedish Americans were better stewards
of American ideals than the Anglo-Americans: "No slave groaned under
the lash of a Swedish slavedriver," and "no 'heretic' languished within
Swedish prison walls on American soil." "In effect," Barton writes,
"Enander maintained that the Swedes were by nature better Americans
than the 'Americans' themselves, that it was their historic destiny to lead
their new homeland to ever higher levels of idealism, in pursuit of all that
was 'great, noble, and beautiful.'"[8]

With the same colony in seventeenth-century Delaware as their point
of departure, writers of Finnish-American popular histories and fiction
have placed the same good American qualities with the Finnish colonists
who, as it were, brought them to America. In these accounts, writes Gary
London, the Finnish colonists are "industrious, harmonious, honest and
fair in their dealings with others, brave, and above all, libertyloving."
They learned the language of the neighboring Indians. Moreover, "cor-
dial relations with the Indians are based upon the fair and honest treatment given them by the Finns." Filiopietistic Finnish Americans, then,
gave their colonial forefathers very much the same characteristics that
filiopietistic Swedish and Dutch Americans gave to theirs. Nevertheless,
the villains in the Finnish-American version of American history are
"Swedes, Dutch, and English." In his *Amerikan ensimmäiset suomalaiset* Salomon Ilmonen compared the Finnish settlers "to the English Puritans, French Huguenots, and other minorities who came to America to
escape 'social injustice.'" Another writer, E. A. Louhi, "saw in the Finnish settlement of the Delaware colony 'the foundation of American civilization.'"[9] Thus Dutch Americans, Swedish Americans, and Finn-

ish Americans not only had American ideals deeply embedded in their character quite independently of the supposed Anglo-American origin of these ideals, but they were, in their different ways, more American than the Anglo-Americans.

Such views of the uniquely American character of a particular immigrant group were in no way limited to those who could relate their nineteenth-century immigration to settlements by fellow nationals in the colonial period. On the contrary, it would be difficult to find a group that did not insist upon an ideological relationship with America since the seventeenth or eighteenth centuries. In 1915, as a war was being fought in Europe for Polish independence, the editor of the *Dziennik Zwiazkowy* wrote an editorial to celebrate the birthday of two great men, Kosciuszko and Lincoln, whose spirits were ruled by "a boundless love of freedom." Looking forward to the independence of the old homeland, the editor pointed out, "The time is near when an indissoluble bond of mutual sympathy between the rejuvenated American people and a free national Poland will be formed, based on the two fraternal spirits of these two defenders of freedom. . . . Great ideals bring nations together. . . . Great men are the heralds who go into the world preaching the ideal and searching for brotherly spirits. They, again, are followed by entire nations, who gather under the banner of the noble brotherhood." Victor Greene has concluded that "Polish nationalists essentially claimed that American and Polish identities were *uniquely* compatible when compared to all other immigrant groups." Paradoxically, however, all such stories had in common the view that the relationship of each immigrant group with America was unique. The Polish pianist and statesman Ignacy Paderewski spoke to a large convention of Polish Americans in Detroit in August 1918 and told them that "the Poles in America do not need any Americanization. It is superfluous to explain to them the ideals of America" since they already knew them.[10] For his listeners this would not have been big news. He said nothing they had not heard many times before from their leaders. What is more, what he said had been told by others to audiences of immigrants from other countries as well.

Stories of ideological relationships are related to what may be called the contributions school of Americanization in the decades around the turn of the nineteenth century, with Jane Addams and Frances Kellor as its most articulate and prominent promulgators. In 1919 Kellor published an article in the *Yale Review*, giving her answers to the question "What Is Americanization?" In a slightly earlier period of intense political debate on immigration, Addams had claimed that far too little was known about immigration and the immigrants. Now Kellor, writing immediately after a period of an intensive war-born government-sponsored program of Americanization in which she herself had been prominently involved, suggested that it was still necessary to consider just what such a program of Americanization should achieve.

Because one third of the population of the United States had "its roots in other soils and in diverse cultures," the challenge was not only enormous but unprecedented: "No nation has had a sufficiently free opportunity with many diverse races to establish its enduring principles and certain procedure." And in America the task was different from in the Old World, which still had not found "a way by which each race living on its own soil, separated by definite national boundaries, can be assured freedom and peace," she wrote. The two main principles Kellor laid down for "race fusion" were "the opportunity to establish a home base in a country and a genuine love for that home" and "identity of economic interest." Both involved, she explained, the equal application of American "political ideals" for all so that they do not "mean one thing for the native-born and another thing for the foreign-born; one thing for men and another for women; one thing for employers and another for employees, one thing for the rich and another for the poor; one thing in one State and another thing in an adjoining State." A prerequisite, however, is a respect for the immigrant, who "has not been permitted to incorporate into the processes of American invention and research the processes of his own genius":

> Nowhere is there a clear authoritative statement of the contribution of the various races as such to America. Nowhere is there an analysis of what they have brought or can bring, and of all that material which we have not used. Nowhere is there information as to what they take or of what they want most from America. Tons of literature are printed and sent out daily by all kinds of agencies, with seldom a consultation with the foreigner as to how it fits the needs of his race. We ignore in most racial meetings the sound principle of race psychology.

Her call was for an Americanization that implied "a recognition of the cultural forces in the various races as expressed in their literature and institutions. . . . It means more than toleration. It means the use for America of the finest aspirations and traditions of these men."[11] The immigrants' own stories, however, of how their "finest aspirations and traditions" harmonized with and contributed to the continued development of American ideals, were not receiving much attention in the schoolrooms where their children were taught. Their children learned not only that all that was good in America was an Anglo-American tradition but that they and their parents were a menace to this tradition.

Throughout the nineteenth century and the early decades of the twentieth century, one way in which immigrant leaders tried to make their people feel at home in America was to insist that the ideals of the United States were an important part of their Old World heritage and that, consequently, they need not feel like foreigners in the land. It was, of course, hoped that such exhortations would also function as arguments for acceptance by the gate-keeping Anglo-Americans. The narratives embodying these arguments could take the form of myths of ideological gifts or contributions, as with the Swedes, Finns, and Dutch, or they could be presented as myths of a close ideological relationship, as those told to the Irish, Czechs, and Poles. As with myths of foundation and sacrifice, there is also a considerable degree of interethnic competition involved in the telling of myths of ideological gifts.

One of the more powerful expressions of such a myth of ideological contributions is from 1854, when the American rabbi and editor Isaac Mayer Wise, in the first issue of his newspaper, the *Israelite,* insisted that "the principles of the constitution of the United States are copied from the words of Moses and the prophets."[12] That this story had an influence is evident in its repetition more than fifty years later by the Chicago rabbi Emil G. Hirsch in his 1905 address, "The Concordance of Judaism and Americanism." "Judaism and fundamental Americanism are one," he said.[13] This was a point Hirsch made on various occasions, for instance, in a debate at the convention of the Council of Jewish Women that same year when the Chicago *Record-Herald* of December 11 reported that he had said, "We cannot be good Jews and not be good Americans. And we cannot be good Americans and not live up to the spirit and teachings of our race and religion." This theme was further embellished in 1930 when Max Goldberg spoke about "The Contribution of the Chosen Race to Civic Progress in America": "Jewish ideals and Biblical influence have played an important part in the foundation of the American Democracy." Among his illustrations were the Pilgrims, who, culturally, "were Jews as much as Non-Jews possibly could be," and Roger Williams, who "preached the doctrine of the separation of the State and the Church, a doctrine dear to the heart of every Jew."

From the earliest times, then, American ideals and Jewish ideals had been identical. In his conclusion Max Goldberg observed that "here in America in the sunlight of our free institutions Jewish qualities have found true self-expression." One speaker at the 250th anniversary of Jewish settlement in the United States had the Jews, together with the Pilgrim fathers and the Dutch ("fresh from having overthrown the tyranny of bigoted Spain"), as the three main sources of the American love of liberty: "Their yearning for religious and political liberty dictated our Declaration of Independence, drafted our Constitution, severed the church from the state, cast into our liberty bell the words of our Bible: 'Proclaim liberty throughout the land, unto all the inhabitants thereof.'" This view, that "some of the ancient religious values found in the Torah and in Talmudic law closely resembled, and thus reinforced, American humanistic, democratic principles," has been called "Hebraism" and was, writes Victor Greene, a common theme with Jewish leaders.[14]

Immigrant stories about participation in and contribution to hallowed American traditions could also be concerned with more colorful and festive details, as when the German-American newspaper *Die Abendpost* reminded its readers on December 20, 1908, that Santa Claus was German. Earlier, in 1890, the organizers of a German-American celebration in Milwaukee had observed that "the German Christmas tree enters year by year also into Anglo-American families." Such stories may in themselves appear insignificant, but they were always part of an argument of momentous proportions: the right to a home in America. Thus the origin of the American institution of Santa Claus was also contested. He came, explained H. I. Katibah in the *Syrian World* in 1929, not "from the blizzards of the dreary North," but "from the East, from a little town not distant from Northern Syria, from whence he went out to conquer the world with his charming kindness and benevolence."[15]

Although people like Frances Kellor and immigrant leaders may appear to be speaking with one voice when asking for national recognition of immigrant "gifts," the important contributions of immigrants to American society, their perspectives were very different, as were their strategies. For Kellor a central question was how to achieve "race fusion." Most leaders of the many ethnic groups, however, were speaking of the acceptance and maintenance of difference. Before World War I, German Americans, in particular, insisted that they were the cofounders of the United States along with the Anglo-Saxons and that to be a German American was as "American" as to be an English American. As one of the prominent academics among the German Americans, Julius Goebel, put it in his speech at the celebration of the tenth anniversary of the United German Associations of New York City in 1912: "Slowly, but with overwhelming clarity we realize that American culture, which is only in the process of entering the highest regions of human nature, has nourished itself on German culture for its best and permanent qualities and that our historical task is to take a creative and formative part in the development of American culture as representatives of German culture."[16]

Such a homemaking argument could also be given a negative slant, highlighting the negative qualities that were of English origin, as in *Die Abendpost* on April 27, 1899. Here readers were told that "long ago it has been proven, even if many Anglo-Americans prefer not to be reminded of it, that our largest supply from the criminal ranks, has been dumped unto our shores by England during the colonial period and even later." Consequently, "real" Americans are warned against excessive pride in their ancestry; the implication is, of course, that German Americans have good reason for pride in theirs. In this story even the hallowed *Mayflower* is a source of American criminality. Seen from such a point of view, the "large number of austere laws, to control crime and vice" was born not of Puritan virtue but of Anglo-American vice. Although other groups did not have the numerical base that made it possible for them to express the confidence that was so typical of German-American leaders before the First World War, their leaders too told stories of how their traditions were American in spirit and of how they had brought American values to America.

Although this book distinguishes between three genres of myths used in the homemaking arguments of European immigrant groups, these genres are not necessarily kept apart in the telling. Stories of ideological contributions may merge with stories of sacrifice because they are often about the defense of ideals shared by a particular immigrant group and the nation. They may also be an inseparable element in stories of foundation because they often are about the ideological roots of the nation. Indeed, stories that demonstrate an ideological foundation may be deliberately presented as more sophisticated rejoinders to stories that argue "we were here first." Although some Greek Americans joined the who-was-first competition by speculating on specific Greek contributions to the discovery of America and even claiming that Columbus was a Greek nobleman, others found more enlightened—and to them more acceptable—ways of insisting on the Greek parentage of the United States.

In an article in the *Aster* (Star) of November 11, 1927, P. S. Lambros, the editor and publisher of this Greek-American newspaper in Chicago, readily acknowledged that "it was Columbus, an Italian, who discovered America." Nevertheless he insisted that "this country is known as the true daughter of ancient Greece, for it has adopted and developed Greek civilization to the point of perfection." Indeed, the "traditional and historical relationship of the two countries" was the reason both for Greek immigration to the United States and that Greek Americans felt at home here. It "was the vital spark that inspired the Greeks to come here and become loyal American citizens."[17] An article in the *Saloniki* for July 23, 1931, makes much the same point, concluding that "the democratic form of government of today and the educational liberation of women owe their origin to ancient Greece." Such ideas of ancient Greece as the cradle of Western and in particular American civilization were of course not novel. They were in fact taught in colleges all over the United States. But it was as difficult for American educators to make the connection between the great men of classical Greece and contemporary Greek immigrants as it had been for Henry James to see the colorful peasants of Italy in the Italian immigrants he observed on returning to New York in 1904 after so many years in Europe.[18] The aim of Lambros and other Greek-American editors was to take the generally accepted story of the greatness of ancient Greece and use it as a homemaking argument for present-day immigrants.

One theme in stories of ideological contributions was the Puritan connection. Thus the Armenians came to the United States as "the Puritans of old, bringing the same earnestness of religious conviction, the same willingness to endure hardships of pioneer life and the same belief ingrained in their minds that they were traveling to a free land." In Chapter 2 we saw that Jewish immigrants had their *Mayflower*, the *St. Catarina*, which arrived in New Amsterdam in 1655. In 1930 the Lithuanian-American newspaper *Sandara* referred to the earliest Lithuanian immigrants to the Americas, who had first settled on Guadeloupe Island in the Caribbean in 1688 and then moved on to New York, as the "Lithuanian Pilgrims": "Like the famous pilgrims who fled from England on the Mayflower, the Lithuanian pilgrims left their homeland to escape intolerable living conditions, persecution, and the tyranny of the Polish landlords."

When German Americans organized the first "German Day" in Chicago in 1906 to celebrate the arrival of the first group of German immigrants in Pennsylvania on October 6, 1683, speeches stressed both the early arrival of the Germans and their contribution to the development of the United States. Again, the ideological parallel with the Pilgrim fathers was made to demonstrate that Germans had brought American ideals to the New World: "Like the Pilgrims who landed at Plymouth Rock so also these had emigrated from the old country following the impulse of free religious conviction in order to be able to serve their God in their own way."[19] In the stories about the early Dutch, Swedish, and Finnish colonists we have seen an obvious element of ideological competition with the Puritans. In *Die Sonntagpost* for January 10, 1919, the early German immigrants too were entered, as it were, in this competition and were placed "on the same level as the Puritans and Quakers." The newspaper also referred to a pronouncement by a prominent academic without "a drop of German blood in his veins" that "the Germans, more than any other American colonists, were guided by personal ideals"; the implication was that they too may have been somewhat better than their equals in colonies to the north.

Liberty, both in the sense of national independence and of individual rights, has been a cornerstone of American ideology—for the immigrant as well as for the native born. The central document for this ideology has been the Declaration of Independence rather than the less inspiring Constitution. Pauline Maier has called this founding document "American Scripture": "It was what the American people chose to make of it, at once a legacy and a new conception, a document that spoke both for the revolutionaries and for their descendants, who confronted issues the country's fathers had never known or failed to resolve, binding one generation after another in a continuing act of national self definition." Immigrants took part in this self-definition by claiming that the Declaration of Independence was their particular document, an expression of their heritage, and thus a document that gave their particular group a right to a home in America.[20]

During the celebration of Polish Day at the Columbian Exposition in 1893, a leader of the Polish National Alliance "reminded his listeners of the close ideological tie between the Declaration of Independence and the Polish Constitution, a link that would be described often," observes Victor Greene. Although the Columbus story tended to overshadow all other Italian-American homemaking myths, much has also been made of the story of the Italian origin of the Declaration of Independence through the influence of Philip Mazzei on his neighbor, Thomas Jefferson. Finnish and Swedish Americans have, as we saw in Chapter 2, both taken responsibility for the adoption of the Declaration with the deciding vote cast by John Morton. In 1932 a Greek American reminded his readers that when the United States decided to come to the aid of "the young Greek nation in her very hour of heroic struggle for political liberation," in 1823, it was "Daniel Webster who poured the honey of his eloquence before the House of Representatives . . . and convinced them that by helping Greece [the United States] was not merely paying their debt to modern Greeks as heirs of their ancient forefathers, but was helping a new nation because it was fighting for mankind, for civilization and for Christianity, and for upholding the very principles set forth in the American Declaration of Independence."[21]

As we saw in Chapter 3, standing up for American ideals, in particular those expressed in the Declaration of Independence, could mean sacrificing your blood for them. This was clear to John Pech, the Czech speaker at a 1911 Decoration Day celebration. He reminded his audience of "the significant sacrifice made by those immigrants who fought in the ranks of the northern army" in the Civil War. The reason for their idealism, he explained, was that they were aware that they were "defending the fundamental law of this great republic, 'that all people are born equal.'" This awareness and this idealism, the speaker implied, inspired not only the members of the first contingent to leave Chicago "for the field of battle in 1861 . . . a regiment composed almost entirely of Czech-Slavs, who chose this land as their country, and took up arms for humanity and civilization." It had also been the inspiration of all immigrants who had stood up for their country in peace as well as in war: "They are deserving of credit for all the growth and progress that America has made since then. It is mainly due to the merits of the immigrants that America has become a great and powerful country."[22]

German Americans too have insisted that the ideas in the Declaration were theirs, that these ideas were of German rather than English origin. The vision of the equality of all human beings, embedded in the Declaration of Independence, was first expressed in the New World in 1688, so goes a German-American story, in Germantown, Pennsylvania, the settlement founded by Francis Daniel Pastorius in 1683. To this "little model colony" America was indebted, according to *Die Sonntagpost* for January 10, 1919, "not only for the beginning of the great industrial development of our country, such as the weaving of linen, the knitting of stockings, papermaking, and book printing, but also for a far greater service, because it involved an ideal—the first protest against the despicable slave trade. No better proof of the German's love of freedom could be found than this protest against slavery." The document, written by Pastorius and other German immigrants in English in 1688 and translated to German for Chicagoans in 1919, was a strong protest, the newspaper reported, "against traffic in men" based on principles later written into the Declaration of Independence: "They are black, to be sure. But we cannot comprehend how that fact could give anybody a better right to enslave them than to enslave whites. There is a saying: 'All things whatsoever ye would that men should do to you, do ye even so to them.' No distinction is made with respect to nationality, origin, or color. . . . In Europe many people are oppressed in matters of conscience; here blacks are oppressed." In 1925 the editor of *Die Abendpost* listed some of the many contributions of German Americans to the growth and development of the Republic as part of his argument for more Germans in public office. He referred to stories of foundation as well as of sacrifice and—at the center of his list—he referred to this German-American story of ideological contribution: "The first declaration of independence originated in Germantown."[23] That the actual Declaration of Independence was not about freeing the slaves is another matter. The "misreading" of the document by German as well as other Americans is an apt illustration of how the Declaration has functioned as American scripture.

In this German-American story, the seventeenth-century German-town "declaration" inspired the Declaration of Independence in 1776. Although the founding of the nation was inspired by German ideals, it failed to heed the German call for freedom for all Americans, including the African slaves. But when the country eventually abolished slavery almost two hundred years after the initiative in Germantown, it was again inspired by German ideals, according to another German story. More specifically, a speaker at the Chicago Lincoln Club in 1924 explained, it was the German revolution in 1848 that "influenced the American unrest, and in the end led to the Civil War." After the failed revolution of 1848, many of the so-called forty-eighters had immigrated to the United States. "Stirred by a tremendous idealism, about 700,000 Germans immigrated to America, all of whom felt inwardly, that they more or less had the call to bring liberty to the world, and who believed, that they also could upset every thing that was old in America and could create new conditions." The "colder thinking Anglo-Saxons" may not have understood that the Germans were "inspired by high ideals," but the fact was, said Dr. H. H. Maurer, that "the unrest of the years before the Civil War were . . . nothing else than the consequences of the bacillers [sic] of the revolution which were brought over by the German immigrants of that time."[24] German Americans were the first to reason against slavery in a public American document, and German Americans were responsible for the war that saved the Union and emancipated the slaves. The context of Maurer's speech, a meeting of a political society named for the Great Emancipator six years after America's war with Germany, underlines the homemaking argument that was implied.

As has been demonstrated, there was scarcely a claim made by representatives of one group that has not also been claimed for another. The Jewish-American *Sentinel* in 1916 observed that

> in the political movements for the abolition of slavery, the Jews took a leading part in creating public opinion. As early as 1853, a fugitive Negro, arrested by a U.S. Marshal, was liberated by a crowd of Chicago citizens led by Michael Greenebaum. In the evening of that day a meeting was held to ratify that act. The first official call to organize the abolition movement was signed by George Schneider, Adolph Loeb, Julius Rosenthal, Leopold Mayer, and a man named Hanson . . . four Jews among the five leaders of the German population of Chicago in a great humanitarian gesture.[25]

Of course, during and immediately after World War I, German Americans had a special need to demonstrate not merely that the central American values also were their values but that these values were of German origin and had been introduced in North America by the first German colonists. Indeed, German Americans had not only brought ideas of liberty with them to the New World, they had also been foremost among those who had taken responsibility for the U.S. Constitution by rallying in its defense. In *Die Abendpost* of September 25, 1927, an article on the making of the Constitution acknowledges that the Constitutional Convention "consisted of ninety per cent of Englishmen, Scotchmen, and Irishmen" but then goes on to note the German influence: "It is true that the Constitution of the United States was not wholly the work of Germans, but was mainly the result of long parliamentarian schooling, as it was inherited from England. . . . But, nevertheless, it was the Germans who pledged themselves with all their might to the preservation of the Constitution."

That German Americans had both contributed to the American tradition of liberty and had always been ready to defend it, however, was neither a new theme in German-American rhetoric nor one that distinguished them from other groups. Moreover, the First World War was by no means the first occasion for German Americans to react to American nativism. They had, for instance, been assisted by Lincoln in making the new Republican Party take a stance against nativism in 1854, as we saw in Chapter 3. In Milwaukee in October 1890 Georg Meyer brought the German American's peculiar love of liberty to the attention of those who were celebrating the "Deutschamerikanischen Tages" festivities: "Another characteristic German-American trait is his sense of liberty [*Freiheitssinn*] that, as we have seen, was as gloriously active when it was necessary to shake off the English yoke as when it was a question of bringing the slavery obnoxiousness to an end." And, he continued with obvious reference to the increasing call for prohibition in many midwestern states as well as to various attempts at English-only legislation, "the German spirit of liberty and independence will not be bent today either when narrow-minded fanatics are trying to bring down the bulwark of individual liberty and lay German behavior and customs in fetters through compulsory laws of prohibition and language." The year before, in 1889, the state legislature had passed a bill on compulsory education bearing the name of its author, Michael J. Bennett. The law's requirement that the obligatory subjects of reading, writing, arithmetic, and the history of the United States all be taught in English had caused an uproar, in particular among the Germans, who made up 37 percent of the state's population.[26] In several midwestern states prohibition was another issue that German Americans tended to see as an Anglo-American infringement on their way of life. Behind the seemingly boastful language of the speaker, then, is his sense of being marginalized, made a foreigner, in the only country he claimed as his own by laws restricting the use of his German language and trying to deprive him of his enjoyment of traditional German beer.

As the maintenance of languages and traditions among immigrants was increasingly questioned and criticized in the years leading up to the First World War, and as the hyphen, originally a symbol of ethnic pride, and the use of languages other than English became symbols of questionable or divided loyalties, immigrant leaders responded by defending their rights as loyal Americans, as Americans of other origins than those of English descent.[27] To the editor of the Czech newspaper *Denní Hlasatel*, little was new in the antihyphen campaign spurred on by the president in 1915. In an editorial, "More About Hyphens," on October 13, he wrote, "It is an old story which pops up every once in a while with new and more or less timely variations." And he explained why "Mr. Wilson has no reason to be afraid of 'hyphenated' Americans": "The much abused hyphen is not a sign of cleavage, but a sign of unity. It is an indication that those who are using it, while not unmindful of their origin, cling firmly to this country, the country they have chosen as their new home."

Irish Americans were among those who would naturally react strongly to an equation of Americanism and anglicism. This would amount to again subjecting themselves to "the English yoke," and some responded by seeking closer ties with German Americans, as did Thomas J. Diven, who published an article (in English) considering the question, "Is This an English Country?" in the German-American journal *Der Zeitgeist*. One of his main points was that the Irish and the Germans in America had consistently stood for Americanism, while all traitors of the American cause had come from English stock. "Without the Irish and Germans of Pennsylvania, we would have had no republic," he wrote. "I have looked in vain for the name of one German who took the British gold and joined the Indians in their raids upon the lonely settlers. . . . There were no traitors, no Tories among the Irish." And now, when the country was again threatened by war, the situation was much the same as during the War of Independence: "The rampant Toryism of the present that would again submit us to the English yoke finds no response in their minds."[28] While voices in all groups insisted at various times that they were the best Americans because of their peculiar national heritage, after war had been declared not many would suggest, as did Diven, that continued resistance to helping the British was an expression of Americanism. On the contrary, German-American leaders, including the editor of *Der Zeitgeist*, were by then busily professing their loyalty and their support of the war effort.

Before war was declared, however, such views as those expressed by Diven were common among German-American leaders. An editorial in Chicago's *Die Sonntagpost* for August 30, 1914, was headlined "We Hyphenated Americans." It speaks for all immigrants from countries other than Britain and claims that they are the true bearers of American ideas, that it was the deterioration of "a strong and genuine Americanism" among Anglo-Americans that created a need for "hyphenated Americanism":

> Because our English language press and the so-called influential social set of our country became less American and more English in tone and attitude, citizens of non-English origin tended to display their descendency, and emphasized their racial stock by referring to themselves as German, Irish, Polish, and Swedish-American, and so on. The war will aggravate this condition, because it revealed the thoroughly British attitude of our English language press, because it proved the allegedly "true" Americanism to be a disguised Anglomania for the most part, displaying a slave-like servility to British interests.[29]

This historical interpretation of the use of the hyphen may be no more sound than most of the historical interpretations in homemaking stories, but it shares an important characteristic with them all: homemaking stories were born of a need to argue against views that stamped one as a foreigner in one's own country.

Although the particular situation in 1914 may have called for a more politicized expression of the homemaking argument than usual, the editor of *Die Sonntagpost* was merely repeating the oft-heard story of how a particular immigrant group was American in its outlook even before coming to America and of why it was at least as American as the Anglo-Americans: "Millions of Germans who crossed the ocean to establish a new home here were, with hardly an exception, ardent admirers of this great and free Republic. They had firmly made up their minds to become good and true Americans. And they became just that—true Americans and not pseudo-Americans. They turned out to be better Americans than their fellow citizens of English blood and heritage because they never tried to put this great Republic in a state of political dependency to Germany."[30] In much the same manner, but without an anti-English slant, the editor of the *Denní Hlasatel*, defending the use of the hyphen on October 13, 1915, explained that immigrants who had come to America "in order to live a life of greater freedom and liberty . . . will remain loyal to her under all circumstances."

Loyalty to the chosen homeland, then, was never to be questioned so far as the immigrant leaders were concerned. To members of the cultural, social, and political elite of this new homeland, however, a real American was, implicitly yet unavoidably, an American of British origin. Loyalty from this point of view was as much a question of descent as of consent. Leaders of some immigrant groups responded to the all-pervasive view of the English as the first-rank founding nationality by claiming a biological as well as an ideological relationship with the English colonists of New England, as did, for instance, Norwegian-American leaders. Others, such as representatives of the Dutch, the Finnish, and the Swedish Americans, countered by insisting on a colonial past that gave their nationalities the status of cofounders, not only of America but, more important, of Americanism along with and not behind the British. Some leaders of the German Americans have also been shown to make use of this rhetorical strategy in their filiopietistic narratives, claiming rights as cofounders through the introduction of American ideals in colonial North America.

As Europe was approaching war, it became equally important for some German Americans to create an American history in which the English were consistently given the roles of traitors and villains. In the propagation of this view they found allies among the Irish. Despite their very different European histories, immigrants from both nationalities at the time of the First World War found reason to bring the Old World conflicts of their former homelands into their New World homemaking arguments. With the English as the enemy, their homemaking narratives would not only have to place eighteenth-century Germans and Irish in the roles of the true American patriots but, equally important, place Englishmen in the roles of traitors to the cause of American liberty. Against such a tradition these spokesmen could then express their twentieth-century Americanism by rejecting an Anglo-American tradition at home and alliances with Britain abroad. Moreover, they could insist that because the United States was not, at least not primarily, a country created by Americans of British descent, they and not the Anglo-Americans were the true arbiters of Americanism.

That members of an immigrant elite gave expression to homemaking mythologies in the so-called foreign-language press and in public addresses or lectures to immigrant audiences does of course not mean that all prominent members of immigrant groups spoke and wrote in this manner, nor that all who read or listened nodded their heads in agreement. For instance, in his autobiography the Norwegian immigrant Andreas Ueland made fun of Rasmus B. Anderson's idealistic notion of medieval Norway as an ideal democracy and the source of American liberty.[31] But even Ueland may seem like an ethnic chauvinist when his minor objections are compared to H. L. Mencken's full-scale debunking of the notion that German Americans contributed anything whatsoever of value to the United States: "As Americans they are mere numbers. . . . The influence of the Germans upon American life is very slight . . . and they have left no impression upon American ideas. . . . In the political field they are as feeble as in the cultural." Indeed, he wrote in a Berlin journal in 1928, their only influence had been upon American cooking and vocabulary. But it should be noted that Mencken was as biased in his way as immigrant leaders were in theirs. An aristocrat of the intellect, he was explaining to fellow intellectuals in the Old World that they had no reason to deplore the loss of the many German immigrants who mainly "belonged to the landworking, handworking and small shopkeeping classes."[32] Although Mencken was distancing himself from the mass of German Americans by insisting on their low station in society on both sides of the ocean, their leaders saw the creation of ethnic pride as a central concern.

All immigrants, according to their leaders—their journalists, public speakers, and historians—were in many and important ways American before they came to these shores. Victor Greene has observed of the many immigrant leaders from different groups that he studied that almost all referred "to the American Revolution and the making of the American state to justify retaining their European culture."[33] Because their values, ideals, and traditions were "American" to begin with, they did not come as foreigners but as ready-made ideal citizens of the Republic. Anglo-Americans, however, who regarded themselves as the only real Americans, did not welcome as their fellow Americans the increasing numbers of citizens of different hues, with different religions and customs, and speaking different languages. This may have caused immigrants at times to be somewhat shrill in their insistence and to express themselves with chauvinist rhetoric. But despite their exaggerations and despite their tendency to glorify themselves, all the immigrants whose stories have been retold here were—in their use of the many ethnically specific variations on the three basic thematic patterns of homemaking myths—engaged in making the United States their rightful homeland and in insisting that "we are not foreigners in this country."

The many immigrant voices insisting on their right to a home in America tend to be less shrill in the 1920s and 1930s than in earlier decades. The wartime experience and the Americanization campaign may have had some sobering effect on the rhetoric as well as the fervor of immigrant leaders. More important, the immigration restriction act of 1924 brought the intense anti-immigration debate of several decades to an end and removed the immediate cause of so much anxiety among Anglo-Americans that their nation was being changed beyond recognition by the "foreign element." Myths of foundation continued to have importance for the identity of members of some ethnic groups and could, as will be seen, even be the ground for considerable emotional involvement in the second half of the twentieth century. A closer look at the chronology of the evidence of the use of myths of foundation and those of ideological contributions, however, suggests that the latter became the more common in homemaking arguments of the 1920s and 1930s. While myths of foundation insist on the separate identity and contribution of a particular group and argue for an exclusive inclusiveness, myths of ideological contributions point to the essential unity of immigrant group and nation. This may be seen in the shift in meaning of the personal pronoun from the "we" in "we were here first" to the "we" in "we have the same ideals." The former refers to the members of one specific ethnic group, pitting them against all others. The latter includes the nation, the people of the United States, regardless of ethnicity.

A similar nonexclusive ideological homemaking argument is implied in some immigrant autobiographies. Typically, the writer of an autobiography is making a case for an individual rather than for a group, as does the immigrant leader, whether writing in a newspaper or speaking at a rally. Paradoxically, the argument for the American qualities of the individual may nevertheless have a more universal potential than the argument made exclusively for a specific immigrant group. One reason for this is inherent in a traditional theme of the autobiographical genre: the life as lesson for the reader. It may also be, however, because of the narrated universality of the experience of immigration as a homecoming: "These immigrants were Americans before they landed," Louis Adamic writes of immigrants with tear-filled eyes holding up their children on first sighting the Statue of Liberty. He may appear unduly sentimental, but he was not making it up. He is reporting, he tells us, on the experiences of many immigrants by whom he has been "repeatedly impressed."[34]

Two Norwegian-American immigrant autobiographies may illustrate how pervasive was the notion of being American before coming to America. In a memoir he published in 1938, Nils N. Rønning told of a childhood experience in rural Norway when he for the first time was told about Abraham Lincoln: "Then and there the heart of the little white-haired, barefooted Norwegian boy went out to the great heart of Abraham Lincoln, and I was baptized with the spirit of America." In *Recollections of an Immigrant,* Andreas Ueland, a successful judge and lawyer in Minneapolis, wrote about how his father, a peasant member of the Norwegian parliament, was familiar with Benjamin Franklin. Ueland's Americanism, he suggested, was quite literally part of his paternal inheritance. What is more, he also made a point of implying that he was well prepared for his American life because the strongest influence on the constitution of his old homeland was the constitution of his new homeland.[35] There could evidently be a two-way traffic of ideological contributions.

That the autobiographical account of an individual experience is often presented as potentially universal is perhaps best illustrated in *The Americanization of Edward Bok* (1920), a rags-to-riches American story of success. In the conclusion of his autobiography the Dutch-born Bok switched from the third person mode of his narrative to the first person and confessed that, "when I look around me at the American-born I have come to know as my close friends, I wonder whether, after all, the foreign-born does not make in some sense a better American . . . whether his is not the deeper desire to see America greater." The question about who makes the better American is clearly not asked on behalf of himself alone, nor is it, as is usual in the stories retold in this book, presented as a claim on behalf of his particular ethnic group, the Dutch Americans. On the contrary, his suggestion is presented as potentially valid "in some sense" for all immigrants, regardless of their country of origin. They are all invited not only to question their Anglo-American neighbors' definition of immigrants as foreigners or aliens but to wonder whether they may not be better Americans than these "native" neighbors. Bok continued his reflection on "how good an American has the process of Americanization made me" with views that have been put forward by so many immigrant leaders, from the Norwegian-American editor Knut Langeland in 1866 to the rabbi Emil G. Hirsch in 1905 to the German-American academic Julius Goebel in 1912, by posing the question: "whether in seeing faults more clearly he does not make a more decided effort to have America reach those ideals or those fundamentals of his own land which he feels are in his nature, and the best of which he is anxious to graft into the character of his adopted land?"[36]

But while the earlier representatives of Norwegians, Jews, Germans, and others explained to their readers and listeners that they had special contributions to make to the quality of their chosen homeland because of the special qualities of their particular nationality, Bok saw the desire to "graft" the "ideals" the immigrant "feels are in his nature . . . into the character of his adopted land" as born of the act and process of immigration. He recognized the vision of a "greater" America as natural to the immigrant—not because he was from a particular country but because he was an immigrant. The immigrant reader of such autobiographies as those by Bok, Antin, or Riis, then, was encouraged to make herself at home in the United States confident that she is in no sense inferior to the native-born American. The Anglo-American reader is advised to see her immigrant neighbor as an American, indeed, as a better American, rather than as an alien.

Although homemaking myths were about the past, they were presented as part of a forward-looking argument for an American future. They were more about ensuring a present and future place in the new American home than about nostalgia for the old home and its past glory. They were about ethnic groups in their new home rather than about their earlier European nationalities. And they were rooted in the new land rather than in the old. Only then could they function in a convincing argument for the right to a home in the new land. This does not mean that they did not glorify the past greatness and achievements of European nations. The homemaking stories of Greek Americans, as of Americans from Italy, Sweden, Poland, and the Netherlands, all glorified the past achievements of their nationalities. The myths of Norwegian Americans tended to focus on the medieval past, as we will see in the next chapter. But while both Greek and Norwegian Americans would point with pride to ancient pasts, the ideals that formed the basis for the ancient greatness of the old homeland were seen as the basis for the present and future greatness of the new one. They were preoccupied with acquiring an acknowledged right to a home in the new land, not with nostalgia for the old one.

5 Norwegian Americans Are Americans

THE STORIES TOLD by immigrants to demonstrate their historical, moral, and spiritual right to a home in the United States were, of course, not deliberately and separately constructed with any thought to the three genres of foundation, sacrifice, and ideological relationship and contribution. A genre, as used in this book, is more a theory of reading than a theory of writing. An awareness of the three genres of homemaking myths is helpful in understanding more clearly the function and subtext of all these stories, regardless of their genre: a homemaking argument. Specific occasions, such as Decoration Day or Columbus Day, could call for stories structured according to a specific genre (for those holidays, the stories would be, respectively, of sacrifice and foundation). On many other occasions an immigrant could present a discourse that integrated all three genres in a narrative that showed the quite special relationship of an immigrant group to its chosen country.

Such an occasion came for a Greek immigrant in 1919 when he wrote to the Chicago newspaper *Saloniki* to express his satisfaction with immigration, both for himself and for his fellow Greek Americans, and his faith that "a wonderful and glorious civilization" would be produced "in the next generation [by] the artistic spirit of the Greeks in the United States, combined with the American practical mind." Greek immigration might be "the newest," he acknowledged, but it was also "the oldest" in that "Pythagoras, who lived in Greece 2,500 years ago, was the first man who discovered that the earth is round." Greek ideas came to

France and Italy, he explained, when Greek refugees from the Turks "produced the European Renaissance. Among the precious knowledge they offered in that time, they promulgated also the Grecian theory about the sphericity of the earth. Columbus took advantage of this theory and discovered America."

But it was not only vicariously, through Columbus's use of a Greek idea, that Greeks were the real discoverers of America. This immigrant's story of a physical Greek presence in America actually predates the Columbus story by several thousand years. He had recently read a newspaper article about the discovery of the "graves and skeletons of giants" in South America. The graves "were of Grecian style" and had the inscription "Alexander, The King's Soldiers." The most reasonable explanation of this mystery, according to the Greek immigrant, was that one of the ships in Alexander's fleet that got lost in a storm off the coast of India eventually "arrived on the shores of South America." Consequently, "Greeks discovered America 2,300 years ago." Moreover, the few Greeks who had arrived in "the seventeenth, eighteenth, and nineteenth centuries" played important roles in the founding of the United States: "the majority of them have [had] a splendid career in letters, science, and the navy."

His main story of sacrifice was about the recent world war in which the "contribution of the Greeks in the United States . . . was wonderful." Not only had an extraordinarily large number served in the armed forces (65,000 of a population of 400,000) but almost as many had worked in munitions factories, and "in the Liberty Loan drives they received honorary positions by their generous contributions." But the main reason this particular Greek immigrant felt at home in his chosen country was not that Greeks had been the first Europeans to discover America or, at the very least, made Columbus's discovery possible, nor was it that Greeks had given their lives for America but that the United States itself was virtually Greek. "I found the shores of the United States very familiar and very hospitable toward me," the man wrote. "I have seen in the port of New York the Statue of Liberty, which was born in Greece many thousands of years ago. I have found the Constitution of the United States copied from the constitution of the glorious Republic of Athens."

The spiritual relationship went further: he had observed Greek architecture "in the most magnificent buildings in every big city" and "reproductions of the Grecian statues in every art museum of the United States." He had seen El Greco's painting of the Virgin in the Chicago Art Institute, Greek books "in every American library," and "Grecian dances revivied [sic] in the United States." With America a Greek discovery, the U.S. Constitution a Greek copy, American victory assured by Greek sacrifice in World War I, and Greek literature and art absolutely everywhere in the country, need we wonder why the United States was the natural home of its Greek immigrants?[1]

The stories used in the immigrants' homemaking arguments did not just happen to be there, ready for use. At some point all were the deliberate creation of individuals. Some stories may have lacked sufficient appeal or may have fallen upon stony places and therefore did not gain the status of a living myth essential to the ethnic American identity of large numbers of immigrants from a particular country. Other stories entered into the common discourse of immigrant leaders and writers and thus became myths shared by many members of a particular group. The point of departure for the creators of these stories could be a newspaper article (as it was for the Greek immigrant who believed that some of Alexander the Great's soldiers had come to the Americas in ancient times) or the work of a professional historian.

Very often, however, the creation of these stories was part and parcel of the amateurish filiopietistic history writing of the immigrants themselves. Although some myths may appear to have the anonymous characteristics of ancient legends, which are somehow attributed to a people rather than to specific individuals, this is merely because their origin has not always been traced. Indeed, because historians have not taken filiopietistic history writing very seriously, they have done little research on the origins of these myths. Understanding how the specific homemaking mythology of one immigrant group came about, was accepted, and was used in agitation may throw light on the homemaking arguments of American immigrant groups in general.

This chapter takes a close look at the creation, development, and widespread acceptance of a Norwegian-American homemaking mythology. This mythology is not singled out because it is special. On the contrary, this book has its beginnings in my realization that the filiopietism of the Norwegian Americans who insisted that they were the first, the most sacrificing, and the best Americans was not so much characteristic of Americans of Norwegian descent as it was of American immigrants in general. Without recognizing it as such, I encountered much homemaking argumentation while doing research for my 1996 book, *The Western Home: A Literary History of Norwegian America*.[2] At first I simply tried to dismiss what I saw as chauvinistic, vulgar boasting; however, I came to see much of immigrant filiopietism as a creative response to immigrants' experience of nonacceptance—indeed, repulsion—by the culturally, socially, and politically dominant group of Americans, those of British descent.

Although the Norwegian-American homemaking mythology seems largely to have been the creation of one individual, Rasmus Bjørn Anderson, a Wisconsin-born second-generation Norwegian American, it was embellished, developed, and used by so many that it may be characterized as a mythology that was widely known and used among Norwegian Americans, especially in the upper Midwest, from the mid-1870s and through the 1920s. As the need to argue for a home in America diminished in the 1920s and 1930s, however, many stories used to promote such an argument were soon forgotten. Those that lingered on, as did the story of Viking discovery, no longer expressed a demand for acceptance in the American home. When a Norwegian American today dons a Viking helmet, she is no longer making a homemaking argument.

Indeed, a homemaking mythology had ceased to be a defining aspect of Norwegian-American ethnicity by the time of World War II, and this was true of most European ethnic groups. Responding to the pressures of Americanization and one-hundred percentism in 1917, a majority of the leadership of the Norwegian Lutheran Church of America (recently created through the merger of three churches) had wished to drop the now offensive national qualifying adjective in the name of the church. This led to a heated debate that lasted several years about ethnicity (or race, the term then used most often), heritage, and homemaking in the United States. When the national adjective eventually was dropped from the name of the church in 1946, it was no longer felt to be a natural qualifier for its members. Indeed, the adjective was retained during World War II in deference to the occupied former homeland. During World War I, immigrant leaders had rallied in defense of their ethnicity; after World War II, American church members, for whom ethnicity had become, at best, a secondary interest, saw no further need to identify the church as an immigrant or ethnic institution.

I am deliberately using the word "mythology," rather than "myth" or "myths," to characterize the complex of stories first presented by Rasmus B. Anderson in the 1870s. From the very beginning the separate stories were so interlinked that they may be regarded as parts of a comprehensive mythology. This mythology soon took on a life of its own. As it developed, it acquired its pantheon of heroes, who, much like the characters in classical mythology, may have originated in very different historical (or mythological) periods but who in the telling of the myths all seem to coexist in one timeless homemaking mythology. This mythology was neither Norwegian nor European. It was not part of the cultural baggage of any immigrant crossing the Atlantic. (Nor is Columbus Day, for that matter, an Italian holiday.) The need to argue for a home in America has been an American experience. Consequently, the telling of stories as part of an American homemaking argument is an entirely American exercise. This does not mean, of course that all narrative *elements* of the Norwegian-American mythology traced and explored in this chapter are uniquely Norwegian American. Nevertheless, whether some story elements are of Old World origin or others refer to events in the historical New World experience of many immigrants, their combination in a comprehensive mythology for use in a homemaking argument makes them as American as the story of the landing of the *Mayflower* at Plymouth Rock.

The beginning of Norwegian immigration is commonly dated as July 4, 1825, when the sloop *Restaurationen* (54 feet long and weighing a mere 39 tons) left Stavanger for New York with fifty-two emigrants, including the crew. When they landed in New York on October 15, fourteen weeks later, the *New York Daily Advertiser* declared them "a novel sight." They were described as a foreign-looking flock, especially because their clothes were made of "coarse cloths of domestic manufacture," such a contrast with the more American-looking clothes worn by New Yorkers that the journalist presumed were made in England.[3] Even though mass immigration would not begin for forty more years, at the end of the Civil War, the early decades were the formative period of Norwegian-American ethnic culture. This was when early institutions were created and basic attitudes took shape.[4] Mass immigration peaked in the 1880s and was over by 1924.

Matthew Frye Jacobson characterizes the decades before the Civil War as a period of "profound cultural reorientation" in the ways Anglo-Americans thought and spoke about immigrants. He relies heavily on Richard Henry Dana's *Two Years Before the Mast*, which was first published in 1840 and "refers to Europeans and Euro-Americans as 'whites' and 'white men.'" Jacobson notes that "the phrases 'English race' and 'Anglo-Saxon race'" are new in the postscript to the 1859 edition. These new terms specifically excluded the Irish, who in 1859 were characterized as a group "with intelligence in . . . small . . . proportion to the number of faces." Jacobson explains, "Whereas the salient feature of whiteness before the 1840s had been its powerful and cultural contrast to nonwhiteness, now its internal divisions, too, took on a new and pressing significance." The new hierarchy of white races that placed the English, or Anglo-Saxon, race at the top was primarily a response to the sudden large influx of immigrants from Ireland, but it was used to categorize all immigrants. This categorization was based on scientific theories of race, quickly became a salient feature of American discourse, and was "reflected in literature, visual arts, caricature, political oratory, penny journalism, and myriad other venues of popular culture."[5]

As I will show, a Norwegian-American homemaking mythology was initially created as a direct and personal response to what was perceived as Anglo-American exclusivity and lack of respect for—indeed, a lack of awareness of—the significant contributions by Norwegians to Western civilization. Moreover, this mythology did not simply argue for the whiteness of Norwegians, which had been questioned. It responded more specifically to the racial theories that placed Anglo-Saxondom, rather than a more general whiteness, at the apex of the human family of races by demonstrating the close historical racial ties between Anglo-Americans and Norwegian Americans.

The immediate reason for the creation of the first expression of a Norwegian-American homemaking mythology at a specific moment and in a specific place may be found in the personality of an extremely proud and touchy young American born of Norwegian immigrant parents in Wisconsin in 1846 and his response to marginalization. Anderson grew up as Norwegian-American institutions were taking shape and in an area where the concentration of Norwegian immigration made possible the formation of an ethnic identity even though the total number of immigrants to the United States still was modest.[6] Moreover, his consciousness of his ethnic identity was formed in the very period that the racial theories of Anglo-Saxons were becoming widely accepted and creating negative attitudes toward foreigners, that is, toward immigrants from countries other than Britain. Anderson's vision of the greatness of his own people, which was embodied in his homemaking narrative, caught on quickly and soon acquired the characteristics of a folk mythology. This suggests that he was responding to a situation and to pressures and challenges experienced by many members of his ethnic group.

One of the earliest American homemaking mythologies was created and used in a homemaking argument within and largely for the Norwegian-American immigrant group. But the myths and the argument were similar to those of other immigrant groups. Some, like the Swedish Americans, were clearly inspired by the Norwegian story for some of their stories; most, like the Italian Americans and German Americans, were quite independent creators of their own myths. Thus the study of the origins, nature, and use of a homemaking mythology among the Norwegian Americans should be of special interest. It will illuminate this peculiarly American genre of filiopietistic historiography and help to create a basis for a better understanding of why homemaking myths were such a prominent feature of European immigrant cultures, especially just before and after the turn of the nineteenth century.

The basic Norwegian-American homemaking mythology was used and referred to in speech and writing for about seven decades, beginning in the late 1860s. Many still actively used and believed in it in the early 1930s, and it may be roughly outlined as follows.

American democracy was of Norwegian origin. The ancient Norse society had fully developed and broadly based democratic institutions. Norwegian democracy was exported to Britain in two different ways, first through the Viking settlement of large areas of England, Scotland, and Ireland, and second through the Normans, who descended from Norwegian Vikings who had taken land in northern France. It was the Norman (that is, Norwegian) lords who created the great document of English democracy, the Magna Carta. The institutions and traditions born of this document were the foundation for the great American democratic charters: the Declaration of Independence and the Constitution—both, then, in effect Norwegian creations.

The Norwegians were the true discoverers of America. That North America was first discovered by Leif Erikson and settled by Norwegians in medieval times were well-documented historical facts. This history made the nineteenth-century settling of the upper Midwest part of a long tradition of colonization: of Normandy, parts of Britain, Iceland, the Faeroe Islands, Greenland, and Vinland.

True Yankees were Norwegians. The seventeenth-century Puritans of New England, the most prestigious founding group in America, largely came from those areas in England that had been most heavily settled by Norwegian Vikings. So, not only were the Norse the first Europeans to settle in the New World but the United States—which was based on Norwegian principles—was founded by English colonists of Norwegian descent.

The Union was *saved by Norwegian immigrants.* The participation of Norwegian Americans in the Civil War, in particular through the Fifteenth Wisconsin Infantry and its commanding officer, Col. Hans Christian Heg, was the central story of sacrifice. This story was integrated with the stories of foundation and of ideological and racial relationship to make a comprehensive homemaking mythology. All elements of this mythology were evident in the argument that the United States was the natural home of its Norwegian immigrants: it was "their land of Leif Erikson."[7] Because the very culture and ideology that made America "American" was Norwegian, it followed that the more you strove to be a good Norwegian American, the better an American you became.

This mythology was not present in the earliest American accounts of immigration from Norway. The first brief history of Norwegian immigration, written in Illinois, was published in 1838, thirteen years after the voyage of "the Norwegian Mayflower" from Stavanger to New York in 1825.[8] Composed in the question-and-answer style of the catechism by an immigrant, Ole Rynning, and published posthumously in Norway as a guidebook for prospective emigrants, *Sandfærdig Beretning om Amerika* (True Account of America) has a brief chapter called "How Did the Country First Become Known?" It begins with the statement that "the credit for the discovery of America is now given to *Christopher Columbus*" and then tells of the Icelandic saga accounts of the medieval Norse settlements in North America. The implication is, it would seem, that those who think of emigrating should be aware of an ancient history of westward migration, but the story has no mythic function, having no implied "we," and no homemaking argument is suggested.[9] Rynning had, after all, arrived in 1837, a few years before the nativism of the 1840s and 1850s, and it is unlikely that he had any experience of those political or cultural conflicts in the New World that created a need for such an argument. The adversaries he and his fellow settlers had in Illinois were soil and climate rather than nativist prejudice.

Another early history of immigration, written by Svein Nilsson, "De skandinaviske settlementer i Amerika" (The Scandinavian Settlements in America), was published in installments in a Wisconsin illustrated journal, *Billed Magazine* (Illustrated Magazine), from 1868 to 1870. It begins with the statement that Columbus discovered the New World and goes on to present a narrative of immigration after 1825, largely based on oral and written material collected from the people (or, rather, men) involved. A later installment retells the story, based on the Icelandic sagas, of the early Norse discoveries, but Nilsson makes no suggestion that this history in some way legitimizes a Norwegian presence in the Midwest. Rather, immigration is legitimized through a narrative of success in the present.

A motif that runs through Nilsson's accounts of the achievements of individual settlers is their success. Of individual after individual we learn that he became prosperous and had a large farm or had left a large farm to his descendants. The concluding words in the last installment are "Both are farmers in Cottage Grove, live in easy circumstances, and are highly respected men." Nilsson does, however, hint at an ideological change in the social environment of the immigrants. Nilsson makes a point of "Yankee" approval of Norwegian immigrants and takes care to distance his group from the Irish. While the Norwegians are settled on prosperous farms, the Irish "prefer town life, and many of the cities in this country are rimmed by several rows of Irish shanties which surround the business district like a frame. Here the sons of Erin live in complete harmony with the habits of their forefathers."[10]

A third history deserves mention here, even though it is a history of the United States rather than of Norwegian immigration. David Monrad Schøyen had a law degree and practiced law before some sort of scandal, apparently involving the misuse of alcohol, led to his emigration in 1869. In Chicago his lowly position as a hack writer is evident in the omission of his name from the title page as well as the colophon page of the first two volumes of his three-volume *Amerikas forenede Staters Historie* (History of the United States, 1874–76), published by the Chicago newspaper *Skandinaven*. His first chapter is "The Original Inhabitants," his second "The Norsemen of Antiquity in America." Here he discusses, in a fairly informed manner, some of the historiographical controversy about the trustworthiness of the Norse sagas and gives a brief account of the known Norse voyages and attempts to settle in North America. Schøyen's versions are rather less fanciful than those found in many contemporary accounts. In his discussion of Columbus and John Cabot, Schøyen makes his claim for the historical importance of the Viking voyages, observing that the existence of both Greenland and North America was traditional and common knowledge in Iceland when Columbus visited the island in 1477. While it was the expeditions of Columbus that had an indisputable impact on world history, he writes, "It is nevertheless of interest to note that one of the most important events in history can be shown . . . to have developed not by the deeds of a single individual isolated from the flow of time, but as a natural and direct consequence of the collective efforts of the generations of mankind."[11]

Schøyen corresponded with Rasmus B. Anderson and may well have known of some of his chauvinistic notions of Norwegian and American medieval history. Anderson's book on the discovery of America, however, was published in the same year as the first volume of Schøyen's history, and the latter does not seem in any way inspired by the young and enthusiastic scholar from Wisconsin. A few years later, however, after Anderson's views had become better known among Norwegian Americans, the working title of a book that Schøyen planned to write but never completed suggests that he too had been converted to Anderson's vision: The Saga of the Norsemen in *Vesterheimen*.[12] As late as 1874, we should note, Schøyen's account of how the New World became known to the Old contains little chauvinism and no homemaking argument. Rasmus Bjørn Anderson would change all that in 1875.

Although the earliest amateur histories of Norwegian immigration may contain some expressions of ethnic pride and even ethnic prejudice, the homemaking mythology that came to characterize so much of Norwegian-American rhetoric around the turn of the nineteenth century did not begin to take shape until the late 1860s when Anderson, then a teacher at Albion Academy in Dane County, Wisconsin, began to give Chautauqua-like lectures to immigrant audiences in the Midwest. In 1869 Anderson became the first native of Wisconsin to win a teaching appointment at the University of Wisconsin and must have experienced his existence there as marginal in almost every way imaginable.[13] His father was of the Norwegian peasant class, and his mother's family was upper class by Norwegian standards. This was the main reason for their immigration. Anderson was a member of the first class of students admitted to the fledgling Norwegian-American Luther College, but a conflict with the school administration and faculty led to his dismissal without a degree. The conflict may be interpreted as a clash between the young student's New World notions of democracy and the faculty's Old World authoritarianism. As a teacher at Albion Academy in a small town in the area in which he grew up, Anderson brought in so many Norwegian-American students that he seemed ensured of success. But he was soon out-maneuvered by other faculty members and felt he had to leave the school. When he began as instructor at the state university, he was also an outsider in an academic sense and had to take some upper-level courses that would qualify him for a bachelor's degree.

In his autobiography he says that part of his problem at Albion Academy was that he was accused of ignoring his ethnic heritage : "I was charged with being too proud to be a Norwegian and with using my position to make the Norwegians ashamed of their nationality and to become 'yankeefied.'" He prepared himself to meet this accusation with the instincts of a scholar:

> I studied the few Scandinavian books I had. I particularly made as thorough a study of Snorre's "Heimskringla" as possible. . . . I found references to the discovery of America by the Norsemen in the tenth century, a fact which was not then mentioned in any text book on American history. I visited the State Historical Society at Madison and found there to my great delight all the works published by the Royal Antiquarian Society of Copenhagen on this subject. I copied everything and immediately prepared a lecture on the Norse discovery of America five centuries before Columbus and sandwiched into it the most enthusiastic eulogies of the viking age, of the Eddas, of the Scandinavian exploits, of the literature, music and art down to present times. I gave under hydraulic pres-

sure a most glowing tribute to both the ancient and modern Scandinavians. This lecture took the wind out of the sails of my accusers.[14]

He delivered this lecture in many places in the Midwest in the winter and spring of 1868. His first motivation, then, in spreading the story of the Norse discovery of America among other Norwegian Americans was to argue that although he was born in the United States, he was also Norwegian and proud of it.

Lloyd Hustvedt, who has studied the manuscripts, gives this interpretation of Anderson's lecture:

> Because Leif Ericson had discovered the New World, the Norwegians had a peculiar right to be in America. The adventurous spirit symbolized by Leif's journey had been expressed again and again in Norwegian history. This had been illustrated anew by the emigrants who had made their way to America in recent years. All that remained for the Norwegians now was to apply the same courageous spirit to new problems on American soil. For the lecturer, Leif Ericson was an overpowering symbol. Norwegians might feel themselves inferior to older and more established American citizens, but their sense of inferiority was unjustified in the light of historical fact.[15]

This is a succinct characterization not only of Anderson's early views but of the homemaking argument as it later was made by leaders from most immigrant groups. To a historian of a more professional kind than this young enthusiast from Wisconsin, the late tenth-century Norse (some would say Icelandic) settlements in Greenland and Newfoundland could not possibly have had any kind of influence one way or the other on the status of nineteenth-century Norwegian immigrants in the United States.[16] But their incorporation in a homemaking mythology made these settlements essential to the American identity of Norwegian immigrants and thus actually did have an influence on their lives.

Anderson was also proud to be an American, although so-called native Americans considered him a foreigner. He later remembered that one of his opponents at the academy said there were "'more Norwegians than white folks at Albion academy' and that was not the kind of school he cared to be connected with." The "Norwegian" upstart was also met with skepticism at the University of Wisconsin, especially when he tried to have Scandinavian languages added to the curriculum. In his autobiography he remembers that his colleagues ignored him when he tried to convince them that Scandinavia was "the cradle of all our liberties and of the laws out of which all modern civilization has poured." His academic credentials were not exactly impressive, and he saw that he needed a book in English that would strengthen both his chances for getting his contract renewed and the status of Scandinavian languages at the university. Moreover, he needed such a book fast, and he later explained that he decided to do a book on the discovery of America because he could base it on his lectures.[17]

America Not Discovered by Columbus was published in Chicago in 1874. It became quite popular, appearing in eight editions, and American reviewers were on the whole favorable. He was generally rejected by British reviewers, however, and in Copenhagen and Christiania he fared no better. A newspaper in the Danish capital "declared the book devoid of academic merit," and a Norwegian newspaper found the book "worthless and superfluous." Present-day readers would no doubt agree with the critic for the *North American Review,* who found "Anderson's lofty prose . . . intolerable." Of greater interest to us here, however, is that while the book was "dismissed . . . as propaganda" in a Norwegian newspaper, the Norwegian-American press was enthusiastic.[18] Of course, the book was propaganda. Anderson was making a homemaking argument that could not possibly be appreciated in Christiania, as Oslo then was named. He was demonstrating that Norwegians were indeed "white folks." In his preface he presented a short version of the homemaking myth that he would develop at greater length the next year: "Yes, the Norsemen were truly a great people! Their spirit found its way into the Magna Charta of England and into the Declaration of Independence in America. The spirit of the Vikings still survives in the bosoms of Englishmen, Americans and Norsemen, extending their commerce, taking bold positions against tyranny, and producing wonderful internal improvements in these countries."[19] Many Norwegian Americans had already heard this version of American history in his lectures, and most were no doubt thrilled to see it in print.

Anderson's lectures and book are among the earliest instances of homemaking mythologizing among American immigrant groups. The Columbus Day celebration of 1870 occurred just as Anderson was beginning his career as a lecturer farther west. According to the *Chicago Times,* the October 12 parade had "gathered Italians, Scandinavians, and American-born—those whose ancestors first discovered America and those who reaped the fruit of that discovery." The spectators were a "motley crowd of many nationalities." The banquet afterward, which was hosted by the Chicago Italian Society, included toasts to the participating nationalities. When the Italians met alone after the banquet, it was "to celebrate a reunited Italy," not to make any special claims to status in the United States because "they" had discovered America. Odd Lovoll observes that this harmonious interethnic fellowship "had a strong class basis. The early Italian community, with its pronounced Genoese and North Italian origin, family character, and prosperity, enjoyed a much greater acceptance than the hard-pressed southern Italians arriving at a later date."[20] Another, and related, explanation of the apparent absence of the interethnic rivalries so characteristic of Chicago in the decades to come is that the "profound cultural reorientation" in terms of racial attitudes, which Jacobson dates to the 1840s and 1850s, still had not taken hold among immigrants in Chicago, at least not among the solidly middle-class participants in this Columbus Day celebration. No homemaking arguments seem to have been made on October 12, 1870, in Chicago.

The propaganda of the Know-Nothings in the decades before the Civil War was not primarily directed at Scandinavian immigrants. Nevertheless, the anti-immigrant attitudes that surfaced during the 1840s and 1850s were an important motivation for establishing the earliest Norwegian-American newspaper (1847), and Norwegians "without exception" opposed Know-Nothingism throughout the 1850s, concludes one historian of the Norwegian-American press.[21] But anti-immigrant attitudes continued to grow after the Civil War as more and more was heard about the relative inferiority of "white" races other than the privileged Anglo-Saxons. Once the competition was declared, Norwegian Americans, along with other immigrant groups, naturally insisted on a place at the top of the scale. At Albion Academy the young Rasmus B. Anderson had been told that he was not included among "white folks," and when his historical research into the medieval greatness of his people made him realize that the English and the Norwegians were closely related, both genetically and ideologically, he made the most of it. Moreover, his insistence that Columbus was not the discoverer of America, and his incorporation of this insistence in an argument for the Norwegians as natural Americans, would make a joint celebration of Columbus Day with Italian Americans, as in 1870, problematic.

Anderson began to lecture on Leif Erikson and the greatness of the Vikings in the spring of 1868, at the same time that Daniel Ullman, a Know-Nothing leader in New York, was giving his lecture, "The Constitution of the United States," throughout his state. In his lecture Ullman defined the "one dominant, leading race" of the United States as "the Anglo-Saxon branch of the Teutonic race of the Caucasian group." In Jacobson's account this "tract detailed a racial myth of the origins of American political institutions" in Britain and that country's four "racial" elements. "The chief element was undoubtedly Germanic. Hence springs the inherent love of freedom of the Anglo-Saxons in England and

America, which has been the hereditary characteristic of the Teutonic or Germanic races from the earliest period." Ullman's views were well known far beyond the State of New York, and Anderson had certainly been exposed to Know-Nothing rhetoric.[22]

Whether Anderson actually read Ullman's tract about the "inherent love of freedom of the Anglo-Saxons" in 1875 or not, the homemaking argument he presented in that year may, as we will see, be read as a rebuttal of that aspect of the racial theories of Ullman and other Know-Nothings that excluded all but those of the Anglo-Saxon race from the best company. Anderson's rebuttal, however, was not directed against the theory as such but merely against the exclusion of his people, the Norwegians. Indeed, Anderson argued that not only were Norwegian Americans family members in this select company of Americans but that it was the *Norwegian* "inherent love of freedom" that had been passed on to the Anglo-Saxons. Anderson's logical conclusion was that, as members of the same family, Norwegians and Anglo-Saxons should share privileged accommodations in their American home.

A Chicago celebration of the fiftieth anniversary of Norwegian immigration on July 5, 1875, gave Anderson an opportunity to present his views to an audience of five thousand at an open-air festival "in a park on the northwest side of the city. It was one of the largest assemblies I ever addressed," Anderson later wrote in his autobiography. "On the platform sat nearly all the then surviving members of the sloop party. I think I made a decided hit with my address, which was immediately printed in a large edition and sold at 25 cents per copy."[23] Anderson's vision was clearly mythic rather than historical. He was bombastic and he was chauvinistic. Indeed, the twenty-seven-page pamphlet demonstrates many of those aspects of filiopietistic historiography that make it intolerable not only for the professional historian but for any reasonably well-informed and sensitive present-day reader. And yet, or perhaps for this very reason, it is a remarkable document for the student of the homemaking mythologizing of American immigrants. I will therefore present its argument in some detail and try to suggest some of Anderson's bombastic style through my translation.[24]

His point of departure was the date of the celebrated event: the Fourth of July, "our dearest day as American citizens because it is America's most beautiful day."[25] After some bombastic words about this "blessed day" of "victory," he reminded his listeners of the other anniversary that was their occasion for gathering in the park: "There is reason to give serious thought to the strange ways of fate that led the first Norwegian emigrants to America to leave Norway on this day." The sloop and its fifty-two passengers "break all chains, bonds, and constraints, weigh anchor in Stavanger harbor and set sail with jubilant cries of liberty for the West of the Stars and Stripes" on the Fourth of July, 1825. They were of course sad to leave behind family and fatherland and apprehensive about the long journey, but "from the far west a friendly star of liberty beckoned." He praised the pioneers who were present at the celebration and reflected on the progress they had experienced since they had arrived. Above all, he thanked them for having "given us as our birthright home and citizenship here in this great, free, and fertile America."

So although Anderson did dwell with some sentimentality on the loss of the old home and the beauty of Norway, this clearly was an occasion to celebrate fifty years in the United States. Indeed, the American-born Anderson spoke of his love of both countries and admonished his listeners that there was no contradiction in being "a loyal citizen of America" and to "retain in your heart and teach your children to love and honor Norway." Despite the losses and hardships of migration, "our lot is in one respect more propitious and enviable than that of our American fellow citizens: We actually have two fatherlands. We are born Norwegians and adopted Americans, and we are proud of both."

All this, however, was but a preamble to the important story Anderson wanted to tell his listeners—the story of the Norwegian origin of American liberty. Medieval Norway may not have had a fully developed democracy, he acknowledged, but in the sagas one will nevertheless find "the germ of the flower that budded at the Eidsvoll convention the 17th of May, 1814," the day the Norwegian constitution was adopted. Anderson's central metaphor was botanical as he traced the seed from the "plant of liberty" in medieval Norway. It was brought to France in 912 by the Norwegian chieftain "Gange-Rolf," or Rollo the Walker, as he is known in English. Here the plant took root and thrived until its seed was carried to England by Rollo's descendant, William the Conqueror, in 1066.

Later "the Puritans took seeds from this same Norwegian plant of liberty with them onboard the Mayflower to America and spread the seed on the virginal American soil before European weeds had been brought here. . . . Here in America our old plant of liberty found the right soil and it grew and thrived, budded, developed blossoms, and bore fruit. In 1765 this wonderful plant of liberty put forth a swelling bud" from which sprouted on the Fourth of July, 1776, "one of the most beautiful blossoms the world has ever seen."[26] After he had dwelled on the effect and "magnetic" attraction of this blossom on the nations of the world in general and on Norway in particular, Anderson noted that the more southerly leaves of the American plant of liberty had long suffered a blight but that this blight had been removed with the "blood of Lincoln": "Our parents nourished and protected this plant of liberty when it grew in Norwegian soil, and there are Norwegians present here today who risked their lives in its defense in our recent Civil War. The ancient Norse spirit is truly still alive in Norwegians of today and our brave ancestors were honored in a fitting manner by our countrymen who fought on the battle fields of the South in order to protect and defend our old Norwegian plant of liberty." Thus the two stories of ideological contribution and sacrifice were welded together into one story. Fighting in the Civil War, Norwegian Americans were defending an idea of liberty that was of Norwegian origin. And Anderson had more for his no doubt expectant audience.

He explained, with reference to reliable sources, that there was "Norwegian blood in the veins of three fourths of the population of England and America" and that "the most intrepid qualities in the American nation may be traced back to the Norwegian Vikings." Again he returned to medieval Norway, where the people had lived in liberty but where their strong sense of independence had led many to emigrate when one of the regional kings or chieftains, Harald Fairhair, made himself autocratic ruler of a united kingdom of Norway. In Anderson's view of history, it was the conclusive victory of this king in 872 that "led the blossom of the Norwegian people to leave their homes and their fatherland rather than to let themselves be cowed by a tyrant." This, however, became a blessing to the world in two ways. One group, under Rollo, "went to France where they settled Normandy," as he had said before. Others settled Iceland where they "created a republic":

> Yes, a fine thread is often spun in the history of the world! Iceland was the point of departure for the voyages of discovery that brought the first information to Europe about Greenland and America and that established a relationship between Europe and the Western World. In truth we have much to thank Harald Fairhair for, even though he was a tyrant whose only goal was to make subjects of a free people. Iceland's, Greenland's, and America's discovery and settlement and the spreading of liberty to England and America are the fruits of Harald's battle at Havsfjord.

After he had talked at great length and with considerable naïveté about the spirit of liberty in Norwegian history and literature, Anderson again turned to the United States. After a brief paean to the Stars and Stripes he addressed why it was not sufficient for Norwegian Americans to love their new country alone and why pride in their Norwegian heritage as well as ethnic solidarity also were essential. "As we should give this land and its constitution our deep-felt devotion and love and show our adopted fatherland true loyalty as its citizens, we must on the other hand take care that our nationality no longer will be shoved aside when rewards and influence are distributed among the citizenry." Anderson made it quite clear that his ethnic group had not made a political impact corresponding to its "numerical strength." And the very reason, he said, "that I have spoken so much about Norway is to show that it is not according to our old memories, our forefathers' way of seeing and doing things, to be neglected in such a manner."

There were two reasons, Anderson explained, that Norwegian Americans and Anglo-Americans should be equals.[27] He had already dealt with one reason at some length—that Norway is "the great and abundant source of almost all popular liberty in the world." The other was that the Anglo-Americans were "descendants of our own family." So it was not only by right of discovery, ideological contribution, and sacrifice but also by being blood relations that Norwegian Americans had the same right as Anglo-Americans to a home in America: "We sought a perfect liberty and independence and found them in a land that had first been discovered by our ancestors under the leadership of Leif Erikson and later been possessed and settled in old Norse fashion by the descendants of Rollo. So when we Norwegians meet with our American brothers the meeting is between brothers that have been separated for a thousand years." So spread the word about our greatness, he admonished his listeners, reiterating some of the reasons they should be admired. And he concluded with a point made by so many other immigrant leaders on behalf of so many other immigrant groups: Norwegians were the best Americans. "Let us move quickly into that future when it will be recognized that the Norseman is America's best citizen from whom deliverance will come when our land is threatened."

Even greater glory than his listeners already had experienced was in store for their chosen land because of their contribution. Just as the Greek immigrant cited at the beginning of this chapter looked forward to the "wonderful and glorious civilization" that would be produced "in the next generation [by] the artistic spirit of the Greeks in the United States, combined with the American practical mind," Anderson spoke of a union of "our creative powers with those of the Americans in order to raise America to a glory that no other country has achieved." True, homemaking myths were for the glorification of the ethnic group. But the ultimate goal—whether the storyteller was a Greek American or a Norwegian American—was the glorification of the United States. Although homemaking myths may at first seem to have been born of a separatist spirit and intention, they were all about entering the United States as fully recognized equals of the Anglo-Americans. As Knut Langeland put it in 1866, with more modesty than typical of later homemaking oratory, if we are able to preserve and develop our identity, "we may be able to place our small contribution to the outcome of the great migrations of the nineteenth century on the altar of our adopted fatherland with the conviction that though our contribution may be small compared to that of other nationalities, it may yet in quality be the equal of any."[28]

Some readers may have recognized one reason for Anderson's lack of modesty: he was doing battle in a nineteenth-century historiographical debate between those we may call classicists, who saw European civilization as growing out of ancient Greece and Rome, and those of what we may call a romantic persuasion, who were convinced that European civilization should be traced to the Germanic tribes and the forests of northern and central Europe rather than to the urban culture of the Mediterranean.[29] In his romanticist view of history Anderson was influenced by the Danish bishop, poet, and educator Nikolai F. S. Grundtvig, in particular through his disciple, Niels Matthias Petersen.[30] So when Anderson was trumpeting Leif Erikson, he was also saying that the discovery of America was a Germanic rather than a Latin contribution to humanity. The reason he made no explicit reference to Italian Americans as his adversaries undoubtedly was that immigration from the south of Europe was not yet significant and that Columbus, as has been demonstrated, would not be appropriated by Italian Americans until several decades after Anderson's Chicago oration. Anderson's vision of world history found expression toward the end of his address:

> Let us not forget that Norway's great advantage is that it is the great and abundant source of almost all popular liberty in the world. The North is the factory where the weapons that cut through the slave chains of the Roman Empire were forged. It was in Norway that the brave Vikings were brought up, they who left their fatherland with the aim of destroying tyrants and slaves and to teach mankind that we are all born free and equal and that there is therefore no reason to acknowledge any other government than that which the people themselves find suitable for their needs.[31]

In using the language of the Declaration of Independence to explain the debt the world owes Norway, Anderson also reminded his listeners that the great founding document of the United States was essentially Norwegian. As other Norwegian Americans used and adapted his homemaking mythology over several decades, however, Anderson's international and historiographical perspective found no place. Anderson's homemaking mythology was passed on in the immigrant culture as a purely American story.

Anderson's version of the Norwegian-American homemaking mythology, with the three elements of foundation, sacrifice, and ideological gifts, soon became widely accepted among Norwegian Americans.[32] One characteristic of a cultural elite is that it leaves behind written records, often published ones in newspapers, journals, pamphlets, and books. For obvious reasons it is more difficult to document the ideas and views of members of social classes less likely to express their views in writing. But we know that Anderson spoke to audiences of farmers, shopkeepers, and laborers in the years he toured the Midwest with his lectures.[33] We also know that the many weekly and some daily newspapers that made references to this mythology entered many homes. As early as 1876 an immigrant farmer in Manitowoc, Wisconsin, referred to the myth of ideological contributions in a crudely composed letter to his family in a Norwegian valley. Much of his letter is a critique of Norwegian society, its monarchy, politics, and class divisions from a liberal and republican American point of view. But he saw signs of change and observed that progress should be expected in the Norwegian people, which "has had such a strong disposition to liberty that it has planted popular liberty in the two most powerful nations on earth, England and America."[34] When one farmer had internalized the myth and could repeat it in a letter, we may assume that he was not alone in having not just listened to Anderson or read him but made Anderson's views his own.

Ethnic celebrations of Norwegian Independence Day, the Seventeenth of May, and of Leif Erikson Day could attract crowds in small midwestern agricultural towns and large cities. Also, national holidays such as the Fourth of July and Decoration Day could, as we have seen, be used as occasions for ethnic celebration and commemoration. Although the Midwest and later the Northwest were the main areas of concentration of Norwegian Americans, they also settled in other parts of the United States, in particular in Brooklyn, New York. There, in 1892 "at least 2,500" people marched in the Leif Erikson Day parade, according to *Nordisk Tidende*. In his book on Brooklyn's Norwegian colony David Mauk notes, "The federal census recorded only 4,500 Norwegian-born residents in the city two years earlier. Even if one makes allowances for the exaggeration that might be expected from a colony newspaper, active participation in the parade was impressively widespread. After all, the journalist claimed to estimate only the number of marchers and did not add Norwegian spectators who must have been in the crowds lining the parade route."[35] Given this kind of gathering several times a year in areas of concentration of Norwegian Americans, a large portion of the immigrant group would, on frequent occasions, be exposed to references to the homemaking mythology originally created by Rasmus B. Anderson.

The mythology was kept alive and developed through several generations in newspaper articles, fiction, and poetry and in speeches at festive occasions. In 1892, almost two decades after it was launched by Anderson, we find the myth expressed in a novel of social protest and utopian vision by Hans A. Foss in North Dakota. Foss was less inspired by the Columbian celebrations of that year than by the populist critique of capitalism, and his title, *Hvide Slaver* (White Slaves), was a common populist metaphor for the victims of capitalism. In this novel Norwegian Americans eventually become accepted as the best Americans both because of their radical politics and because of their racial and cultural excellence. At a political rally after some of the battles for a better society have been won, the main speaker, a German-American lawyer, thanks the Norwegians for their contribution to "the liberation of our country [from capitalism]. One day history will tell us that the people who set her leaders on the English throne, who gave new lifeblood to the nerve-racked French people, and who erected Norman towers in France, also were a powerful factor in the liberation of this, their land of Leif Erikson."[36]

One element frequently mentioned in this mythology was not included in Anderson's 1875 oration in Chicago: the Magna Carta. It was part of his argument in his 1874 book on the discovery of America, however, and in the lectures he gave around in the Midwest he would constantly talk about the Magna Carta as the first document of the spirit of liberty brought to England from Norway via Normandy and as the forerunner of the Declaration of Independence.

Almost a half century later the Magna Carta pedigree showed up in another novel of inconsiderable literary merit by one of Anderson's students. James A. Peterson wrote his amateurish autobiographical novel, *Hjalmar; or, The Immigrant's Son*, in English but it was published by a Minneapolis publisher whose trade in 1922 was still mainly in the Norwegian language, and the book was addressed to an ethnic audience. When the protagonist, Hjalmar, arrives as a student at the University of Wisconsin, he is ashamed of his ethnic background and keeps it a secret from all except his Anglo-American roommate. Then he comes under the tutelage of Professor Anderson and becomes increasingly proud of his Norwegian heritage. Lloyd Hustvedt has paraphrased the episode in which Hjalmar repeats Anderson's homemaking mythology to his fellow students: "On an outing with some American comrades at Picnic Point on Lake Mendota, he engaged in a debate with a group of doubting Thomases.

He convinced them that the seeds of democracy had been brought from Norway when Rollo the Walker conquered Normandy. William the Conqueror had later brought them to England, where the concepts of freedom were tangibly expressed in the Magna Carta. But, Hjalmar argued, the final flowering took place in the American Declaration of Independence and in the American Constitution."[37] In the novel, as in the history of so many immigrant groups, one purpose of the teaching of homemaking stories is to combat a negative self-image. From being ashamed of his own ethnic origin, Hjalmar, a second-generation American, becomes an exemplar of the ideal Norwegian American called for in his mentor's 1875 address when he said that not only should Norwegian Americans "listen to our American brothers with attention when they tell us of what they have achieved in the cause of mankind and liberty" but that they should also reveal to these brothers Anderson's remarkable vision of Norwegian history.

This vision must have struck many bright but uneducated immigrants as a revelation of the greatness of a heritage unknown to them before emigration. The vision was to remain with and affect all the work of an immigrant who arrived in 1896, the novelist and educator Ole E. Rølvaag. We may now be in a better position to appreciate why he would choose as his text for a Seventeenth of May speech in Sioux City in 1926, "You are the salt of the earth. You are the light of the world." We will also recognize the mythology created by Anderson in the report of Rølvaag's speech (which I also quoted in my prologue):

> He gave an outline of the social system in ancient Norway and demonstrated how our people from as far back as we have historical records had a fully developed popular democracy in self-governed counties. This is precisely the same democracy that the Norwegians brought with them to England, either directly with the Vikings or indirectly through the Normans, and that the Pilgrim fathers in their turn brought with them to America. Later research has disclosed that the early colonists came from those parts of England that had been settled by the Vikings.

Just as Anderson taught this vision to his students at the University of Wisconsin in the 1870s and 1880s, Rølvaag taught it to his students at St. Olaf College in the early decades of the twentieth century.

Toward the end of his life Rølvaag's fiction became increasingly ideological and didactic. In his last novel, *Their Father's God* (1931), the concluding volume in the trilogy that begins with *Giants in the Earth* (1927), one of his characters, a Lutheran minister, tells the same story that Rølvaag used to tell his students.[38] We may perhaps imagine that the skepticism voiced by Peder in the novel had also been voiced by some of Rølvaag's students in the classroom. The occasion is a Christmas party on the Holm farm, and Peder is embarrassed by a guest, the Reverend Kaldahl, whose "English was downright terrible" and who "insisted on talking Norwegian." The conversation leads the clergyman "into a discussion of how 'the race' (he used the phrase often) had lived in olden times," and this again leads another character to speak in praise of the Vikings. The pastor has a lot to say on this topic: "Their expeditions, to be sure, show forbidding, gruesome aspects, and plenty of them, but I am convinced that never in all the world's history has man's courage spanned higher and overcome greater odds." But the "Americanized" Peder is skeptical: "And what on earth did they accomplish?" This really gets the pastor going. First he admonishes the young man on his duty to preserve his heritage, and then he begins to lecture on the Vikings, paying much attention to Iceland, "the world's oldest republic. . . . Their own race it was who laid the foundation and who built upon it. They could do that because since time immemorial the spirit of democracy had glowed in the Norsemen's hearts." His "lecture" on history is blended with one on the need to be "true to their traditions," and this becomes more and more irritating to Peder, who finally says, "We're Americans here!"

The pastor's example of a people who have survived because they retained their traditions is the Jews who, he says, show that you serve America best by retaining your distinctive traits. But Peder is not to be daunted by the learned clergyman and responds, "It would be folly to try to build up the different European nations over here. The foundation is new, the whole structure must be new, and so it shall be!" And with this Peder has given Kaldahl his cue. The pastor's text, which his author had used for his Seventeenth of May speech in Sioux City and in his classes at St. Olaf College, is straight out of Rasmus B. Anderson:

> The foundation is not quite as new as you think. . . . Where did the Puritans come from? Mostly from eastern England. Was that mere accident? Not at all; there, too, cause and effect worked hand in hand. It was in that part of England that the Scandinavians, and not least the Norwegians, exerted their greatest influence. By nature the Puritans were nonconformists; an imposed system of worship was to them unthinkable, just as it was to your own forefathers. Suppose you look at this a little more closely: What did the framers of our Constitution have to work with? First and foremost two priceless documents which supplied the very groundsills for their structure, the *Magna Charta* and the *Bill of Rights*. Where do you suppose the basic principles set forth in these two documents came from? The seeds came from the Scandinavian penin-

sula, some directly to eastern England, others through Normandy, and still others, perhaps, by way of the Western Isles. There is no getting away from the fact that in no place on earth has the desire for liberty and individualism glowed brighter and more impelling than in the Scandinavian north.[39]

By 1931 this was a familiar story indeed to large numbers of Norwegian Americans. But although the story may have been familiar, the argument was no longer the same. By now few Norwegian Americans felt they were regarded as foreigners in the only country they knew as home. The Reverend Kaldahl is no longer arguing for the acceptance of his flock as Americans. Rather, he is trying to convince the "Americanized" second-generation Peder Holm that he should not forget that he is not simply an American but a special sort of American, a Norwegian American. In a way it is no longer a homemaking argument but a don't-forget-the-home-of-your-parents argument. But it took some time before the argumentation shifted, and much had happened along the way.

Although Anderson's interpretation of history may strike present-day readers as rather naive, he was well within a historiography that included respected professional historians. He may have been an enthusiast, but it would hardly be fair to label him a crackpot. However, some myth elements that a few other Norwegian-American promoters tried to make part of the Norwegian-American homemaking argument may more readily be dismissed as what Michael Musmanno in an angry moment has called "Scandiknavery."[40] One such myth was mentioned in Chapter 2, that George Washington was of Norwegian descent.[41] Another was a complex of myths related to stories of Viking settlement and exploration of the interior of North America. Some spoke of legends of white Indians, reports of Norse influence on Indian languages, and the many alleged Viking Age artifacts, such as the Kensington rune stone, that have been found in Minnesota and other states.[42] Even such wild tales, however, should be taken seriously by the historian as born of an immigrant group's need to claim America as home.

Aspects of the homemaking mythology first created by Anderson are mentioned in many publications from the mid-1870s through the 1920s; evidently, the mythology was so well known that speakers and writers could make references to bits and pieces of it and expect listeners and readers to make the necessary connections to the larger mythology. Indeed, many such references would hardly have made sense to an audience unfamiliar with the mythology. For example, in a speech he gave in 1926, Julius E. Olson, a professor at the University of Wisconsin, reminded his audience that "our instruments of government were largely shaped by men of our blood." A 1928 essay by the sculptor Oskar J. W. Hansen, "Why a Colossal Monument to Leif Erikson?" is obviously inspired by Anderson, not only in its title but also in its Germanic romanticist interpretation of European history: "From the granite walled fastnesses of the Norwegian fjords the descendants of this race went forth and gave strength to the weakening bloodstream of the decaying classical empires. . . . Those Northmen who conquered Normandy, three generations later laid the foundations of the present British Empire."[43]

Other book titles, such as *From the Norwegian Normandy* and *From the New Normandy*, suggest that Norwegian immigration to the United States in the nineteenth and twentieth centuries should be understood in the perspective of the medieval migrations to northern France.[44] That the Norwegian settlement of the Midwest was related to the migrations of the Vikings is also suggested in a poem by Simon Johnson, "Det nye vikingetog" (The New Viking Expedition).[45]

A more subtle manifestation of how many saw their midwestern achievements in this perspective is the Norman Gothic architecture introduced to the St. Olaf College campus with a new power and heating plant in 1922. A more prominent structure in the style adopted for future use was Holland Hall, built in 1925 and modeled on the Gothic monastery La Merveille of Mont-Saint-Michel on the Normandy coast. This is how an article in the yearbook, the *Viking*, introduced the "New Norman Gothic 'Mount St. Olaf'":

> About a thousand years ago, a group of Scandinavian invaders settled in northwestern France and became in time a part of the French people. These Normans, as they were called, were a remarkably gifted race, excelling not only in military and organizing ability, but in scholarship, and artistic and religious achievements as well. Their greatest talent along artistic lines lay in the field of architecture and building construction, in which they produced a style which has given us a large number of the most beautiful buildings of the world.

The yearbook gives two reasons for choosing this particular architectural style not only for this building but for the St. Olaf campus. The first is historical, that both the college and the Norman Gothic style "are the products of the same race in streams far separated by time and place but largely identical in character and aspirations" and the second ideological, "that the old mediaeval buildings were the home of much the same ideas and ideals as those which the modern Christian institution of learning stands for."[46] Yet another instance of Norwegian-American celebration of the "Norman connection" is the 1912 statue in Fargo, North Dakota, of Rollo, the Viking chieftain who supposedly led the exodus to northern France. The statue was yet another project initiated by Anderson.[47] In the context of the larger Norwegian-American mythology, in which the Norwegian Normans are the bearers of the spirit of democracy and the virtual creators of the Declaration of Independence, these medieval Norman cultural references on the prairies of the Midwest symbolize the Norwegian foundations of the United States.

Many Norwegian-language poems celebrate the Viking discoveries of North America and use Viking imagery to speak of the pioneers on the plains and prairies. One of the many poems about Leif Erikson concludes:

> We who are the descendants of Leif Erikson
> Live here with the right of the first to arrive.
> He kindled the daylight of history for this country.
> The calling of our people is to be its light.
> True, we are few among its millions.
> But thus should a chieftain's clan always stand.
> As he was the first to find the land,
> We shall be the clan who won it in spirit.[48]

The poet claims not only the legal right of Norwegian Americans to their country—a kind of squatter's right, "the right of the first to arrive"—but also that America is the special creation of their ancestor, that it entered into history with Leif Erikson (not, it is implied, with Christopher Columbus).

Some poems bring together myths of foundation and of sacrifice, as, for example, "Vinland" by Julius Baumann, the most beloved of all American poets who wrote in Norwegian. The opening stanzas are about the Viking discoveries and conclude that the "darkness of oblivion has fallen over the graves of the Vikings." Then a transitional stanza reminds us that the same ocean that carried the Vikings to Vinland also carried those "who still carve their runes in this country." Among several stanzas about the immigrant pioneers is one on the ultimate sacrifice to the chosen land:

> In the War Between the States, before peace came to the land,
> Many of our fathers went armed to battle
> As they carried the banner in the front lines
> And died as heroes in defense of our country.

The argument in these stanzas is that Norwegian Americans have earned the right to speak of America as "our land," not primarily because of the long-forgotten Viking explorations and settlements but because of their own exploits and contributions to their chosen homeland: the pioneering efforts of the early nineteenth-century immigrants and settlers, their contributions to American politics through the prominence of "Norse-men" who "interpret our constitution" in Congress, and the excellence of their religious and educational institutions "on American soil." Above all, however, the land is theirs because of the sacrifice of the many young men in the Civil War:

> Our land, under the shining row of stars,
> To you we have dedicated our lives and our songs.
> Here shine our hope, our endeavor, and our faith
> And here we will live in happiness and freedom.[49]

The Norse discoveries and the Norse origins of American democracy were distant and abstract notions of which most Americans were sadly ignorant. But the Civil War was close and real, and many regarded the sacrifices of the Norwegian-American Fifteenth Wisconsin Infantry, as well as of individual Norwegian-American soldiers and officers, as a more solid foundation for the claim that no better American than the Norwegian American existed.

The desire to cultivate the memory of the Fifteenth Wisconsin Infantry is evident in the many books about this volunteer regiment.[50] The first appeared in 1869. When the author, John A. Johnson, used immigrant newspapers to appeal to regimental members for firsthand information shortly after the end of the war, he explained that it would be up to the Norwegian Americans to write the history of their regiment because there "was reason to fear that the regiment's Scandinavian character" would not be stressed by American historians.[51] Ole Buslett, a prolific writer of poetry and fiction, dedicated his 1894 book on the regiment to "The Norwegian People in America," and in his preface he insisted that on the basis of this history his people deserved to be counted in the first rank of Americans: "Of one thing we may be quite certain: in relation to the size of the population, no other nation was as greatly and as bravely represented in the war as the Norwegian one."[52]

Hans Christian Heg was the central hero of the Norwegian-American myth of sacrifice. Heg had come to Wisconsin as a child with his parents in the 1840s. He entered state politics and at the outbreak of the Civil War he organized the Fifteenth Wisconsin Infantry with Norwegian as the language of command. When Colonel Heg died with many of his regiment at the battle of Chickamauga, he was the highest-ranking Norwegian-American officer in the U.S. Army. As the Viking-helmeted Leif Erikson was the main symbolic character in the Norwegian-American myth of foundation, the Union-uniformed Col. Hans Christian Heg became the corresponding symbolic character in the myth of sacrifice.

In 1925 the centennial of Norwegian immigration to the United States was celebrated in the Twin Cities of Minnesota. This was a spectacular event, graced by the presence of the president, Calvin Coolidge, and culminating in a historical pageant at the Minnesota state fairground in St. Paul performed by fifteen hundred before eighty thousand spectators. The celebration took place just a few years after the antiforeign and anti-immigrant sentiments of the World War I period had peaked. Indeed, the Johnson-Reed Act, which signaled the end of mass immigration from Europe, had been signed by Coolidge the year before, in 1924. After a difficult period in which the loyalty of Norwegian Americans and even their right to the name "American" had been questioned, the organizers of the centennial celebration had a need to assert that Norwegian Americans were indeed Americans. In April R. Schultz's convincing interpretation, the pageant performed on the state fairground argued "that not only were Norwegians entitled to equal status in the culture with 'Yankee' Americans, but also were actually *better* Americans."[53]

Pageants were a prominent feature in national and local celebrations in this period, and the organizers of the centennial had appointed a professional pageant writer and director, Willard Dillman. As his synopsis of the "Pageant of the Northmen" reveals, this professional outsider had fully grasped the intentions of the centennial organizers and the mythology that had by then gained currency among Norwegian Americans:

> The theme of the pageant is to suggest for the present generation some hint of the story of the fathers, those hardy descendants of the Vikings, who laid the foundation of the splendid achievements of their race in the new world. The story does not follow history with too much exactness. The dramatic form cannot do this. Events must be telescoped. The story must form a dramatic entity. There must be a central current, from which no overflow may spread too far afield. To this end the story concerns itself particularly with the life of one man, Hans Christian Heg, a type of all that is best and noblest in a citizen. The story commences with his childhood, and while it does not close with his death, his spirit and the effects of his sacrifice extend through to the end.[54]

The Norwegian-American myths of foundation and of sacrifice, what we may call the Viking story and the Civil War story, had been presented as parts of the same homemaking mythology fifty years earlier by Rasmus B. Anderson in Chicago in 1875, upon the hundredth anniversary of the same 1825 event that was celebrated in St. Paul in 1925. The two stories are quite different in point of departure, content, and strategy: the one claims that all that made America great was Norwegian before it became American; the other insists that Norwegian Americans earned a right to be American because they were among the first to stand up in defense of their chosen homeland in a time of national crisis.

In the 1925 pageant, as in Anderson's 1875 speech, both stories are presented as central elements in one homemaking mythology. The pageant dramatized the connection between the Viking explorers and the nineteenth-century immigrants by presenting medieval scenes, one of which depicted Leif Erikson discovering America and defeating hostile Indians, as the narratives told to Hans Heg by his grandparents. Interpreting the pageant, Schultz has explained that "just as these stories linked Heg to an organic, heroic Norwegian past, the statue of Heg unveiled at the end of the pageant would connect contemporary Norwegian Americans through Heg to that same past—not an American past, but a Norwegian past."[55] I would argue, though, that this Norwegian past had long been incorporated in a more recent American past and that the pageant, in its way, presented Leif Erikson and St. Olaf as part of a Norwegian-American past much as Anglo-American history books and literary histories would present the Magna Carta and Shakespeare as part of an Anglo-American past.

Although the 1925 pageant highlighted the story of Hans Heg, the Civil War, and blood sacrifice, the most visible and prominent symbols of the centennial were those associated with the Viking Age. An advertisement for the Dayton Department Store shows a settler resting by his plow, hat in hand, looking over his fields and home at a vision of a Viking ship. The souvenir medal for the Norse American Centennial has a Viking, probably intended to be Leif Erikson, walking, with drawn sword raised, from a Viking ship and the dates 1825 and 1925. On the other side is a Viking ship under sail and with the oars out. Below the ship appears the legend "A.D. 1000"; above it is inscribed "Authorized by the Congress of the United States of America." Clearly, what was claimed to have been authorized and sanctioned here was a view of American history that connected the years that initiated the two great periods of Norwegian settlement in North America, 1000 and 1825. A medieval Viking ship rather than a nineteenth-century immigrant ship was selected as its most telling symbol.

This view of American history was also authorized by the U.S. government in the two souvenir stamps issued by the U.S. Post Office, and here the nineteenth century was more explicitly expressed. The five-cent stamp showed a Viking ship, whereas the two-cent stamp carried a representation of the 1825 sloop *Restaurationen*. Both had the legend NORSE-AMERICAN CENTENNIAL, 1825–1925.[56] It would seem from the five-cent stamp that the 1925 centennial somehow commemorated an event involving a Viking ship. A juxtaposition of both stamps would bring out the close connection between the discovery suggested by the Viking ship and the Norwegian immigration suggested by the sloop: ours by the right of discovery but also ours by the right of immigration, of dedication, hard work, and sacrifice.

In the 1920s, as in the 1870s, both the Civil War story and the Leif Erikson story were used to strengthen ethnic self-confidence and to convince the dominant Anglo-America that Norwegian Americans should be accepted as equals. This is why both Vikings and Hans Christian Heg were so prominent in the St. Paul pageant, and this is why Norwegian Americans have taken the initiative to raise statues of both Leif Erikson and Colonel Heg in the United States. These two historical characters have been used to represent the two basic but very different components of a homemaking mythology that claims the United States as the true home of Norwegian Americans.

Rølvaag became the most prominent promoter of the Norwegian-origins-of-America story. His friend and fellow novelist, Waldemar Ager, at least in this respect more of a realist than Rølvaag, took up the other story, writing a history of the Fifteenth Wisconsin Infantry in 1916 and giving it a central place in his novel, *Sons of the Old Country*, in 1926. In the history of the Fifteenth Wisconsin Ager found "the most obvious evidence that the most nationalistically-minded Norwegians over here are also actually the best Americans—that is the most self-sacrificing— the first to report for duty when the war alarm sounds and their new country is in danger," as he wrote in his preface to his 1916 regimental history.[57] Ager also successfully campaigned to have Wisconsin officially recognize the contribution and the sacrifice of Norwegian Americans as epitomized by Hans Christian Heg. If you visit the grounds of the Wisconsin State Capitol in Madison, you will see the monument to Colonel Heg that Ager regarded as his greatest achievement. The monument is unique, both as the only monument in honor of an individual in the park surrounding the State Capitol and as the only one bearing the name of a specific ethnic group. With the good help of Waldemar Ager, Hans Christian Heg, many decades after his death in battle, became the officially recognized homemaker for Norwegian Americans in Wisconsin.

The centennial celebrations and the dramatization of the Norwegian-American homemaking myths in 1925 no doubt served to boost the confidence of the celebrants in their ethnicity and in their right to a place in American society. But even at this early date and even as the open doors of immigration were closing on their European relatives, the ethnicity of most Norwegian Americans was undergoing changes and acquiring new functions. A marked Norwegian-American identity was no longer central to their American lives nor was their right to be counted American seriously questioned. The language that had served to distinguish them and to keep their institutions quite separate from other American institutions was rapidly being silenced, less because of Anglo-American nationalist and political pressure than because of natural attrition. Indeed, as the homemaking myths of this ethnic group came together in a major cultural event in 1925 and achieved their fullest expression and their widest acceptance as the central ethnic narrative, the need and the pressure that gave rise to the myths ceased to be a concern for most members of the group. And as they lost their distinguishing language, Norwegian Americans also lost the complex web of myths of foundation, ideological contribution, and sacrifice created in and for this language. In the generation after that of the organizers of the ethnic celebrations of 1925, it would be difficult to find a significant number of Norwegian Americans for whom these myths were essential to their claim to be recognized as Americans. This may be a measure of the success of their homemaking myths—but it is probably a better measure of the success of America for these and other immigrants.

Epilogue:
Three Twentieth-Century Stories

Anglo-American Americanism has tended to be exclusive, in particular in the period considered in this book. What we may call immigrant or ethnic Americanism has at times been no less exclusive in its competitiveness. The competition has been for recognition as Americans, at times even as the best Americans. The vision of many middle-class ethnic leaders has, as we have seen, all too often been that of an exclusive place in the American home for their particular group rather than of a shared home of many races and nationalities, all with an equal status in one nation. In a country with a long and strong yet deplorable tradition of a hierarchy of ethnic groups and races, the aim of ethnic leaders has frequently (and, we may add, naturally) been for their particular group to climb to a higher place in this hierarchy, not to abolish it for a common American identity for all. In this they have of course followed the lead of the Anglo-American elite, which not only placed their "founding" group at the top of the hierarchy but defined them as *the* Americans. Immigrants have had a choice of two main strategies for countering their exclusion from the best and most desirable rooms in the American home: applying for acceptance as "Anglo-Americans" or insisting on the equal American value and quality of their own culture and traditions.

Many convincing arguments have been made for retaining ethnic cultures and their languages within a larger all-encompassing American society. Whatever one may think of these arguments, however, history has in most cases decided the issue in favor of those who have spoken for an integrationist vision or Americanization. This is certainly true of those nineteenth-century immigrant groups that are the focus of this book.[1] It may be that the ethnicity of most Americans of European origin is today largely symbolic, as the sociologist Herbert Gans has argued. Nevertheless, despite the successful integration of the descendants of nineteenth-century European immigrants, ethnicity continues to be a complementary component of their American identities.[2] The ethnicities that now may find expression in playful celebrations, however, were in an earlier period under so much pressure, both from within and from the dominant, largely Anglo-American society, that expressions of immigrant leadership may best be appreciated as responses to threats against the distinguishing identity of their people.

The combination of American nationalism with ethnic separatism—even chauvinism—so typical of the views of leaders in most immigrant groups at the turn of the nineteenth century has not been understood or appreciated by the representatives of what John Bodnar has called the official culture. In particular, in the aftermath of the Americanization campaigns of World War I there were attempts to bring the many ethnic groups together in collective manifestations and celebrations of their common Americanism. However, as Bodnar has demonstrated, such attempts could as often reveal the tensions as express the desire for harmony. His illustration, among "numerous" examples, is the "America's Making Festival" in New York City in 1921, where "an explicit attempt was made by educational officials and civic leaders to direct the commemoration of the ethnic past toward a wider audience and the need to reinforce national loyalty." Such a manifestation of unity, however, faced many obstacles. The Irish representatives on the committee wanted a representation of St. Brendan and his explorations of the continent "as far west as Ohio" that predated both Columbus and Leif Erikson. Meanwhile, Dutch representatives withdrew in protest when the others did not agree to place them first in performances and exhibitions, a priority they no doubt felt was theirs because they had been first to settle New York. Other disputes arose between Scottish and Irish representatives about the correct ethnic identification of Thomas McKean, a signer of the Declaration of Independence, as well as of Robert Fulton, the inventor of the steamboat.[3] Because homemaking arguments have tended to be exclusive, it follows that they also have tended to be disputed: the homemaking argument of one group would often be in opposition to the argument made by another.

The competition for the symbol that would give a right to the better room in the American home was particularly acrimonious between Scandinavian Americans and Italian Americans, who promoted two different stories of "discovery" and foundation. History was not the issue in this quarrel. For historians, who are usually not concerned with how the past defines their status in the present because of their real or imagined descent, the Norse voyages, however admirable, are an episode in history, whereas the voyage of Columbus in 1492 inaugurated the modern age. As homemaking myths, however, the stories of these voyages were equally vital to the identities of those who claimed the myths as essential to their homemaking arguments. Any official recognition, however perfunctory, of one story of discovery could be an affront to those who identified with another.

In Chapter 2 we saw how the Italian-American journal *Vita Nuova*, as late as October 1930, characterized the placing of a bust of Leif Erikson, "pretended explorer of these lands," in New York City as a "perfidy" committed to "satisfy the fanaticism and jealousy" of "the Swedish people." The journal also found "perfidous" all attempts to "dispute the Italian origin of the bold Italian navigator." The author, who was president of the Sezione Columbiana of New York, in 1930 evidently still was sufficiently insecure in regard to the place of his ethnic group in American society that he saw this bust as an attempt to undermine the status of Italian Americans. Anglo-Americans, on the other hand, have until recent decades been so secure in their privileged position as the native or real Americans that they have at best been bemused by the homemaking controversies between the many "foreign" groups in the United States. The fervor with which homemaking stories could be supported and the corresponding resentment with which the stories of others could be attacked or belittled, however, shows that, for those involved, a group's identity as "American" could be at stake in such controversies.

The homemaking wars between ethnic groups had countless skirmishes but no decisive battles. Gradually, members of European ethnic groups have ceased to see themselves as outsiders, and some descendants of immigrants from Europe have themselves become guardians of an America that cannot accommodate all "foreign"-looking or "foreign"-speaking newcomers. But as late as 1936 the competition between European ethnic groups for the best rooms in the American home could still be fierce. Again, the competition was between Italian Americans and Scandinavian Americans for the status as discoverers of America. In that year the governor of Illinois and the mayor of Chicago issued proclamations recognizing October 9 as "Leif Erickson Day." The date alone is ample demonstration that the Scandinavian-American leaders who sought such official recognition were in competition with the Italian Americans, who had long had October 12 recognized as Columbus Day.[4] In the *Bulletin Order Sons of Italy of Illinois* Franco D'Amico attacked the notion of a competing discoverer and ironized about the "Nordic Superiority Theory": "But the imposing and elaborate structure erected to screen the emptiness within, lacked the 'sine qua non' of its very existence. The foundations could not withstand the mere ripple of a laugh to be flattened and when the people of the South learned to laugh at it, the idol of the North became a myth and merrily relegated to mythology." The "bespectacled professor" was implored "to find a new idol on which to pin their hope to regain the lost prestige," and thus, said D'Amico, the myth of Leif Erikson was born. But lacking "historical bases" on which their idol could stand, "a group of the most fanatic among the believers intrigued to have their idol sanctified through an official recognition."

Although D'Amico characterized as "blessed ingenuity" the belief that a mayoral proclamation was all that was "necessary to create an imaginary hero in juxtaposition to [the] historical being, greatness, and value of Washington or Lincoln," he clearly found it necessary to take action. The Sons of Italy sent letters to the governor and mayor, asking whether it was true that they had "substantiated and convalidated the strange and fantastic assumption advanced by a local group of Norwegians that America was discovered by Leif Erickson instead of Columbus," explaining that "historical facts cannot be changed or denied to suit chauvinistic idealogies [sic]," and respectfully asking the two officials "to give us your version of the truth in the matter in order to assuage the painful impression created among the Italian constituency."

The *Bulletin* quoted in full the replies from the mayor and from the governor's secretary. The mayor limited his comments to the question of "official recognition" and refrained from entering "into any controversy" pertaining to historical claims: "Needless to say, I am always happy, as Mayor of Chicago, to recognize the courage and enterprise of any person regardless of nationality." He also assured "the members of your splendid organization that I have only the friendliest of feelings toward your group and the Italian people in general—a race which I am proud to have the privilege of honoring at any time, for their valor and outstanding achievements." In the governor's absence, his secretary merely sent a copy of the proclamation with a covering letter. Franco D'Amico could then assuage his fellow members of the Sons of Italy that the documents show "that neither the governor nor the mayor make any allusion that Leif Erickson was the discoverer of America."[5] Although the two Illinois politicians were most likely bemused by the affair, they could not but take seriously a letter from so large a "constituency," as the letter writer had pointedly characterized those on whose behalf he was writing. But the Italian Americans of Chicago and other cities wanted more than mere political clout—they were demanding recognition as a founding nationality. Surely, the experience of the governor and the mayor of the ethnic politics of state and city should have prepared them for the reactions they got.

Such rivalries were by no means limited to Americans of Italian and Scandinavian descent, nor did they cease to engage ethnic spokesmen (as observed in an earlier chapter, they tended to be men) after the period discussed in this book came to an end around 1930. Ethnicity, as Rob Kroes has reminded us, persists even when language and other close ties with the homeland have been lost.[6] To illustrate that homemaking myths and the arguments they make have continued to engage the emotions of Americans of various descent, I will, as an epilogue, give accounts of three very different controversies about foundation stories at intervals of about thirty years in the twentieth century, in 1938, 1965, and 1998.

The three-cent U.S. postage stamp issued in commemoration of the New Sweden tercentenary in 1938 shows, as the legend on the stamp has it, the "Landing of the Swedes and Finns." The harmony between these two peoples suggested by the stamp, however, was far from characteristic of the often acrimonious struggle between them for attention before the celebration eventually found its final, official form. The picture of men in early seventeenth-century attire on a shore with a ship, presumably the *Kalmar Nyckel* (the "Swedish *Mayflower*"), in the background was in the original version but was called "Landing of the Swedes." The change in the caption was made at a late stage in the manufacturing process after a highly placed presidential adviser of Finnish descent convinced the stamp-collecting Franklin Roosevelt that it had to be done.[7] The Finnish and Swedish governments were eventually given equal billing by the United States in the official program, and Americans of both Swedish and Finnish descent shared in the glory of recognition. Max Engman, a Finnish historian of Swedish descent, has characterized the events leading up to the tercentenary celebration as a "tug of war."

New Sweden, with a brief history from 1638 to 1655, when it was taken in war by the Dutch, is a small and insignificant episode in the history of the New World. Yet it looms large in the mythology developed to bolster the self-image of both Finnish and Swedish Americans, whose histories begin with nineteenth-century migrations. Yet their central myths of foundation, sacrifice, and ideological contributions all converged in a concept of a seventeenth-century settlement that was largely a creation of a nineteenth-century ethnic imagination. As H. Arnold Barton observes, "Perhaps the greatest significance of New Sweden has been the central role it has played in forming the self-image of Swedish—and Finnish—Americans from the late nineteenth century onward." In 1888 the Swedish-American celebration of the 250th anniversary was a local and ethnic midwestern affair in Minneapolis. The two main speakers were William Widgery Thomas, a Swedophile and former U.S. minister to Sweden, and Johan Enander, who, inspired by the Norwegian-American Rasmus B. Anderson, was the foremost expounder of the Swedish-American homemaking mythology. No official representative from either Stockholm or Washington, D.C., attended. Indeed, in Sweden as in other European countries, the official attitude toward both emigration and emigrants was a negative one, and there seemed little reason to take part in emigrant celebrations.

As emigration from Sweden declined, however, official attitudes toward Americans of Swedish descent began to change. The first official participation in the celebration of an immigrant institution occurred in 1893 when a Swedish bishop represented the Church of Sweden at the Augustana Synod's celebration of the three-hundredth anniversary of the adoption of the Augsburg Confession in Sweden. But Sweden and Swedish Americans and their institutions had little contact until the visits of Archbishop Nathan Söderblom in 1923 and of the crown prince and princess in 1926. These trips inaugurated an official recognition of what, from a Swedish point of view, now was a Swedish diaspora.[8]

The 1938 celebration of the three-hundredth anniversary of New Sweden was from the outset intended as a very different event from that in Minneapolis fifty years earlier. The initiative was taken by people far more centrally placed in American society than even the prominent Hans Mattson, who had served as a colonel in the Civil War and as Minnesota's secretary of state and who was the main organizer of the 1888 celebration. As Max Engman has observed, the initiative in the early 1930s was "plainly under the direction of representatives from Sweden, even though they preferred to remain in the background." Thus the proposal sent by the highly placed businessmen and academics of the Sweden-America Foundation in January 1935 to the Swedish foreign ministry was passed on to the Swedish ambassador in Washington, D.C., who invited representatives for several Swedish-American organizations to a meeting that established the Swedish Tercentenary Association. Engman's main sources are Swedish and American government archives; in his account the planning and organization of the tercentenary was largely in the hands of officialdom in Stockholm and Washington, D.C., with some participation from the governors of Delaware and Pennsylvania, and with the Swedish-American Tercentenary Association on the sidelines.

Or at least that was how it was before Finnish Americans got into the act. Although Swedish Americans were well aware that New Sweden was as central to the identity created by citizens of Finnish descent as it was to their own, they excluded Finland and Finnish Americans from the early planning of the tercentenary. Under the direction of Swedish officialdom as well as Swedish business interests, the event was, by February 1937, "on the way to becoming a vigorous Swedish presentation of modern Sweden in the United States and of the history of the country as well as its early contributions to America, thereby lending powerful support to Swedish-American aspirations." The first signal that a third party wished to take part had come in July 1936 when the Pennsylvania legislature, evidently influenced by its considerable Finnish-American constituency, decided that the state "was to conduct the celebration in cooperation with the governments of the United States, Sweden, and Finland."[9] The official Swedish view was that because Finland did not exist in the seventeenth century, the Finnish government could not be recognized as a successor of the government of New Sweden. But things looked very different from American points of view.

It may be, as the Finnish historian Auvo Kostiainen has suggested, that "the 1938 Delaware celebration came to Finnish Americans by accident and certainly much too soon." In the mid-1930s the Finnish-American Historical Society was still dominated by a naively romantic and filiopietistic view of history and led by Pastor Salomon Ilmonen, the author of *Amerikan ensimmälset suomalaiset* and many other books, all except one on John Morton and in Finnish. They planned a Finnish-American celebration of Finns in America rather than of New Sweden. For that reason they had decided to celebrate their tercentenary in 1941 rather than in 1938, since 1641 was the first year for which they had been able to determine the arrival of a significant number of ethnic Finns in the colony. They had taken no initiative to involve the national governments of Finland or the United States in their parochial celebration. When pressure from outside the traditional Finnish-American ethnic organizations was brought to bear on Washington to include the Finnish government in the official invitation, Finnish-American newspapers and organizations responded immediately and with ardor. They were, however, to remain on the sidelines.

Two developments may serve to illustrate how the world had changed

by the 1930s, leaving behind immigrant spokesmen like Salomon Ilmonen and similarly parochial leaders in both ethnic groups. First, a new
group of Finnish Americans, all firmly integrated in American society,
convened in New York and formed the Delaware Tercentenary Committee, effectively taking control of things on the Finnish-American side.
Two of the group were professors, at Columbia University and City College, but another member personified the distance that had been traversed
in this change of the guard. Emil Hurja was an influential figure in Washington and in the Democratic Party. He was a friend of Roosevelt's and a
trusted presidential adviser, and he worked closely with James F. Farley,
the postmaster general, in the 1936 election and had considerable influence over patronage. In 1936 he was on the cover of *Time* magazine.
When Hurja spoke, most members of Congress would at least listen.
Second, although their significant role in the early history of the United
States was central to the concerns of traditional Finnish-American leaders, the one factor that made it difficult to bypass Finland and Finnish
Americans in 1938 was not their glorious past or the efficacy of their
homemaking myths but, as the Finland-based historian Michael Berry
pointed out in 1988, the immense contemporary popularity of the little
country that paid its debts. After 1933 Finland was the only country that
punctually continued to pay its debts to the United States, and in 1937
public and popular praise of Finland was at its height.

When the question of including Finland in the official invitation was
debated in the U.S. House of Representatives, Pehr G. Holmes, a Republican from Massachusetts who had been born in Sweden, made formal
and historical arguments against Finnish participation. Holmes's rhetoric was no match, however, for the words of Robert Gray Allen, Demo-
crat of Pennsylvania: "We are extending the invitation to a nation that
has been very friendly to the United States in recent years, and whose
sense of honor and responsibility stands out above all others in the pay-
ment of its national debt to us." Other representatives from areas with a
significant Finnish-American constituency made the same point. One
member of Congress suggested that Finland should be "invited to every
celebration held in the United States," another that not only should they
be invited but there should a "special celebration for" *them.* The decision by the House to invite Finland was unanimous.[10] Both the forum in
which the matter was finally decided and the main argument used in
support of the Finnish side suggest that neither group had much need for
homemaking narratives or arguments.

When the time for the tercentenary celebration came, with representatives of the three governments and ethnic organizations in place in

Wilmington, Delaware, from June 28 to 29, 1938, peace and harmony reigned. The celebration, which included local as well as specifically ethnic events in many places in the United States, signaled that both the older type of ethnic competition for recognition had ceased to have much relevance and that current events were more important in image building than past glory, imagined or real.

For an earlier generation of Swedish Americans it had been important to argue that Swedes (and not the Finns) were one of the founding groups in the colonial history of the United States. For an earlier generation of Finnish Americans it had been equally important to argue that through their numerically strong presence in New Sweden, Finns too were among the founding groups. But in 1938 it turned out that Americans of Swedish and Finnish descent had little reason to continue to argue their right to the home in America they had long since achieved. Increasingly, the grandchildren and great-grandchildren of immigrants from the two countries looked to the culture and politics of contemporary Sweden and Finland, rather than to sixteenth-century New Sweden, to fortify an American ethnic identity. The 350th anniversary of New Sweden was celebrated in 1988, but by then it was a formal exercise and the ethnic competition for attention was friendly, as becomes competition between confident members of the same American family. A central event on this occasion was a conference for professional historians.[11]

And yet ethnicity persists. And yet myths of foundation proved to be an integral part of people's sense of being American as late as the 1960s. Although no one who could be taken seriously would at midcentury question the right of Americans of either Italian or Norwegian origin to their American identities, the homemaking myths of Christopher Columbus and Leif Erikson still carried an emotional appeal in 1965. Norwegian Americans continued to strive to have Leif Erikson recognized as the "real" discoverer of America. Although several statues have been erected in honor of the Viking from Iceland who made Greenland his home, a stamp with a Viking ship issued, and an official Leif Erikson Day, October 9, established, the hold of the Columbus story on the American imagination has never been challenged. And to many Italian Americans in 1965, Columbus was and remained their hero and, above all, their claim to a special place in the American home. So when Yale University Press announced on October 11, the eve of Columbus Day 1965, the publication of an authentic medieval map of Vinland, the name Leif Erikson had given to the area of North America that he visited, Italian Americans responded with indignation.[12]

The publishers had of course chosen a date that they believed would give *The Vinland Map and the Tartar Relation* the maximum publicity. They may not, however, have reckoned with the fury they created, nor with the quite special reaction to be expected in New Haven, not only a city with a large Italian-American population but the city where the Knights of Columbus had been founded in 1882 and where the Catholic fraternal organization still has its architecturally imposing headquarters. There is no reason to believe that the Yale University Press and the scholars involved in the project had other than scholarly motives for making the book. Scholarship was indeed an issue from the very beginning, and all reviewers were not equally impressed. Luckily, we need not concern ourselves here with the still unresolved controversy about the authenticity of the map.[13] Regardless of the scholarly issues involved, many Italian-American leaders saw the publication of the Vinland map, especially given the timing, as an assault on their central homemaking myth and a threat to an American identity closely linked to their story of the *Italian* discovery of America in 1492, even though Italian Americans in 1965 were by almost any measuring stick imaginable a successful and well-integrated American ethnic group.

The timing had the expected effect, and the sensationalist manner in which many newspapers presented the story may have helped to market the book. But it certainly did not improve relations between Yale University and Americans of Italian descent. The *New Haven Register* began its notice of the book on October 11 with this question: "Should a Lief [sic] Ericson Day Replace Columbus Day?" and concluded by rubbing it in: "The map will be put on public display in the Yale Library Tuesday—Columbus Day." "Sorry, Chris, We MAY Have to Call Off the Holiday," the *Boston Globe* proclaimed across the top of its front page that same day. Although the *Globe*'s actual story (from wire service reports by the *Washington Post* and *Los Angeles Times*) was a factual account based on the publisher's press release, the headline clearly demonstrated that the desk had risen to the bait.

Italian Americans paused in their preparations for the next day's celebrations to respond, some in fury, others with derision. The Columbus Day issue of the *New Haven Register* had a front-page story headlined "Yale's Release of Ericson Map Raises Protest":

> This is a Columbus Day that will be long remembered. The news from Yale that Leif Ericson reached these shores before Columbus has set off a flood of angry words from Italian-Americans here.
> In a calm voice, but obviously concerned by the turn of events, attorney John Ottaviano Jr., chairman of a committee to make Columbus Day a national holiday, had this to say: "Whatever happened before Colum-

bus had sunk into oblivion. His voyage was the significant one, the one that provided the first direct life line to the New World." . . . To Frank Amato, venerable of Sons of Italy No. 37 of New Haven, the news was "one of the most ridiculous things" he has ever heard. . . .

"This is very serious," said John N. La Corte, president of the Italian Historical Society. He told a gathering of 600 Columbus rooters, "They're trying to change history." He said Yale would come to regret its claim that Columbus was a johnny-come-lately to the New World, and that it actually was discovered by the Viking adventurer Leif Ericson.

"We're going to give Yale University something to think about," La Corte told a pre-Columbus day observance in Brooklyn. "We will dispel this new claim very fast." . . . He said the university's announcement will have "no effect on school children," who have been taught that Columbus discovered America.

The timing of the map's publication also paid off in the sense that far more people than generally are interested in scholarly publications about the Middle Ages became not merely aware of the event but were sufficiently interested to go to see what it was all about: "Record 1,300 Jam Beinecke for View of Vinland Map" was a front-page headline in the *New Haven Register* for October 13.

The following Sunday, the *New York Times* could not take the event altogether seriously, saying it had "produced a tempest in the melting pot":

Italian-Americans rose to the defense of Columbus. Irish-Americans upheld St. Brendan whose less substantial claim dates from about A.D. 500. The Spanish alternately backed Columbus and berated the Italians for claiming him as their own. A Madrid paper raged, "To credit the Italians with Columbus's voyage is tantamount to crediting Germany with victory in World War II only because Dwight D. Eisenhower was of German descent." Eric the Severeid summed up the hubbub when he signed off a Washington telecast as reporting "from the District of Ericsonia."

According to the *New York Times*, reactions to the Vinland map were not limited to those with positions of prominence in the Italian-American world. "On Columbus Day, there was scrawled on a wall in an Italian-American section of Boston: 'Leif Ericson is a fink.'" One reason the *Times* could not take it all too seriously was that although the phrase "new evidence" was used in the headline, the reporter observed that the map "was not necessary to prove the Vikings' presence in North America before Columbus" and told of the Helge Ingstad discoveries of medieval sites of Norse origin in Newfoundland.[14]

Some Italian-American leaders, such as Victor A. Arrigo, chairman of the Chicago Columbus Day parade, took the high ground of humor and derision: "Frankly, this Nordic myth makes its appearance around every Columbus Day. It happens all the time. But Italian-Americans have become tolerant of these Scandinavian claims. I don't blame them for wanting to come into the shadow of Columbus' accomplishments."[15] Similarly, Alfred E. Velluci, a city council member in Cambridge, Massachusetts, the following year made fun of the notion of a competing discoverer at the marker for the house that Leif Erikson supposedly built for himself in Vinland in 1000. "'Every year near Columbus Day,' he sighed to the *Boston Herald*, "they turn over this old Leif. Why, why, why? This marker is a fraud, even the stone is a fraud. The stone's been moved half a dozen times since they started building the rotary. I remember when the stone was down by Gerry's Landing."[16] Even when Velluci turned aggressive, there was more play than anger in his words, as when he took an initiative for the Cambridge council to "ask Harvard to stop playing in any athletic contest with Yale."[17] In the same vein, in Chicago Jimmy Durante and Richard Daley supported their constituencies with a glint of humor. "I know Columbus was first, because I was there to meet him," quipped the comedian. The perennial mayor of Chicago, while proclaiming it "a great day for Columbus and the Italians," also made a plug for his own ethnic group: "After the Huns overran Europe and destroyed all the records, the Irish kept the books of history. These books show unequivocally that Columbus discovered America."[18]

Many Italian-American leaders, however, were far too furious to be facetious about what they considered the outrageous behavior of Yale University Press. The violent rhetoric of John N. La Corte, head of the Italian Historical Society of America, suggested that the press had touched deep emotions when he "accused Yale of 'stabbing 21 million Italian Americans in the back' . . . and vowed to call in the Vatican and the National Geographic to help 'force Yale to the Wall.'"[19] One who took the publication of the map very seriously was Michael Musmanno, justice of the Pennsylvania Supreme Court and trustee of the Italian Historical Society of America. He was quick to characterize the map as a fraud, and exactly one year later he published a book to prove his conviction, *Columbus Was First*.[20] The author of a dozen books and an experienced justice, Musmanno scathingly and with considerable literary elegance took apart the evidence presented by the Yale scholars. For his work he was honored by the Italian Historical Society of America. The society's members were probably no more objective in their evaluation of the scholarship of Musmanno and the Yale scholars than was the American Scandinavian Foundation (ASF) when it decided to print a special edition of the Vinland map and mail it "free of charge, together with the Autumn issue of *The American-Scandinavian Review,* to all ASF associates and subscribers."[21]

In an editorial on October 12, 1966, the *Boston Globe* suggested "that those engaging in this controversy are missing the point. They are arguing about who was the first European to come to this country and report back." The *Globe's* well-meaning attempt to clarify the issue also missed the point, however, for the argument was not about past discoveries at all but about present recognition and status. One who seems to have understood this was a member of Congress from New York City, Benjamin Rosenthal, who introduced legislation to make Columbus Day a legal national holiday. This would, he explained, recognize the "enormous contribution made to this country by Americans of Italian descent."[22]

Scholars are still divided in their evaluation of the map. The Italian-American reactions in 1965 and 1966, however, were a last ethnic hurrah. When a new edition of the book was released in 1996, no uproar ensued. This may be because the Ingstads' discoveries in Newfoundland had become generally accepted as evidence of a Norse settlement, but it may be more likely that a new generation of Italian Americans does not see its identity threatened by the possibility that Columbus may not have been first. This does not mean, however, that foundation stories are no longer contested, as my account of a third controversy will demonstrate.

The geographic area that is today the United States was settled by people from Spain before British, Dutch, Swedish, and French colonies were established on the Atlantic coast. Since 1598, people of European descent have made their homes in what today is New Mexico. The oldest American church building is in Santa Fe, and it too predates Jamestown. Nevertheless, the 1998 celebration of the four-hundredth anniversary of the first settlement of European Americans in New Mexico was not a national affair as was, for instance, the three-hundredth anniversary of New Sweden in 1938. This may have been because the view that the founding group came from Britain and was supplemented by colonists from some other northern European countries was so entrenched that the 1598 arrival of some conquistadors and their followers had to be regarded as relatively unimportant. It may also have been because the view that the history of the United States began in the east, on the Atlantic, and that the frontier had moved steadily westward, bringing civilization to New Mexico as late as 1848, has had so powerful a hold on the American imagination that incorporating a southwestern foundation story—and a Spanish one to boot—in an acceptable account of the history of the United States was simply impossible.

Should one, despite these conceptual difficulties, still attempt to incorporate a southwestern foundation story in a narrative of the making of the United States, it would probably be too unpalatable for popular consumption. It would have to include the imperialistic war with Mexico and the 1848 Treaty of Guadalupe Hidalgo as central elements and somehow incorporate a narrative of the founding nationality as not only conquered but disinherited. So the 1998 celebration was local and not much noticed outside New Mexico.

In the view of a thirteenth-generation Santa Fe resident, "We are saddled with the history that England was the mother country—well, Spain was also a mother country." "Who wrote the history?" asked the Washington, D.C., correspondent for a Spanish weekly magazine. The Spanish reporter also answered the question: "The Anglos. . . . Their history starts with the Mayflower."[23] Apparently, Congress and the federal government found the three-hundredth anniversary of the abortive New Sweden far more important in 1938 than the four-hundredth anniversary of still vital New Mexico in 1998. The U.S. Postal Service did issue a 1998 postage stamp marking the arrival of the Spanish, just as one marking the arrival of the Swedes and Finns was issued in 1938. Perhaps the federal government became involved in 1938 because Swedish Americans and, after some pressure, Finnish Americans were perceived as more worthy of attention than Hispanic Americans were sixty years later.

It should not be difficult, then, to appreciate the Hispanic-American expressions of resentment at the dominant version of American history. However, it turned out that by 1998 the greatest distance was not that between the different foundation perceptions of the dominant American culture, which now included both Swedish and Finnish Americans, and the Hispanics of the Southwest, but that between the historical perception of Native Americans on the one side and those of all Americans of European descent on the other. At issue was not merely the question of what European nationality was here first but who they had conquered and how, as well as the larger question of how both points of view could be incorporated in one historical account acceptable to all.

The quite specific problem in New Mexico of contrasting views of the past surfaced in November 1997 when the Albuquerque Arts Board debated a proposal to erect a monument in Old Town Albuquerque to Don Juan de Oñate, the conquistador who established and led the 1598 settlement.[24] The apparent incompatibility of the two views of history was dramatized when it was eventually discovered one January morning that someone had sawed off the right leg of the statue of Oñate in Española, New Mexico. No one had apparently been looking very closely at the statue, and the media had to be notified before any attention was paid. A letter to the *Santa Fe New Mexican* said that it had been done "on behalf of our brothers and sisters at Acoma Pueblo" and "in commemoration of [Oñate's] 400th anniversary acknowledging his unasked for exploration of our land."[25]

The grievance was old but real. The mission of Don Juan de Oñate into the region was hardly a great success—except that it did become the beginning of Spanish, later Mexican, and eventually American settlement and government in the region. Oñate came north with soldiers, settlers, and Franciscan friars from Sacatecas in Mexico, where he had been born to immense wealth based on silver from the mines there. After ten frustrating years he gave up his governorship of the settlement. He probably should have spent more time at administration and leadership than on long expeditions in search of precious metals and salt. A mutiny immediately after his arrival was dealt with harshly. His party tortured and hanged Indians, in particular their chieftains, in attempts to force them to provide the colonists with corn and submit to baptism. Resistance from the Indians in Acoma Pueblo was especially strong, and after they had been subjugated in battles that left several hundred Acoma and thirteen Spaniards dead, he punished the Acoma by cutting off the right foot of twenty-four men. Ergo the equestrian statue's sawed-off leg four hundred years later.

The vandalism of the statue was not a promising start to a celebration that turned out to have more ambiguities than the planners had envisaged. Writing in the *New Mexican,* columnist Ray Rivera drew parallels with the protests against the Columbus quincentennial in 1992, the debunking of Jefferson for having had a slave mistress and of Kit Carson for his military campaign against the Navajo, and against the recent change of the name of a New Orleans elementary school from George Washington to Charles Richard Drew because the former had been a slave owner. Rivera did not like any of it. Nor did the two New Mexico historians with whom he spoke. Tom Chávez told Rivera, "We're suffering the fallout of political correctness and the ethnic chauvinism of the '60s," and Oñate's biographer, Marc Simmons, declared, "If we fail to honor Oñate this year because we're intimidated by crackpots, we not only disgrace Oñate, we disgrace ourselves." For a while it looked as if the celebrations might have to be called off. But Rivera also quoted a voice of moderation, that of Albert Hale, president of the Navajo Nation. Some days earlier Hale had written in the *New Mexican* that "it's time to remember there are two stories to every conquest. Until now only one story has been told. This year, it is time to tell the other story."[26] He did not sound at all like a crackpot.

In surprisingly short time, gestures, compromises, and efforts on both sides to understand conflicting points of view gave New Mexico a four-hundredth anniversary celebration that was more about healing and reconciliation than about claims and counterclaims. In Albuquerque the arts board decided in March to change the focus of the memorial from the conquistador Oñate to the settlers who with great sacrifice and suffering established the settlement that begat New Mexico and to include in the celebration the Pueblo Indians and their obviously central position in the early history of New Mexico.[27] Important roles in the process leading up to the celebration were played by the Spanish government, which sent representatives, including Vice President Francisco Alvarez-Cascos, to meet with Pueblo Indian leaders in early March. On the Native American side, Governor Earl N. Salazar of San Juan Pueblo (Oke Owingeh) initiated a meeting of the Spanish politicians and the Pueblo Indian leaders.[28] Salazar himself is a bridge—his father is of Hispanic descent, his mother is a native of San Juan Pueblo, and he is fluent in English, Spanish, and Tewa, the language of Oke Owingeh. His letter of invitation to the Spanish government asked for "a discourse to heal the wounds and pain of the past, reaffirm and acknowledge the surviving sovereigns and to shape the framework for our future relationship and that of our children."

So when the time came for the first of 185 events and projects to celebrate New Mexico's Spanish origins—including the unveiling of a new bronze statue of Don Juan de Oñate in Madrid, New Mexico, by one of the conquistador's descendants from Madrid, Spain—Americans of Hispanic and Indian descent were for the most ready to party with their Spanish guests. At a "reconciliation" ceremony with Spanish diplomats and most of the nineteen pueblo governors at San Juan Pueblo, also the site of the first Spanish village, on Sunday, April 26, Governor Salazar reminded his listeners that both the Pueblo Indians and the Spanish had let much blood without apologies from either side. And on Monday, after a dinner hosted by New Mexico's Governor Gary Johnson for the Spanish officials and the governor of Acoma Pueblo, Reginald T. Pasqual, the *New York Times* reported that Pasqual "turned to the Spaniards and invited them to visit Acoma. 'It was enormously moving,' Mr. Gullón, the Oñate descendant said. 'It was such a generous, open attitude. It seemed incredible after all that Juan de Oñate did to his people—the massacre, the feet.'"[29] The remaining area of contention for many of New Mexico's Hispanic Americans would seem to be with the still dominant "English-centric" view of the country's past, which made the remembrance of the historic event in 1598 a largely local affair.

Other important aspects, however, made the celebration of the Spanish foundation of New Mexico different from earlier celebrations and different from the uses of the other foundation stories considered in this book, including the official Anglo-American ones. As things turned out, New Mexicans were far less concerned with their mythic uses of the past than with serious efforts to remember and to understand the several different stories (different because of different experiences and different points of view) that merge in what we may call the early history (as distinct from the separate ethnic filiopietistic stories) of New Mexico. What began with an act of violence against a bronze masculine figure on a bronze horse and a squabble about whose story was the true one continued with diplomacy and conversation and concluded with a celebration that aimed at bringing people together in the present rather than holding them separate and apart because of their real or imagined pasts. In earlier times Lithuanian Americans refused to celebrate Kosciuszko/Koscinsko together with Polish Americans, and Swedish Americans did their best to exclude Finnish Americans from celebrations of New Sweden. And no one ever imagined making Native Americans participants rather than adversaries in European-American foundation stories (with some exceptions such as Pocahontas, the providers of corn and turkeys for the first Thanksgiving, and the sellers of Manhattan).

It may be that the United States has come so far in making one nation out of the many ethnic groups that ethnic leaders have a diminishing need to hold on to mythologies that may serve as exclusive arguments for a right to an American home for their people. It may be that the individuals in the many groups that make up the nation are becoming not only so interrelated but also so willing to say a heartfelt "brothers, sisters" to their kin of various colors and religions that the sense of being an excluded "foreigner" in the American home is becoming less and less acute among Americans, regardless of background.[30]

It may also be, however, that the many Americans who because of class or color still not only feel excluded but *are* excluded from the American family and its family comforts have despaired. Immigrants from Europe at the turn of the nineteenth century were peoples of hope. One way they had of confronting the frustration of exclusion was by telling homemaking myths. One of the more purposeful and practical homemaking arguments today as we enter the twenty-first century may simply be to register as a voter. The half of the nation that does not feel sufficiently at home in American society to do this needs far more than stories to argue for its right to decent accommodations in the American home—and far more than myths actually to achieve them. Indeed, home-making myths have never been enough to make a home in the United States. They have nevertheless served important functions.

Homemaking myths were, however indirectly, addressed to the culturally and socially dominant American group at the turn of the nineteenth century, middle-class Americans of primarily English descent. These Anglo-Americans, however, did not read the "foreign language press," nor did they attend Polish-American, German-American, or other ethnic rallies, banquets, and picnics where these myths thrived. Clearly, the stories considered in this book largely failed to reach their Anglo-American audience. To the extent that mainstream America was aware of the homemaking arguments and disputes of the country's motley mass of immigrants, these arguments and the stories that bolstered them were, at best, shrugged off. Indeed, it may be said that the homemaking myths of the European immigrant groups have not been so much forgotten as they have never been much known or, at least, cared for outside the narrow and closed ethnic societies in which they were created and celebrated. They have nonetheless been important in American history.

Homemaking myths have been separatist yet unifying: their most important functions have been to create ethnic pride and, paradoxically, pride in belonging in the United States. "No people can claim to be civilized unless it leaves behind testimonials to its history," Knut Langeland insisted in the Chicago newspaper *Skandinaven* in 1866. His notion of history was filiopietistic—primitive and naive from our more enlightened point of view. Yet, as we have seen, the history of their country, as taught to the immigrants' children in the late nineteenth-century public schools, was no less filiopietistic, and it certainly did not include the parents and grandparents of immigrant children in the national narrative. If Italian Americans may have seemed to insist too much on the crucial role "they" played not only in the discovery of America but in the making of the Declaration of Independence and the success of the War of Independence and other American wars, this was more than balanced by their exclusion from the history texts of their children, whether they attended public or parochial schools.

But while the intention of those who told these filiopietistic stories clearly was to create pride in a specific ethnicity, the stories of all immigrant groups told similar tales of immigrants' contributions to the United States and of immigrants' participation in the country's history. Homemaking myths were part of arguments for the right of immigrants to enter the United States as fully acknowledged members of the American family. The argument was not merely for acceptance but for acceptance on their own terms. Homemaking myths were stories told by immigrants who insisted on being welcomed into the American home with the recognition of their achievements and their part in American history and not merely as uprooted, lost masses in a country purely the creation of immigrants from Britain.

The stories and their arguments were, then, about creating group identities—not to resist the pull of the new land but to enter it with pride and dignity. In his 1866 editorial in the first issue of *Skandinaven,* Langeland wrote that if the immigrants could preserve and develop their identity, "we may be able to place our small contribution to the outcome of the great migrations of the nineteenth century on the altar of our adopted fatherland with the conviction that though our contribution may be small compared to that of other nationalities, it may yet in quality be the equal of any." For all their narrowly ethnic filiopietism, the homemaking myths so prevalent among European immigrants in the United States at the turn of the nineteenth century have been less about ethnic separatism than about being American.

These stories have contributed to an American rather than to an ethnic nationalism, however, because they were factors in the pride essential to ethnic cohesion. Consequently, the America of which they spoke and to which they contributed was a multicultural America. It should also be obvious that those who created and used homemaking myths—the immigrant leadership largely made up of professionals, clergy, small businessmen, and journalists—may have had mixed motives for this, as for other aspects of their work. For without ethnic cohesion and pride, they would be without flocks to lead, without parishioners who would fill their churches, without customers who would choose their banks and businesses, and without subscribers to their newspapers. But to concentrate on this limited aspect of the motivation for the creation of homemaking myths would be to distort immigration history in general and the role of the immigrant leadership in particular.

The historian who looks closely at one aspect of the past—as I have done in this book—is necessarily guilty of some degree of distortion. This book has, for instance, not been about the hard work, struggles, and denials, nor about the losses and the victories, that eventually made so many of the descendants of immigrants at home in America. Although the immigrants' myths certainly had a mission, they remained myths. Nor has this book been much about those immigrants for whom these myths never had any meaning. It has clearly been more about immigrants with middle-class aspirations than about those immigrants and working-class Americans who were given a voice in Hamilton Holt's 1906 collection of as-told-to accounts, *The Life Stories of Undistinguished Americans as Told by Themselves,* originally published by the *Independent,* the New York progressive weekly. The anonymous Lithuanian immigrant who told his story to the journalist Ernest Poole for this series worked in the stockyards of Chicago. He appreciated attending a Lithuanian society with two picnics in the summer and as many "big balls" in the winter and going "one night a week to the Lithuanian Concertina Club." On these occasions he would probably have heard speeches that presented homemaking arguments with stories of the kind we have considered in this book. His main social center and his main provider of the pride and identity essential to his socialization, however, was the Cattle Butchers' Union, a local of the Chicago Federation of Labor. One reason for his pride in his union was that

> it is combining all the nationalities. The night I joined . . . I was led into the room by a negro [*sic*] member. With me were Bohemians, Germans, and Poles, and Mike Donnelly, the president, is an Irishman. He spoke to us in English and then three interpreters told us what he said. We swore to be loyal to our union above everything else except the country, the city and the State—to be faithful to each other—to protect the women-workers—to do our best to understand the history of the labor movement, and to do all we could to help it on.[31]

Obviously, this too is an essential aspect of the American experiences of immigrants in the period covered in this book. Moreover, such experiences may eventually have been far more important for the creation of American homes in the real rather than in the metaphorical sense in which the word has been used in this book.

This, then, has been a book about certain aspects of American multiculturalism in the decades around the turn of the nineteenth century. The study of American multiculturalism should be as concerned with the multicultural nature of American society and of American culture as a whole as with the culturally and ethnically specific ingredients of a multicultural United States. By leading to a recognition of the shared American themes of ethnicity-specific experiences, multicultural studies may also lead to a new understanding of what makes the many one. All the stories considered in this book, while insisting that there is as much reason to be proud of being Armenian American or German American as of being Anglo-American, also insist on a common right to be—simply and proudly—American.

Notes

Author's note: All translations to English from publications only available in Scandinavian languages or German are mine.

Prologue

1. The American dictionaries I consulted are *Merriam Webster's Collegiate Dictionary*, 10th ed. (Springfield, Mass., 1995), *The American Heritage Dictionary*, 2d college ed. (Boston, 1985), *Webster's Third New International Dictionary of the English Language Unabridged* (Springfield, Mass., 1966), *A Dictionary of American English on Historical Principles* (Chicago, 1940), and *A Dictionary of Americanisms* (Chicago, 1951). *The Oxford English Dictionary*, 2d ed. (Oxford, 1989), however, does note a parallel usage of "foreign" in British English: "the word is in British use not applied to parts of the United Kingdom, nor, ordinarily, to (former) colonies chiefly inhabited by English-speaking people."

2. Philip Gleason, *Speaking of Diversity: Language and Ethnicity in Twentieth-Century America* (Baltimore, 1992), 164.

3. As late as 1966, *Webster's Third New International Dictionary* does not record "American Indian" as a meaning of "native American."

4. This practice is not limited to European holidays, of course, as witnessed by the large-scale Chinese New Year celebrations in several U.S. cities. This book, however, focuses on immigrant and ethnic groups of European origin.

5. Except where noted, references to Chicago newspapers in languages other than English are to the translations in the Works Progress Administration project, *The Chicago Foreign Language Press Survey*. These translations of selections from the Chicago press are organized thematically and chronologically by language. The entire collection is available on microfilm; I used the copy at the Immigration History Research Center, University of Minnesota, St. Paul.

6. In his *The Promise Fulfilled: A Portrait of Norwegian Americans Today* (Minneapolis, 1998), Odd S. Lovoll gives illustrations of how May 17 celebrations

in heavily Norwegian-American communities have taken on characteristics of general American celebrations with the participation of many with no claim to Norwegian descent. They have, he observes, "in some regions been transformed into local community celebrations" (262). See also p. 54.

7. Jon Gjerde, *The Minds of the West: Ethnocultural Evolution in the Rural Middle West, 1830–1917* (Chapel Hill, N.C., 1997), 61.

8. The report by Kristine Haugen, "Syttende mai i Sioux City," appears in the June 1926 edition of the journal *Norsk Ungdom* (Norwegian Youth). Her son, Einar Haugen, later a professor of Norwegian language and literature at the University of Wisconsin and Harvard University, served as master of ceremonies.

9. Jacobson goes on to say that "in the interest of an accurate historical rendering of race in the structure of U.S. culture and in the experience of those immigrant groups now called 'Caucasians,' we must listen more carefully to the historical sources than to the conventions of our own era; we must admit of a system of 'difference' by which one might be both white *and* racially distinct from other whites" (*Whiteness of a Different Color: European Immigrants and the Alchemy of Race* [Cambridge, Mass., 1998], 6).

10. Ole E. Rølvaag, *Concerning Our Heritage,* translated and with an introduction by Solveig Zempel (Northfield, Minn., 1998), 72. Zempel uses italics for words written in English in the original Norwegian text.

11. Victor R. Greene, *American Immigrant Leaders, 1800–1910: Marginality and Identity* (Baltimore, 1987), 20–21. So successful have the Irish been in making an American celebration of St. Patrick's Day that Finnish Americans in Minnesota have created their own Finnish-American saint, St. Urho, "in large measure patterned after St. Patrick's Day observances," reports Matti Kaups, "A Commentary Concerning the Legend of St. Urho in Minnesota," *Finnish Americana: A Journal of Finnish American History and Culture* 7 (1986): 13. March 16 has been officially recognized as St. Urho's Day in all fifty states, says Kaups, adding that Finland has no St. Urho legend and that it is entirely an American creation.

12. Michael A. Musmanno, *The Story of the Italians in America* (Garden City, N.Y., 1965), 7–8, 12.

13. David Mauk, *The Colony That Rose from the Sea: Norwegian Maritime Migration and Community in Brooklyn, 1850–1910* (Northfield, Minn., and Urbana, Ill., 1997), 42–43; Marcus Lee Hansen, "Immigration and Puritanism," *The Immigrant in American History* (New York, 1964), 101–2; Musmanno, *The Story of the Italians in America,* 89.

14. Patrick J. Gallo, *Old Bread New Wine: A Portrait of the Italian-Americans* (Chicago, 1981), 4.

15. Mirta Ojito, "Two Rival Parades and One Enigmatic Hero," *New York Times,* October 14, 1996.

16. An example of the many writings on Welsh discoveries is Benjamin F. Bowen, *America Discovered by the Welsh in 1170 A.D.* (Philadelphia, 1876). This book has another feature that is an element in homemaking mythology: the naming of members of an ethnic group who played central roles in early, preferably colonial, American history. The final chapter, "The Welsh of the American Revolution," relates that the captain of the *Mayflower* was Welsh, as were Roger Williams and eighteen of the signers of the Declaration of Independence, including

not only John Adams and Thomas Jefferson but also John Morton. Homemaking myths of both Swedish Americans and Finnish Americans claim Morton.

17. One example of the many books on pre-Columbian voyages across the Atlantic is Michael Bradley, *The Black Discovery of America: Amazing Evidence of Daring Voyages by Ancient West African Mariners* (Toronto, 1981).

18. Alfred E. Hudd, "Richard Ameryk and the Name America," reprinted from the *Proceedings of the Clifton Antiquarian Club, 1909–1910*, part 19, vol. 7, part i; and Brian Dunning, "The Man Who Gave America Its Name," *Country Life*, June 20, 1963, pp. 1507, 1509. I am indebted to Ian Richmond for these references.

19. John R. Chávez, *The Lost Land: The Chicano Image of the Southwest* (Albuquerque, 1984), 8, 22, 92, 93. With the relaunching of the ancient myth of Aztlán at the First Chicano National Conference in Denver in 1969, the claim to an American home was again based on the claim of being indigenous. See, for instance, Armando B. Rendon, "The People of Aztlán," reprinted in Livie Isauro Duran and H. Russell Bernard, eds., *Introduction to Chicano Studies: A Reader* (New York, 1973).

20. Jacobson, *Whiteness of a Different Color*, 22–23, 141.

21. Booker T. Washington, *Up from Slavery* (1901; reprint, New York, 1986), 217–25.

22. Paul Laurence Dunbar, "At Shaft 11," *Folks from Dixie* (New York, 1898), 208, 214, 231; Washington, *Up from Slavery*, 217–25. Although industrialists sometimes used African Americans as strikebreakers in this period, they rarely rewarded black workers for their services. When strikes were broken, and white workers could be brought back at lower wages, the desperate black workers, whose situation was worse and whose bargaining position was weaker, were sent away.

23. Gary Hartman, "Building the Ideal Immigrant: Reconciling Lithuanianism and 100 Percent Americanism to Create a Respectable Nationalist Movement, 1870–1922," *Journal of American Ethnic History* 18 (Fall 1998): 59; Carol Poore, "Whose Celebration? The Centennial of 1876 and German-American Socialist Culture," in Frank Trommler and Joseph McVeigh, eds., *America and the Germans: An Assessment of a Three-Hundred-Year History*, vol. 1 (Philadelphia, 1985), 186–87. An editorial in the *Chicago Vorbote* on July 1 recommended this celebration but explained that Germans "had no reason to commemorate the centennial of a republic that was the political instrument of the 'monied aristocracy.' . . . For *us* it is not a republic, not a fatherland" (Poore, "Whose Celebration?" 177). According to Hartman, Lithuanian-American socialists claimed that because they were "striving to improve the situation for workers at home, rather than pursuing political interests abroad . . . they were 'really the best patriots' of all" (59).

24. The letter from Ueland is quoted in Nina Draxten, *Kristofer Janson in America* (Boston, 1976), 148–49; Frederick C. Luebke, *Bonds of Loyalty: German-Americans and World War I* (De Kalb, Ill., 1974), 49. Draxten also gives an account of the ball. Ueland seems to have forgotten that Anderson had not merely been a spokesman for the views expressed by Julius Olson but that Anderson, as will be demonstrated, had introduced them. Olson was a professor at the University of Wisconsin.

25. David Lowenthal, *The Heritage Crusade and the Spoils of History* (London, 1997), ix, 151, 122, 120, 2.

26. Oscar Handlin, *The Uprooted*, 2d ed. (Boston, 1973), 253.

27. The account of Rabbi Hirsch's address comes from the *(Chicago) Record-Herald*, November 25, 1905. The emphasis is added.

28. In my pamphlet, *Home-Making Myths* (Odense, Denmark, 1996), I discuss some troubling affinities between the celebratory expression of homemaking myths among Norwegian Americans in the 1920s and European expressions of fascist and Nazi nationalism in the same period (17).

29. Georg Meyer, *Die Deutschamerikaner. Festschrift zur Feier des Deutsch-amerikanischen Tages in Milwaukee, Wisconsin, am 6. Oktober, 1890* (Milwaukee: Herausgegeben von dem Festausschuss, 1890). The statement appears on the title page and on p. 54, where it concludes a chapter, "Bedeutung und Einfluss des heutigen Deutschthums." Implied in the statement is that the German language is not foreign "in this country."

Chapter 1: Contexts and Contests

1. Daniel Soya, "Between Two Worlds: The Jewish *Landsmanshaftn* and Questions of Immigrant Identity," *American Jewish History* 76, no. 1 (September 1986): 5–24. The entire issue is devoted to studies of the *landsmanshaftn* in America. See also Odd S. Lovoll, *A Folk Epic: The Bygdelag in America* (Boston, 1970). In his introduction to his *For God and Country: The Rise of Polish and Lithuanian Ethnic Consciousness in America, 1860–1910* (Madison, Wis., 1975), Victor Greene has a very useful discussion of the various levels of ethnic and national awareness among immigrants.

2. Horace M. Kallen, *Culture and Democracy in the United States* (1915; reprint, New Brunswick, N.J., 1998), 86–87, 94.

3. Orm Øverland, *The Western Home: A Literary History of Norwegian America* (Northfield, Minn., 1996), 188–89.

4. From Frank Thistletwaite's 1960 address to the 21st Congrès des Sciences Historiques, "Migration from Europe Overseas in the Nineteenth and Twentieth Centuries," to Mark Wyman's *Round-Trip to America: The Immigrants Return to Europe, 1880–1930* (Ithaca, N.Y., 1993), historians have pointed to the problems of determining the relative volume of return migration. (Wyman quotes Thistletwaite on p. 9.) On the basis of previous scholarship and available statistics, Wyman attempts some estimates for the period 1880–1930. The return rate for Italian immigrants to the United States was quite high, about 50 percent, while percentages for other countries could vary from 20 percent for Finland to 36 percent for Croatia and Slovenia combined (10–12).

5. In American English, the more common meaning of statements such as "I am Polish" or "I am Irish" is "I am an American of Polish origin" or "I am an American of Irish origin." In European languages adjectives such as "Polish" or "Irish" more commonly refer to nationality than to ethnicity. Typically, dictionaries do not register this Americanism. Thus the *Random House Webster's College Dictionary* (1992) has this entry for Polish: 'pertaining to Poland, its inhabitants, or the language Polish' and does not mention the quite common American meanings, one of which may be described as "pertaining to an American ethnic group with its origin in Poland."

6. Matthew Frye Jacobson, *Special Sorrows: The Diasporic Imagination of Irish, Polish, and Jewish Immigrants in the United States* (Cambridge, Mass., 1995), 1, 3, 121.

7. Gary Hartman, "Building the Ideal Immigrant: Reconciling Lithuanianism and 100 Percent Americanism to Create a Respectable Nationalist Movement, 1870–1922," *Journal of American Ethnic History* 18 (Fall 1998): 37.

8. Dorothy Burton Skårdal, *The Divided Heart: Scandinavian Immigrant Experience Through Literary Sources* (Lincoln, Neb., 1974); Ferdinando P. Alfonsi, *Dictionary of Italian-American Poets* (Bern, Switzerland, 1989), 16. This view was dominant in the 1950s and 1960s when historians took their cue from Oscar Handlin's *The Uprooted* (Boston, 1951).For instance, Maldwyn Allen Jones writes: "For all immigrants immigration was a traumatic experience, resulting in a sense of alienation and isolation. It was nearly always the fate of the first generation to remain a 'marginal man' suspended between two cultures but belonging to neither" (*American Immigration* [Chicago, 1960], 127).

9. Jon Gjerde, *The Minds of the West: Ethnocultural Evolution in the Rural Middle West, 1830–1917* (Chapel Hill, N.C., 1997), 8, 60. See also p. 63. Marcus Lee Hansen has argued that because of their involvement in the Civil War immigrant groups ceased to "perpetuate the atmosphere of the motherland" and began to see themselves primarily as American ("Immigration and American Culture," *The Immigrant in American History* [New York, 1964], 140).

10. Greene, *For God and Country*, 133. These loyalties were, however, seen as contradictory by many within the church who were not yet ready to accept ethnic pluralism "within a religious unity" (134).

11. The terms "ethnic" and "immigrant" are at times used interchangeably in this book. Depending on the point of view and context, individuals and the groups to which they belonged were, of course, both. Historians and social scientists speak of immigrants of second and third generations and also count immigrants of the first generation in statistics of American ethnic groups.

12. There seems to be little place for this peculiar kind of ethnicity and nationalism in Anthony D. Smith's *Theories of Nationalism*, 2d ed. (London, 1983).

13. Rudolph J. Vecoli has shown that the Italian-American neighborhoods in Chicago were to a great degree based on the region and village of origin and that some such neighborhoods "remained intact for several decades" ("The Formation of Chicago's 'Little Italies,'" *Journal of American Ethnic History* 2 [Spring 1983]: 17). The process of acquiring a more general Italian-American identity was not necessarily completed within one generation. Similar patterns of settlement in the rural and small-town Midwest have been described by Jon Gjerde, *Minds of the West*, 79–131.

14. Dag Blanck, *Becoming Swedish-American: The Construction of an Ethnic Identity in the Augustana Synod, 1860–1917* (Uppsala, Sweden, 1997).

15. Jerre Mangione, *Mount Allegro: A Memoir of Italian American Life*, with an introduction by Herbert J. Gans and a new, final chapter by the author (1942; reprint, New York, 1981).

16. Kallen, *Culture and Democracy*, 97–98.

17. John Higham, "Leadership," in Stephan Thernstrom, ed., *Harvard Encyclopedia of American Ethnic Groups* (Cambridge, Mass., 1980), 642–47. In an earlier book Higham poses the hypothesis that "ethnic groups in an open society are,

in some degree yet to be specified, the creation of their leaders" (*Ethnic Leadership in America* [Baltimore, 1978], ix).

18. Victor Greene, *American Immigrant Leaders, 1800–1910* (Baltimore, 1987), 4, 141.

19. Higham, "Leadership," 642.

20. Hansen, *Immigrant in American History*, 148–49; Kallen, *Culture and Democracy*, 91.

21. Kallen offers a deliberately provocative comparison of the immigrant "vernacular dailies and weeklies with the yellow American newspapers which are concocted expressly for the great American masses. The content of the former, when the local news is deducted, tends to be a mass of information, political, social, scientific; sometimes translations into the vernacular of standard English writing, sometimes original work of good, often high literary quality. The latter, when the news is deducted, consist of the sporting page and the editorial page" (*Culture and Democracy*, 99).

22. Many more instances could be cited. The quotations are from John G. Moses, *Annotated Index to the Syrian World, 1926–1932* (St. Paul, Minn., 1994).

23. I am thankful to Professor Najwa Nasr of the Lebanese University for providing me with a copy of Gibran's text.

24. Matthew Frye Jacobson, *Whiteness of a Different Color: European Immigrants and the Alchemy of Race* (Cambridge, Mass., 1998), 223, 239–40.

25. Julius Goebel, "Gedanken über die Zukunft des Deutschtums in Amerika," *Der Deutsche Kulturträger: Monatschrift für die Kulturarbeit des Germanentums deutscher Zunge* (January 1913), 4. The author was a professor at the Urbana campus. The journal was published in Fredericksburg, Texas. The First World War, it may be noted, was about to deal a severe blow to German-American self-confidence.

26. Her address was published in *The Commons* 10 (January 1905) and reprinted in Philip Davis, ed., *Immigration and Americanization: Selected Readings* (Boston, 1920), 3–22. The account of the young woman who committed suicide is on pp. 12–13. With her tongue-in-cheek characterization of immigration as a neglected field at a time rife with debates on immigration, Addams was criticizing the tendency to study immigration as a social and political problem and to disregard the lives and traditions of actual immigrants.

27. Louis Adamic, *A Nation of Nations* (New York, 1945), 2. In an earlier book, *My America* (New York, 1938), Adamic quotes at length from a letter he received from a second-generation Swedish American who tells of his sense of inferiority because of his ethnicity (224–26). The dating of the Norwegian immigrant's story of humiliation may be wrong because such campaigns were more likely in the heyday of Americanization during and immediately after the First World War. The American Speech Committee of the Chicago Woman's Club, for instance, produced a "Pledge for Children" in 1918: "I love the United States of America. I love my country's flag. I love my country's language. I promise

1. That I will not dishonor my country's speech by leaving off the last syllables of words.

2. That I will say a good American 'yes' and 'no' in place of an Indian grunt 'um-hum' and 'nup-um' or a foreign 'ya' or 'yeh' and nope" (Dennis Baron, *The English-Only Question: An Official Language for Americans?* [New Haven, Conn., 1990], 155–56).

28. Daniel Santoro and John A. Rallo, *Italians: Past and Present* (New York, 1955), 80–82. In his new concluding chapter, "Finale," for the 1981 edition of *Mount Allegro*, Jerre Mangione writes about the "intensity of the hatred and abuse directed against the immigrants in the years when they were pouring into the country by the millions." He claims that both the first and third generation were better able to handle "such maligning" than the second. "The grandchildren of the immigrants . . . have a far easier time than their parents" because they have "become more objective about their ethnic situation" and "can relate to the culture of the immigrants without any sense of conflict" (306, 307). This, of course, is a restatement of the so-called Hansen thesis.

29. Baldo Aquilano, *L'Ordine Figli d'Italia in America* (New York, 1925), 19. Aquilano quotes from contemporary textbooks to illustrate the negative self-image Italian-American children acquired in school, for instance: "They don't conquer the world anymore as did their ancestors, but they are filthy and work on the railways and sell bananas and nuts" (20). He concludes, "There is to our detriment, a continuous belittling of every elevated Italian thing, undertaking or happening" (21) and counters, in the manner of Michael Musmanno (*The Story of the Italians in America* [1965]), with a chapter entitled "The Italian Contribution to American Society." My translation is based on a crib by Sissel Henriksen.

30. Ole E. Rølvaag, *Peder Victorious* (New York, 1929), 155.

31. Dorthea Dahl, "The Seventeenth of May," *North Star*, no. 4 (May–June 1921): 224–25. The title refers to Norway's Constitution Day. Dahl, who lived most of her life in Idaho, wrote fiction in both Norwegian and English.

32. Ole E. Rølvaag, *Concerning Our Heritage*, translated and with an introduction by Solveig Zempel (1922; Northfield, Minn., 1998), 72–73. Rølvaag did not actually write "ethnic pride" but *racial* pride or feeling. See *Omkring fædrearven* (Northfield, Minn., 1922), 44. It is an error to pretend that American intellectuals in the nineteenth and early twentieth centuries were merely talking about cultural differences between nationalities. Nationalities were races, and the perception of the superiority of some races and the inferiority of others was based on theories of anthropology and genetics.

33. Addams, "Immigration," 11; *Denní Hlasatel*, March 5, 1918. The report in the *Chicago Daily Tribune* is quoted in the Czech newspaper.

34. See Orm Øverland, "Waldemar Ager: Untiring Crusader," *Western Home*, 324–45, and Einar Haugen, *Immigrant Idealist: A Literary Biography of Waldemar Ager* (Northfield, Minn., 1989). Ager's essay, "Smeltedigelen" [The Melting Pot], was published in 1916. A 1905 essay, "Vore kulturelle muligheter" [Our Cultural Possibilities], argues for an ethnic culture independent of that of the old homeland, and in "Om at bevare vort modersmaal" (1905) and "Det vigtigste" (1908) [Preserving Our Mother Tongue and The Language Is Most Important, respectively], he insisted that an American ethnic culture would have to be based on the immigrant language. He elaborated his views on the melting pot and the World War I "Americanization" drive in a series of essays, "Den store udjævning" [1917–1920, The Great Leveling]. These and other essays are collected in translation in Odd S. Lovoll, ed., *Cultural Pluralism Versus Assimilation: The Views of Waldemar Ager*, introduction by Carl H. Chrislock (Northfield, Minn., 1977).

35. Werner Sollors, "Theory of American Ethnicity, or: '? S Ethnic?/TI and American/Ti, De or United (W) States S S1 and Theor?'" *American Quarterly* 33

(1981): 257–83, discusses the A + B + C = D (pluralist) and the A + B + C = A (assimilationist) interpretations of the melting pot. A revised version of this article is used as the introduction to Sollors's *Theories of Ethnicity: A Classical Reader* (New York, 1996).

36. One of Ager's illustrations in making this point is music. "In no field does the melting pot have greater possibility of success than in music," he writes. But even if the material conditions, such as "a piano in almost every home," are greater than in Europe, there is still not "a single great musician" with American roots: "No musical training is considered complete without one's having been in Europe to learn some foreign national element or other in music" ("The Melting Pot," 80). Other quotations in this paragraph are from pp. 77–79, 85. The German term translated as "Germanness" is *Deutschtum*. Similarly, Polish Americans spoke of *Polskosc*, or Polishness.

37. Waldemar Ager, *On the Way to the Melting Pot*, trans. Harry T. Cleven (Madison, Wis., 1995); it was originally published as *Paa veien til smeltepotten* (Eau Claire, Wis., 1917). Quotations are from pp. 173, 197–98, of the new translation. I have also discussed this novel in "From Melting Pot to Copper Kettles: Assimilation and Norwegian-American Literature," in Werner Sollors, ed., *Multilingual America: Transnationalism, Ethnicity, and the Languages of American Literature* (New York, 1998), 50–63.

38. Ole E. Rølvaag, *Their Fathers' God* (New York, 1931), 208.

39. This letter of December 20, 1922, by John Heitmann is in the Ole Edvart Rølvaag Papers at the Norwegian-American Historical Association, St. Olaf College, Northfield, Minn. The images of mother and bride were in common use, as in Carl Schurz's statement, "I love Germany as my mother. America as my bride" (Gjerde, *Minds of the West*, 61).

40. The reference to *Skandinaven* is to a microfilm copy of the weekly edition and not to the *Chicago Foreign Language Press Survey*, which also includes selections from this newspaper.

41. In 1919 Frances A. Kellor included in her program of Americanization "a recognition of the cultural forces in the various races as expressed in their literature and institutions." It was particularly important to make the immigrant's "religious beliefs and experience of use. This means more than toleration. It means the use for America of the finest aspirations and traditions of these men. It means an appreciation of their literature and of the art which has come out of these beliefs" ("What Is Americanization?" *Yale Review* [January 1919], quoted in Davis, *Immigration and Americanization*, 637–38). This view is also expressed in Kellor's concluding chapter, "Principles of Assimilation," for *Immigration and the Future* (New York, 1920). In his discussion of "immigrant gifts," John Higham suggests that it was the "settlement founders" who taught the immigrants to think of their culture as a "gift" to America (*Strangers in the Land: Patterns of American Nativism, 1860–1925*, 2d ed. [New York, 1963], 121, 251). But in fact this was an idea independently expressed by immigrants. Every immigrant group had leaders who urged their compatriots to take care of their old heritage in their new lives and tried to instill them with a sense of pride in their old culture as their contribution to their new country.

Higham has a brief sketch (see pp. 239–41 and 243–44) of the career of Frances Kellor, who had a law degree from Cornell and played an important role in U.S.

political life in the early decades of the twentieth century because of her involvement in crucial social issues of the day. Her concern with urban poverty led to her involvement with the social conditions of immigrants, immigration policy, and Americanization. After her work on the 1908 New York Commission on Immigration, she was appointed head of the new state Bureau of Industries and Immigration. This, as well as her active role in local and national organizations for the education and integration of immigrants into American society, led to her leading role in the World War I–era National Americanization Day Committee and her appointment as assistant to the chairman of the immigration committee of the U.S. Chamber of Commerce. Although this could hardly be said of the many people and organizations she worked with, Kellor seems always to have had a genuine interest in immigrants and their just place in U.S. society.

42. Hans Mattson, *Reminiscences: The Story of an Emigrant* (St. Paul, Minn., 1891), 300.

43. Johannes B. Wist, *Jonasville: Et kulturbillede* (Decorah, Iowa, 1922), 113–14. The two earlier volumes are *Nykommerbilleder: Jonas Olsens første aar i Amerika* (1920) and *Hjemmet paa prærien: Jonas Olsens første aar i nybygget* (1921).

44. Higham, *Strangers in the Land.* Keep in mind that xenophobia and hatred of other ethnic groups (even when accounting for the evil of slavery and the genocidal wars against the native population) have been less pronounced in the United States than in countries and cultures on other continents. It may be fair for a European to note that while the United States has not practiced genocide since the 1880s, European, Asian, and African countries have been active in such horrors in the 1990s.

45. Oscar Handlin, *The Uprooted,* 2d ed. (Boston, 1973), 240; Merle Curti, *The Roots of American Loyalty* (New York, 1946), 81 (Curti too points to the irony of nativists' questioning of the loyalty of immigrants who speak in praise of their chosen land); Clyde Haberman, "A Proud Day on Island of the People," *New York Times,* January 6, 1998.

46. Sacvan Bercovitch, *The Rites of Assent: Transformations in the Symbolic Construction of America* (New York, 1993), 368, 369.

47. Mary Antin, *The Promised Land* (Boston, 1912), xi, 364; Jacob Riis, *The Making of an American* (New York, 1901). Images of the experience of America as the true homeland are common in immigrant autobiographies. Visiting Sweden, Ernst Skarstedt found consolation in a botanical garden where "a few languishing specimens of Douglas fir from the Oregon and Washington Territories and of California's mammoth [redwood] trees made me dream of the peaceful primeval forest on the shores of the Pacific Ocean and of a home of one's own under their sheltering branches" (*Vagabond och redaktör: Lefnadsöden och tidsbilder* [Seattle, 1914], 291, quoted in H. Arnold Barton, *A Folk Divided: Homeland Swedes and Swedish Americans, 1840–1940* [Uppsala, Sweden, 1994], 63). "It was not unusual for Americans traveling abroad to be thrilled at seeing the Stars and Stripes or a Yankee ship or even a Connecticut-made machine or a bale of cotton," writes Curti of the early decades of the Republic in *Roots of American Loyalty* (145).

Horace Kallen reminds us that "the biography of an individual, particularly of a literary individual, [is not] the history of a group." He expresses skepticism of the conversion stories by such autobiographers as Antin and Riis, arguing that they "protest too much; they are too self-consciousness and self-centered, their 'Americanization' appears too much like an achievement, a *tour de force,* too little like a growth" (*Culture and Democracy,* 78).

48. Anonymous, *Nordlyset,* no. 3 (1847), my prose translation. The reference is to the microfilm copy of the newspaper. For a discussion of this poem and a more complete translation see Øverland, *Western Home,* 36.

49. Quoted in Werner Sollors's introduction to Mary Antin, *The Promised Land* (New York, 1997), xxxvii.

50. St. Louis in 1900 may serve to illustrate that the Anglo-Americans could be dominant even though they were in the minority. From 1860, when about 60 percent of the city's population was foreign born, the percentage of immigrants had dwindled to a mere 19 percent by 1900. Sixty percent, however, had foreign-born parents, and German Americans alone of first, second, and third generation "constituted fully 56% of the city's population." Nevertheless, the "majority of city fathers were native-born residents of English heritage" (Margaret LoPiccolo Sullivan, "Ethnic Elites and Their Organizations: The St. Louis Experience," in Timothy Walch, ed., *Immigrant America: European Ethnicity in the United States* [New York, 1994], 215–16).

51. Nina Baym, "Early Histories of American Literature: A Chapter in the Institution of New England," in Gordon Hutner, ed., *The American Literary History Reader* (New York, 1995), 81–82, 84.

52. Michael Singer, "Research of German-American History," *Der Zeitgeist* 2 (February 9, 1918): 31. This article is in the journal's English-language supplement.

53. Baym, "Early Histories," 104, n. 12.

54. Quoted by Frances FitzGerald, *America Revised: History Schoolbooks in the Twentieth Century* (New York, 1980), 78. FitzGerald observes that this and other textbooks "portrayed the immigrants as nothing more than a problem."

55. The most comprehensive study of the Americanization movement of World War I is still Edward George Hartman, *The Movement to Americanize the Immigrant* (New York, 1948). Speeches by the president and former president to immigrant audiences are Woodrow Wilson, "Address at Convention Hall, Philadelphia, May 10, 1915," and Theodore Roosevelt, "Americanism," an address delivered before the Knights of Columbus, Carnegie Hall, New York, October 12, 1915 (both appear in Davis, *Immigration and Americanization,* 611–14, 645–60).

56. Adamic, *Nation of Nations,* 6.

57. Gary London, "The Delaware Finns and John Morton: Seeking to Legitimize the Immigrant Experience in America," *Siirtolaisuus/Migration,* no. 3 (1978): 16. The Polish and Lithuanian competition for Kosciuszko is discussed in chapter 3.

58. At this time Swedish Americans in Chicago seem to have felt that they were losing the competition with Polish Americans for recognition; another newspaper, the *Svenska Amerikaneren* (Swedish American), complained on June 14, 1917, that the English-language newspapers were paying undue attention to Polish-American celebrations at the Kosciuszko monument. See Anna Williams, *Skribent i Svensk-Amerika: Jacob Bongren, journalist och poet* (Uppsala, Sweden, 1991), 156–57.

59. Kathleen Neils Conzen, "The Stories Immigrants Tell," *Swedish-American Historical Quarterly* 46 (January 1995): 50–52. An often repeated motif in Norwegian-American fiction is that the protagonist wins the approval of a Yankee by standing up for Norwegian values and traditions. See, for example, Øverland, *Western Home*, 269.

60. C. Carnahan Goetsch, "The Immigrant and America. Assimilation of a German Family, Part 1," *Annals of Iowa* 42 (Summer 1973): 20–21.

61. John Bodnar, *Remaking America: Public Memory, Commemoration, and Patriotism in the Twentieth Century* (Princeton, N.J., 1992), 70.

62. Øverland, *Western Home*, 10.

63. Greene, *For God and Country*, 10, emphasis added. The core of his book is a detailed discussion of this controversy.

64. Adamic, *Nation of Nations*, 1–2, 6, 11.

Chapter 2: Foundations and Refoundations

1. Isolated, that is, compared to the impact of the Columbian voyages. The four centuries of voyages between Iceland, Norway, and Greenland, including regular use of Labrador as well as areas farther to the north for timber and furs, involved not only the people of the far north of Europe but also the Church of Rome. Until the last bishop arrived in Greenland in 1368, the pope sent bishops there and collected revenue. Although the bishopric itself was forgotten, bishops of Greenland continued to be appointed until the Reformation, that is, after the voyages of Columbus. See Kirsten A. Seaver, *The Frozen Echo: Greenland and the Exploration of North America, ca. A.D. 1000–1500* (Palo Alto, Calif., 1996), 111–12, 237–38, 309.

2. Franco D'Amico, "To Our Brothers in 'The Melting Pot[,]' the Norwegians," *Bulletin of the Order Sons of Italy of Illinois* 8, no. 11 (1936).

3. "Our son attends the English school," wrote one immigrant to Norway in 1835 (see Theodore Blegen, *Land of Their Choice: The Immigrants Write Home* [Minneapolis, 1955], 21). In Ole E. Rølvaag's *Peder Victorious* (New York, 1929) the eponymous protagonist goes off to "*English* school among the *Norwegians*" because of his mother's fear of the consequences of mixing with the Irish (151). "They accommodate to the english [*sic*] manners and customs when they think it is for the good, but retain their German customs, when they think the english are bad ones," wrote an immigrant in 1893. Another, in 1892, spoke of wearing "English dress" (Jon Gjerde, *The Minds of the West: Ethnocultural Evolution in the Rural Middle West, 1830–1917* [Chapel Hill, N.C., 1997], 62, 231).

Other illustrations of this usage may be found in Herbert J. Brinks, ed., *Dutch-American Voices: Letters from the United States, 1850–1930* (Ithaca, N.Y., 1995), 114, 116 (letter from 1866), 124 (1870), 166 (1897), 258, 259 (1873), 266 (1874), and more; and Walter D. Kamphoefner, Wolfgang Helbich, and Ulrike Sommer, eds., *News from the Land of Freedom: German Immigrants Write Home* (Ithaca, N.Y., 1991), 213, 278, 452, 460.

4. The German immigrant is quoted in Gjerde, *Minds of the West*, 113. In 1871 the *Illinois Staats-Zeitung* objected to the view that "English . . . is the language of the country," insisting it was merely "one of the languages of the country that is recognized as official because it is the native language of a majority of the in-

habitants. And that is all!" After giving some statistics for a variety of languages used in the United States and insisting on "their good right on the side of English," the newspaper acknowledged in its edition of July 21, 1871, that "the numerically weakest nationalities have dissolved into the by far stronger English, but that does not mean that all other nationalities must follow the same course. The Germans at any rate will not do so."

Two years later (March 3, 1873), the same newspaper again reacted strongly to attacks in Chicago's *Times* on the teaching of German in the public schools, insisting "that the German language is no foreign language but is one of the authorized languages of the country. And the American State consists of citizens speaking different languages of which the German language is one of the most important." On March 5, 1893, arguing against a proposal "to discontinue German language instruction" in the public schools, the newspaper insisted that "the German and German-American population of Chicago is much larger than the Anglo-American one. The German language is spoken by about a half million people, and it is just as indispensable in every day social and business affairs as English."

5. Johannes B. Wist, *Hjemmet paa Prærien: Jonas Olsen's første Aar i Nybygget* (Decorah, Iowa, 1921), 98. Marcus Lee Hansen has observed that this was true not only of the Yankee but of the recently arrived English immigrant as well: "Possessing greater initial resources than the Continental immigrant, he made a quicker start at independent farming; and this fact, together with his prior knowledge of the language, placed him on a higher level in community affairs. He did not assert himself belligerently; nor did he suffer from an inferiority complex. His presence created no problem, social or political" (*The Immigrant in American History* [New York, 1964], 148–49).

6. Michael Singer, "'Der Zeitgeist' und dessen Ziele," *Der Zeitgeist,* October 23, 1917, p. 1. The quotations from Diven are on pp. 35–36.

7. One who has included Native Americans in stories of immigration is Louis Adamic. One chapter, "Americans from Russia," in Adamic's *A Nation of Nations* (New York, 1945) begins with the immigration of the first "Indians" across the Bering Strait from Siberia: "Thus, going as far back in the story of American immigration as is possible at present, we can say that the first Americans came from a territory now part of Russia" (144).

8. Swedish Americans would say a Scandinavian (and, of course, "we") discovered America. Leif Erikson was Norwegian in the limited sense that his allegiance, such as it may have been, was to the Norwegian king. He was an Icelander in the sense that he grew up on that island. He was a Greenlander, however, in the sense that he migrated to Greenland along with his father, Erik the Red, and settled there. An on-line discussion about the nationality of Leif Erikson in the Web site of the Oslo newspaper *Aftenposten* (Evening Post) in the early winter of 1998 had 189 participants in a few days from Norway, Denmark, Sweden, and Iceland (<http://www.aftenposten.no/debatt/debatt.cgi>).

9. Armando B. Rendon, "The People of Aztlán," in Livie Isauro Duran and H. Russell Bernard, eds., *Introduction to Chicano Studies: A Reader* (New York, 1973), 28–34; "El Plan de Aztlán," in Richard A. Garcia, ed., *The Chicanos in America 1540–1974: A Chronology and Fact Book* (New York, 1977), 108–9; David G. Gutiérrez, *Walls and Mirrors: Mexican Americans, Mexican Immigrants, and the Politics of Ethnicity* (Berkeley, Calif., 1995), 184–87.

10. Theodore Saloutos, *The Greeks in the United States* (Cambridge, Mass., 1964), 237–38. The three different categories of homemaking myths are not necessarily pure and distinct; this particular story includes a myth of ideological contribution or kinship.

11. M. Vartan Malcom, *The Armenians in America* (Boston, 1919), vii, x; H. Arnold Barton, *A Folk Divided: Homeland Swedes and Swedish Americans, 1840–1940* (Uppsala, Sweden, 1994), 69.

12. Vereinigten Deutschen Gesellschaften der Stadt New York, *Nachtrag zur Festschrift zur Feier des Zehnjährigen Bestehens der Vereinigten Deutschen Gesellschaften der Stadt New York* (New York, 1912), 8.

13. A will to take up competition with Italian Americans is implied in a report in *Die Abendpost* of October 18, 1925, on a lecture on "the history of the German elements in the United States." Although Amerigo Vespucci may have been Italian, "a German scholar gave the name of the true discoverer of America . . . to the country"; the report was referring to the 1507 pamphlet in which Martin Waldseemüller named the New World "America."

14. John Higham, *Strangers in the Land: Patterns of American Nativism, 1860–1925*, 2d ed. (New York, 1963), 218.

15. Albert Welles, *The Pedigree and History of the Washington Family . . .* was published in New York by Society Library in 1879. Because the early thirteenth-century saga of the Norwegian kings, *Heimskringla* by Snorri Sturlason, begins by tracing the descent of the medieval Norwegian kings from Odin, all Albert Welles had to do was relate the Washington family to one of these kings through a Viking settler in Yorkshire. Welles also traces the relationship between George Washington and Snorri Torfinson, "the first birth of European parentage in America" (xviii). Welles was probably thinking less of glorifying Scandinavian Americans than of glorifying the Republic by giving its founder a divine lineage like that of many kings and emperors in Europe as well as in Asia.

16. "Washington a Scandinavian," *Northern Review* 3, no. 10 (January 1918): 3–8. Other articles in this issue are "John Hanson, A Delaware Swede: First President of the Confederation Congress" and "John Morton, a Delaware Swede: He Cast the Vote That Pledged Pennsylvania to Freedom" (9–10). The politics of the journal were undisguised. The September 1916 issue, for instance, had an article entitled "Why Deutschland Is Unconquerable: The Culture of Race and National Unity" (3–5). Another use of the Washington story to promote the idea of Norwegians as true Americans comes from the novelist and journalist Simon Johnson, "Glimt av norsk foreningsliv i Amerika," *Nordmands-Forbundet* 18 (April 1925): 191.

17. Angelo Flavio Guidi, "Washington and the Italians," in Richard C. Garlick, Jr., Angelo Flavio Guidi, Giuseppe Prezzolini, Bruno Roselli, and Luigi Russo, eds., *Italy and the Italians in Washington's Time* (New York, 1933), 29–46. Originally published by Italian Publishers, the book was reprinted in 1975 by Arno Press.

18. A related story is the German-American one of Lincoln as a German American. As Chicago's *Die Abendpost* reported on February 26, 1901: "There are many proofs existing that Lincoln's ancestors had the German name 'Linkhorn,' and that his progenitors came from a German settlement in Virginia. . . . Besides, it is not difficult to trace the Linkhorns. They lived in Berks County, Pennsylvania, the most predominantly German country of that state, where the German language is still in popular use, although it is mixed with some English expressions." In

conclusion the newspaper observed that "the Anglo-Americans, perhaps will never admit that Lincoln is of German descent, but so many reasons and pieces of evidence seem to prove this point that it can be reasonably accepted as a fact, of which all German-Americans certainly can be proud."

One of the German-American characters in E. Annie Proulx's *Accordion Crimes* (New York, 1996) is a firm believer in the Linkhorn story, which he had from "a German paper that came weekly by mail . . . and from it [he] ordered a perforated cardboard portrait of the dead president for Gerti [his wife] to work up in colored wools." "It's the Germans making this country great," says one of his neighbors (73).

19. Matthew Frye Jacobson, *Whiteness of a Different Color: European Immigrants and the Alchemy of Race* (Cambridge, Mass., 1998), 79, 147, 230–31.

20. David R. Roediger, *The Wages of Whiteness: Race and the Making of the American Working Class* (London, 1991), 138, 148; Jacobson, *Whiteness of a Different Color*, 49, 55; the *Atlantic Monthly* is quoted in Jacobson.

21. Booker T. Washington, *Up from Slavery* (1901; reprint, New York, 1986), 221–22; Paul Laurence Dunbar, *Folks from Dixie* (New York, 1898). These texts are discussed in more detail in the prologue.

22. The rabbi's speech, as reported in the *Chicago Tribune*, April 20, 1891, is included in the Jewish section of *The Chicago Foreign Language Press Survey*.

23. Although one may understand the sentiment expressed by the *Daily Jewish Courier*, the statement is not accurate. Jews held places of prominence in, for instance, German-American and Polish-American ethnic associations and publications.

24. Barton, *Folk Divided*, 64.

25. The statue of Leif Erikson (1887) on Commonwealth Avenue in Boston was the result of Ole Bull's campaign. The monument committee consisted of the governor, the mayors of Boston and Cambridge, and many of the best-known intellectuals of the time and place, such as Henry Wadsworth Longfellow, Oliver Wendell Holmes, John Greenleaf Whittier, Robert Lowell, and Charles W. Eliot (president of Harvard). See R. B. Anderson, *Life Story* (Madison, Wis., 1915), 206–7. In Cambridge, near the Eliot Bridge, is a stone inscribed: "On this spot in the year 1000 Leif Erikson built his house in Vinland." Here, near what used to be called Gerry's Landing, Eben N. Horsford, who was a very active member of the monument committee, was satisfied he had found evidence of medieval Norse habitation. See Eben Norton Horsford, *The Problem of the Northmen* (Cambridge, 1889); Cornelia Horsford, "Vinland and its Ruins: Some of the Evidence That Northmen Were in Massachusetts in Pre-Columbian Days," an offprint (in the Widener Memorial Library, Harvard University, Cambridge, Mass.) from *Appleton's Popular Science Monthly*, December 1899; and Elizabeth G. Shepard, *A Guide-Book to Norumbega and Vineland; or, The Archæological Treasures Along Charles River* (Boston, 1893).

26. Anita Libman Lebeson, *Jewish Pioneers in America, 1492–1848* (New York, 1931), 13; Julian W. Mack, "The Pledge of the American Jew," in New York Co-Operative Society, *The Two Hundred and Fiftieth Anniversary of the Jews in the United States: Addresses Delivered at Carnegie Hall, New York, on Thanksgiving Day MCMV Together with other Selected Addresses and Proceedings* (New York, 1906), 144; Peter Wiernik, *History of the Jews in America from the Period*

of the Discovery of the New World to the Present Time (New York, 1912); Max Goldberg, *The Contribution of the Chosen Race to Civic Progress in America: An Address Delivered Under the Auspices of the Essex Institute on February 10, 1930, at Academy Hall, Salem, Massachusetts,* 1, 2. The story of Jewish participation in the 1492 voyage also appears in the opening pages of Miriam K. Freund, *Jewish Merchants in Colonial America: Their Achievements and Their Contributions to the Development of America* (New York, 1939); Joseph Krauskopf, "The Jewish Pilgrim Fathers," in New York Co-Operative Society, *Two Hundred and Fiftieth Anniversary,* 125.

27. Seraphim G. Canoutas, *Hellenism in America: The History of the Greeks in America from the Early Days to the Present Time . . .* (New York, 1918), 19–21; Canoutas, *Christopher Columbus: A Greek Nobleman . . .* (New York, 1943). Parts of the 1918 book appear in Paul Koken, Theodore N. Constant, and Seraphim G. Canoutas, *A History of the Greeks in the Americas, 1453–1938* (Ann Arbor, Mich., 1995), a book said to be written by these three "between 1935 and 1938."

28. Adamic, *Nation of Nations,* 266. He adds that Canoutas was not the first to argue that Columbus was a Greek and refers to a 1937 book by "Spyros Cateras of Manchester, New Hampshire," *Christopher Columbus Was a Greek Prince and His Real Name Was Nikolaos Ypshilantis from the Greek Island Chios.*

29. Miecislaus Haiman, *Polish Past in America, 1608–1865* (1939; reprint Chicago, 1974), 5–6; Adamic, *Nation of Nations,* 287; "Poles in the United States," *Chicago Society News,* July 1926, p. 8, in *Chicago Foreign Language Press Survey,* Polish. Haiman's book is based on an earlier version in Polish, *Z Przeseszlosci Polskiej w Ameryce* (Buffalo, N.Y., 1927). The Polish-American historian Sigmund H. Uminski is convinced that this story "must be relegated to the limbo of legends" and omits it in his *Poland Discovers America* (New York, 1972), xi. John J. Bukowczyk has called Haiman "the ideologue of Polish America" and characterizes his "singular message" as "where America happened, Poles were there" ("Polish Americans, History Writing, and the Organization of Memory," in John J. Bukowczyk, ed., *Polish Americans and Their History: Community, Culture, and Politics* [Pittsburgh, 1996], 14). Kirsten A. Seaver agrees with Samuel E. Morison that a voyage of discovery by the two Hanseatic adventurers Didrik Pining and Hans Pothorst (in the company of a Danish, Norwegian, or Polish Jon Scolvus) in all probability never took place (*The Frozen Echo,* 199–202).

30. The Croatian historian is Jurica Bjankini, "Yugoslavs in the United States: Their Contribution to American Culture and Civilization," in the program book for the "First All-Slavic Singing Festival. Given by United Slavic Choral Societies, Sunday, December 9, 1934," Chicago, p. 9, *Chicago Foreign Language Press Survey,* Croatian; Adamic, *Nation of Nations,* 234–35. Although Yugoslavia has since broken apart, it is evident that Adamic identified himself as much with Yugoslavia as with his then province of Slovenia.

31. Although it is only natural for descendants of peoples who lived in the Americas at the time of the voyages of Columbus (or of the Norse, for that matter) to have resented the notion that they were discovered, it is equally natural from a European point of view to speak of such discovery. That something or someone is discovered does not mean that it, she, or he did not exist before discovery, merely that those who made the discovery were ignorant of such existence.

32. David Humphreys, *A Poem on Industry. Addressed to the Citizens of the United States of America* (Philadelphia, 1794), 8, 12, 16, 22.

33. Joel Barlow, *The Columbiad. A Poem, with the last corrections of the author* (Washington, D.C., 1825), xi–xii, 358–61. Quoted from the facsimile edition, William K. Bottorff and Arthur L. Ford, eds., *The Works of Joel Barlow*, vol. 2 (Gainesville, Fla., 1970), emphasis added.

34. Alvin J. Schmidt, *The Greenwood Encyclopedia of American Institutions: Fraternal Organizations* (Westport, Conn., 1980), 176; Timothy J. Meagher, "Why Should We Care for a Little Trouble or a Walk Through the Mud?": St. Patrick's and Columbus Day Parades in Worcester, Massachusetts, 1845–1915," *New England Quarterly* 58 (March 1985): 23.

35. The *Sacred Heart Review* is quoted in John Marcus Dicky, comp., *Christopher Columbus and His Monument Columbia. Being a Concordance of Choice Tributes to the Great Genoese, His Grand Discovery, and His Greatness of Mind and Purpose* (Chicago, 1892), 178, 180–82.

36. Ellen M. Litwicky, "'The Inauguration of the People's Age': The Columbian Quadricentennial and American Culture," *Maryland Historian* 20, no. 1 (1989): 50. Tammany was organized in 1789 and incorporated in 1805 as the Society of Tammany, when it also became identified with the Democratic Party; Dicky, *Christopher Columbus*, 73; "The Columbian Celebration," *Harper's Weekly*, October 22, p. 1014. The journalist was of course mistaken in believing that New York was such a special case. Had he looked more closely, he would have found a majority of first- and second-generation immigrants in many cities and counties.

37. "Columbian Celebration"; Dicky, *Christopher Columbus*, 92–93; 281. The monument in Boston may still be seen in the enclosed private park in Louisburg Square where it was originally placed. Other monuments are described on pp. 247–50, 250, 272–75, 277, 279, 280, 281, 311.

38. "Columbian Celebration"; Litwicky, "'Inauguration of the People's Age,'" 52–54.

39. Anthony James Delpopolo, Sr., "The Making of a Holiday," *Ambassador* (Spring 1992): 14–15; *L'Italia*, October 15, 1887. The newspaper noted that "this is an old festival which the Italian colony celebrates once a year in honor of Christopher Columbus and the discovery of America."

40. *L'Italia*, April 2 and September 24, 1892, and October 7, 1893; Margaret LoPiccolo Sullivan, "Ethnic Elites and Their Organizations: The St. Louis Experience, 1900–1925," in Timothy Walch, ed., *Immigrant America: European Ethnicity in the United States* (New York, 1994), 219.

41. Hoover's proclamation designates Columbus Day specifically as a day for "his compatriots" (see *Bulletin Order Sons of Italy in America—Grand Lodge of Illinois*, October 1932, p. 2, *Chicago Foreign Language Press Survey*, Italian; Delpopolo, "Making of a Holiday," 16–17).

42. Dag Blanck, *Becoming Swedish-American: The Construction of an Ethnic Identity in the Augustana Synod, 1860–1917* (Uppsala, Sweden, 1997), 192.

43. Meagher, "Why Should We Care?" 24.

44. The Italian section of *The Chicago Foreign Language Press Survey* gives ample illustration of the efforts of Italian-American leaders to have Columbus recognized as their particular American hero. See especially the material under thematic groupings IC and IIC.

45. *L'Italia,* October 10, 1908; *Bulletin Italo-American National Union,* March 1935, p. 1440. Amerigo Vespucci is not given much prominence in Italian-American foundation stories, probably because of the major role played by Columbus.

46. Frances Kellor, *Immigration and the Future* (New York, 1920), 259–60.

47. *L'Italia,* November 17, 1912.

48. *New Haven Register,* October 9, 1998; Mireya Navarro, "Columbus Returns as a 600-Ton Tourist Magnet," *New York Times,* December 21, 1998. The other annual ethnic celebrations in New Haven were St. Patrick's Day, the African-American Freddy Fixer Parade, and Connecticut Puerto Rican Day.

49. Bjankini, "Yugoslavs in the United States," 95. That Bjankini was a Croatian rather than a Croatian American does not alter the homemaking function the story had for the readers of this American "all-Slavic" publication.

50. Adamic, *Nation of Nations,* 235. Immigrant groups usually lacked strong central institutions, and memory was often both short-lived and local. The authors of a 1921 pamphlet, *The Yugoslavs in the United States of America* (New York, 1921), were not acquainted with the Roanoke story, nor was their Croatian story apparently known by the editors of the 1934 festival program in Chicago: "The town of Croatan, in the state of North Carolina, was founded about 1800, by ship-wrecked sailors from Croatia who established a little colony. The descendants are, of course, totally Americanized, but the name of the town recalls the race of the original settlers" (14). The so-called Croatan Indians were believed to be descended from the Roanoke colonists, and an account from 1709 claims that "their language is the English of three centuries ago. They do not have any Indian names or words." Ethnological scholarship, however, gives a less spectacular but more credible account. See Hugh Talmage Lefler, ed., *North Carolina History Told by Contemporaries,* 4th ed. (Chapel Hill, N.C. 1965), 7.

51. David Lowenthal, *The Heritage Crusade and the Spoils of History* (London, 1997), 149.

52. Krauskopf, "Jewish Pilgrim Fathers," 125–27, and Mack, "Pledge of the American Jew," 144–45, in *Two Hundred and Fiftieth Anniversary.*

53. For information on church organization among Dutch immigrants in the nineteenth century, see Rob Kroes, *The Persistence of Ethnicity: Dutch Calvinist Pioneers in Amsterdam, Montana* (Urbana, Ill., 1992). The negative reference to the Dutch of New York was made in a speech at the Holland Society of Chicago and published in B. T. Van Alen, ed., *Year Book of The Holland Society of Chicago, 1897, 1898, 1899, 1900* (Chicago, March 1901); it also was included in *Chicago Foreign Language Press Survey.* See *Onze Toekomst* for February 25, 1921, April 24, 1908, July 2, 1909.

54. Blanck, *Becoming Swedish-American,* 186–87; Hans Mattson, *Reminiscences: The Story of an Emigrant* (St. Paul, Minn., 1891), 313; C. F. Peterson, "Amerikas första svenskar," *Förenta staternas historia i sammandrag* (Chicago, 1890), 75–87.

55. Barton, *Folk Divided,* 64–65, 67. Barton quotes from a speech Enander gave in 1890. Enander's version of medieval Swedish-American history is quite fanciful and includes a Vinland visit by a bishop from Iceland in 1121. He is called "America's first ordained bishop," and Vinland at this time seems to have been a thriving city.

56. When "Sweden's Day" at the 1893 World's Columbian Exposition was cel-

ebrated with a parade and speeches, for instance, no mention was made of the Viking discovery. See Dag Blanck, "Swedish Americans and the 1893 Columbian Exposition," in Philip J. Anderson and Dag Blanck, eds., *Swedish-American Life in Chicago: Cultural and Urban Aspects of an Immigrant People, 1850–1930* (Uppsala, Sweden, 1991), 283–95.

57. Blanck, *Becoming Swedish-American*, 169–70, 206. The Enander quotation is from a speech he made in 1892.

58. Blanck, *Becoming Swedish-American*, 207, 206, n. 104; Gary London, "The Delaware Finns and John Morton: Seeking to Legitimize the Immigrant Experience in America," *Siirtolaisuus/Migration*, no. 3 (1978): 21–22, n. 21; Auvo Kostiainen, "Delaware as a Symbol of Finnish Immigration," in Auvo Kostiainen, ed., *Finnish Identity in America*, Turun Historiallinen Arkisto 46 (Turku, Finland, 1990), 49.

59. London, "Delaware Finns and John Morton," 16, 18. In referring to early Delaware settlement as "the foundation of American civilization," London is quoting E. A. Louhi, *The Delaware Finns* (New York, 1925). Estonia was part of Sweden at the time of the colony; although some Estonians were among the colonists, they have not been used in Estonian-American myth making as were the Finnish and Swedish Americans. See Jaan Pennar, *The Estonians in America, 1627–1975: A Chronology and Fact Book* (Dobbs Ferry, N.Y., 1975), 1. On Salomon Ilmonen see Raymond W. Wargelin, "Salomon Ilmonen: Early Finnish Historian," *Siirtolaisuus/Migration*, no. 3 (1987): 3–11.

For his 1998 doctoral dissertation, "Finnish American Ethnicity as Measured by Collective Self Esteem" (Joensuu University, Finland), Chris Susag measured the responses to "symbols of Finnishness" on the basis of 134 questionnaires returned from rural northern Minnesota. Here John Morton tops the list of "most unknown symbols of Finnishness ranked by frequency of response 'I don't know.'" Susag is rather vague about Morton's identity as well, characterizing him as both "founding father of the New Sweden colony . . . and signer of the Declaration of Independence," thus giving him a central role in 1638 and 1776! More important, Finnish Americans at the turn of the twentieth century seem to have little use for the homemaking myths of the turn of the nineteenth century. See Chris Susag, "Ethnic Symbols: Their Role in Maintaining and Constructing Finnish American Culture," *Siirtolaisuus/Migration* 25, no. 4 (1998): 3–8.

60. "Poles in the United States," *Chicago Society News*, July 1926, p. 8; Haiman, "Polish Colonial Immigration," *Polish Past in America*, 11–28; "Lithuanians Were Among the Early Settlers of the New World," *Sandara*, October 10, 1930; John O. Evjen, *Scandinavian Immigrants in New York, 1630–1647* (Minneapolis, 1916); Bruno Reselli, "Francesco Vigo, Savior of the Midwest," 77–111, in Garlick et al., *Italy and the Italians*, and John Borza, Jr., "Two Romanians in the Civil War," *New Pioneer* 1, no 1 (1942): 5.

61. Although *Staats-Zeitung* was magnanimous to Americans from other countries of northern Europe, it did object to Italian immigration as it began to increase in the late 1880s (see the edition of August 11, 1888).

62. Goebel and Kern are quoted in Vereinigten Deutschen Gesellschaften der Stadt New York, *Nachtrag zur Festschrift*, 18, 8. The German form of Arminius, chief of the Germanic tribe known as the Cherusci, is Hermann. The late nineteenth-century celebration of Arminius as a German national hero may not be

historically sound, but, then, neither are many other celebrations typical of homemaking mythology. The German-American Order of the Sons of Hermann contributed to the erection of the "Hermann's Monument" (1897) in New Ulm, Minnesota (Kathleen Neils Conzen, "German-Americans and the Invention of Ethnicity," in Frank Trommler and Joseph McVeigh, eds., *America and the Germans: An Assessment of a Three-Hundred-Year History* [Philadelphia, 1985], 142).

63. Wllll Paul Adams, "Ethnic Leadership and the German-Americans," in Trommler and McVeigh, *America and the Germans.* vol. 1, 153.

64. Barton, *Folk Divided,* 69; Mattson, *Reminiscences,* 312–13.

65. Blanck, *Becoming Swedish-American,* 194–96.

66. Gary London, "Delaware Finns and John Morton," 19.

67. See Herbert Gans, "Symbolic Ethnicity: The Future of Ethnic Groups and Cultures in America" (1979), reprinted with a new epilogue, in Werner Sollors, ed., *Theories of Ethnicity: A Classical Reader* (New York, 1996), 425–59.

Chapter 3: Sacrifice

1. Miecislaus Haiman, *Polish Past in America* (1939; reprint, Chicago, 1974).

2. Le Pen is quoted in David Lowenthal, *The Heritage Crusade and the Spoils of History* (London, 1997), 57. This talk of fatherland and blood smacks of the fascism so powerful in Europe, particularly in the 1930s and 1940s, but so does much of extreme filiopietism, including that of U.S. ethnic groups.

3. Hans Mattson was quite specific, insisting that Ericsson "saved the navy and the great seaports of the United States" (Mattson, *Reminiscences: The Story of an Emigrant* [St. Paul, Minn., 1891], 313).

4. O. E. Djerf, *Ensimmäiset suomalaiset Amerikassa* (Ashtabula, Ohio, n.d.). See Gary London, "The Delaware Finns and John Morton: Seeking to Legitimize the Immigrant Experience in America," *Siirtolaisuus/Migration,* no. 3 (1978): 17, 18–19.

5. During the World War II, my father was a pastor in the Norwegian Seaman's Mission in Montreal, and I have in my possession a letter sent from Bergen, Norway, on October 10, 1939, to him and the other pastors affiliated with the mission on the Continent. The letter refers to conversations with J. A. Aasgaard, president of the Norwegian Lutheran Church in America (NLCA), and explains that the NLCA will take financial and administrative responsibility for the mission, should the home office be unable to function. Thus an American church body was ready to take responsibility based on ethnic bonds, but the assistance was clearly offered by a U.S. institution and without any compromising of its primary loyalty or national identification. See also A. N. Rygg, *American Relief for Norway* (Chicago, 1947), on the World War II involvement of Norwegian-American ethnic organizations in wartime assistance.

6. Not only immigrants denied citizenship suffered, of course, but also their descendants, who were U.S. citizens by birth.

7. John Borza, "Two Romanians in the Civil War," *New Pioneer,* November 1942, pp. 5–7. Also typical is the secondary theme of the article: the perfidy of the Hungarians in general and their hero, Kossuth, in particular. Old World rivalries were not easily forgotten in the New.

8. Vladimir Wertsman, *The Romanians in America and Canada: A Guide to*

Information Sources (Detroit, 1980), 67–71. The remaining section on U.S. history concerns ethnic organizations.

9. Michael Musmanno, *The Story of the Italians in America* (New York, 1965), 22. An earlier history made the same point: "in all the wars waged by the United States up to the Great War, the Italians residing in the United States served always with enthusiasm and bravery" (Angelo Flavio Guidi, "Washington and the Italians," in Richard C. Garlick, Jr., Angelo Flavio Guidi, Giuseppe Prezzolini, Bruno Roselli, and Luigi Russo, eds., *Italy and the Italians in Washington's Time* (New York, 1933), 45. The same focus on foundation and sacrifice may also be observed in Francis Dvornik, *Czech Contributions to the Growth of the United States* (Chicago, 1962). Here the first two chapters (of eight) are on the sixteenth and seventeenth centuries (including participation in the War of Independence) and the fifth is "Czechs in the Civil War" (and includes participation in wars with Mexico and Spain and World War I). Similarly, when the Swedish-American Historical Society began to publish its *Year-Book* in 1907, the first volumes were very much in the filiopietistic vein, with a focus on foundation and sacrifice. In the first volume the only article is "John Morton: En af revolutionens svensk-amerikaner" (John Morton: One of the Swedish Americans of the Revolution). The third volume (1910) has articles on the Civil War, on Vinland, and on the Kensington Stone (supposedly a relic of fourteenth-century Scandinavian exploration of the United States). Soon, however, the influence of Johan Enander wanes and professional historians dominate the pages of the *Year-Book*.

10. The biographical dictionary of immigrants and ethnics in the Confederacy by Ella Lonn is aptly named *Foreigners in the Confederacy* (Chapel Hill, N.C., 1940).

11. A notable exception is John Ford's film *Drums on the Mohawk* (1939) in which the actor playing General Herkimer (or Niklas Herchheimer), who had such a heroic role in protecting the Mohawk Valley, an area of early German settlement, speaks with a pronounced German accent. Such stage German may often have an intended comic effect, but here this is dispelled by the character's stoic behavior in the face of pain and death. Considering the year of production, this German-American hero in a war against the British is a contrast with the usual Hollywood presentation of Germans as a new war with Germany was looming.

12. Dag Blanck, *Becoming Swedish-American: The Construction of an Ethnic Identity in the Augustana Synod, 1860–1917* (Uppsala, Sweden, 1997), 206. In a Finnish-American version the soldiers from Delaware are Finnish Americans and are organized by the Finnish-American John Morton on Washington's request to fight the British in Boston (London, "Delaware Finns and John Morton," 19). Both stories are of course equally fictitious.

13. Guidi, "Washington and the Italians," 46.

14. Bruno Roselli, "Francesco Viga, Savior of the Midwest," in Garlick et al., *Italy and the Italians*, 77–111; "A Banquet in Recognition of Their Efforts," *Bulletin of the Order of the Sons of Italy in America—State of Illinois* (March 1936), *Chicago Foreign Language Press Survey*, emphasis added; "Begrüssungsansprache des Herrn Dr. Albert J. W. Kern," *Nachtrag zur Festschrift zur Feier des Zehnjährigen Bestehens der Vereinigten Deutschen Gesellschaften der Stadt New York* (New York, 1912), 8.

15. This does not mean that the memory of sacrifice did not have to be kept

alive for new generations. The *Abendpost* for August 14, 1927, had an article under the headline "A Distinguished Page in German-American History: General Niklas Herchheimer." A brief biographical sketch, including the deplorable change of his name to Herkimer, is followed by an account of the 1777 battle for the Mohawk Valley, largely, it would seem, a German-American affair on the side of the Republic. Such reminders of a heroic past were standard features of immigrant newspapers.

16. Joseph Krauskopf, "The Jewish Pilgrim Fathers," in *The Two Hundred and Fiftieth Anniversary of the Settlement of the Jews in the United States: Addresses Delivered at Carnegie Hall, New York, on Thanksgiving Day MCMV Together with Other Selected Addresses and Proceedings* (New York, 1906), 128, emphasis added.

17. Goldberg gave his address under the auspices of the Essex Institute at Academy Hall, Salem, Massachusetts, on February 10, 1930. A copy of the pamphlet containing his address may be found at the Widener Memorial Library, Harvard University, Cambridge, Massachusetts.

18. *(Chicago) Greek Press*, January 29, 1931.

19. The difference between the filiopietistic use of history in homemaking arguments and current historical scholarship is significant. The names of these two heroes, so central in earlier ethnic celebrations, addresses, and popular historical accounts, are not mentioned in the index to John J. Bukowczyck, ed., *Polish Americans and Their History: Community, Culture, and Politics* (Pittsburgh, 1996). But by not considering their later *use* in the creation of a Polish-American sense of community, historians may have thrown out the baby with the bath water.

20. Victor Greene makes this point in *American Immigrant Leaders, 1800–1910: Marginality and Identity* (Baltimore, 1987), 106. He also gives several other illustrations of the homemaking use of Kosciuszko and Pulaski.

21. Victor Greene, *For God and Country: The Rise of Polish and Lithuanian Ethnic Consciousness in America, 1860–1910* (Madison, Wis., 1975), 95. The situation was in no way unique for Polish Americans. In 1873, in Madison, Wisconsin, Rasmus B. Anderson took the initiative for the raising of a Leif Erikson monument on the university campus. The committee advertised in the Norwegian-American papers. "It seems incredible,—but the truth must be told—this call for voluntary contributions to so magnificent a cause did not produce one single response. Not one cent was received from anybody" (Anderson, *Life Story* [Madison, Wis., 1915], 190).

22. "From the Kosciuszko Festival Committee," *Dziennik Chicagoski*, June 20, 1896; Jon Gjerde, *The Minds of the West: Ethnocultural Evolution in the Rural Middle West, 1830–1917* (Chapel Hill, N.C., 1997), 61.

23. Greene, *For God and Country*, 162.

24. "The Unveiling of the Thaddeus Kosciuszko Monument in Chicago," *Narod Polski*, September 14, 1904. It should be noted that the monument committee was motivated by its members' desire to preserve a Polish identity in the United States and affirm their ties to the old homeland as well as by the wish for acceptance in the United States. On concluding its activities the following year, the committee reported that it had "worked, mutually, to accomplish a deed, incontestably difficult, but admirable and great, which has turned the attention

of the American world to all of us in general, and at the same time, fastened the ties with our brothers in the far off but always beloved fatherland, by forming a golden bridge joining all of us with that traditional worship of our great men—that worship given with the whole heart, the same in Poland as in America. The monument is proof that, although we have left our native land, we still have in our hearts, our fatherland and all that is connected with it, that brings it to our thoughts, and we ardently desire, that our love of that which is Polish will be conveyed likewise to the hearts of our progeny. It was this kind thought, besides other motives that was primary in our minds when we conceived the idea of building the Kosciuszko monument" ("To the Honorable Public and Polish Organizations in Chicago," *Narod Polski*, August 2, 1905).

25. Gary Hartman, "Building the Ideal Immigrant: Reconciling Lithuanianism and 100 percent Americanism to Create a Respectable Nationalist Movement, 1870–1922," *Journal of American Ethnic History* 18 (Fall 1998): 40–41; *Sandara*, October 10, 1930; *Lietuva*, April 22, 1893, and April 2 and 23, 1909. A notice in the *Lietuva* on October 19, 1917, may help to explain why there was little Lithuanian participation in the Kosciuszko celebrations organized by Polish Americans. Here a Lithuanian who participated in the one-hundredth anniversary commemoration is branded as a "traitor": "But is it not only a shame but really a sin for Lithuanians to place themselves voluntarily under the yoke of the Poles? Lithuanians, is it not enough that our people have been tortured and oppressed by the Poles for five hundred years? Why should we continue to be their slaves?" The newspaper suggested that this Lithuanian, who was a printer, should not be given any Lithuanian business in the future.

Before the First World War and the Russian Revolution, Lithuania and eastern Poland were part of the Russian Empire. After its unification and independence, Poland annexed part of Lithuania, including the present capital, Vilnius, leaving a truncated Lithuanian Republic. Surely, this did not improve relations between Polish and Lithuanian Americans.

26. See Wilhelm Kaufmann, *Die Deutschen im amerikanischen Bürgerkriege* (Munich, 1911).

27. *Svenska Tribunen*, October 9, 1878. The translation error of "offer" instead of "sacrifice" is a common one because the Scandinavian word for sacrifice is *offer*.

28. John Hawgood had an entirely different and negative account of German Americans and the Civil War: "Neither in the North nor in the South could the German farmers, busy clearing their land and needing more labour, relish the demands of the War upon manpower. The draft was often resisted. . . . When the average German fought in the Civil War, or lent his active support to it in any other way, on either side, he was usually following the mob and the line of least resistance rather than his own inclinations" (*The Tragedy of German-America: The Germans in the United States of America During the Nineteenth Century and After* [New York, 1940], 51). A lack of patriotic fervor for the Union as well as its opposite can be found in all ethnic groups, depending on what kind of evidence the historian is looking for. Merle Curti found unpatriotic attitudes among Americans of British descent. See Merle Curti, *The Roots of American Loyalty* (New York, 1946), 160–64.

29. J. M. Rogers, "Jewish Soldiers in the Union Army," *North American Review* 153 (December 1891): 762.

30. The Hebrew Veterans of the Wars of the Republic, with members who had fought in many wars, including the Boxer Rebellion and the Spanish-American War, was organized by Civil War veterans in the 1880s "when the Jew was assailed as a coward, and as one who reaps all the benefits and privileges from a liberal government; but never aids nor offers his life or fortune to defend his country in time of war" (*Chicago Chronicle*, July 2, 1920).

31. *Chicago Chronicle*, November 25, 1905, *Chicago Foreign Language Press Survey*, Jewish. This is an early instance of the antihyphen rhetoric made popular by Theodore Roosevelt and Woodrow Wilson during World War I.

32. *Reform Advocate*, April 19, 1930, *Chicago Foreign Language Press Survey*, Jewish. The story is quite literally retold, repeating a text also used in the *Chicago Chronicle*, March 30, 1923. In both cases the source is a B'nai B'rith publication.

33. *Rassviet* (Dawn), November 20, 1934.

34. Mattson, *Reminiscences*, 312–13.

35. *Denní Hlasatel*, May 31, 1913, and May 31, 1915. The annual reports on Decoration Day celebrations are very similar. See, for instance, May 31, 1911, and May 31, 1922. The letter to the editor of the *Chicago Tribune* is also in the Bohemian section of the *Press Survey*.

36. Thomas Capek, *The Čechs (Bohemians) in America* (Boston, 1920), 267–68.

37. J. N. Lenker, "The World after the War," *Northern Review*, September 1916, p. 5.

38. Selections translated in the *Chicago Foreign Language Press Survey* from the Chicago newspapers of immigrant groups with roots in dependent and independent countries involved in the war give ample illustration of how attitudes toward the war before U.S. entry were dependent on ties to Europe rather than to the United States. There were objective reasons for American anxiety about immigrants' loyalties, priorities, and national identification in the period before war was declared.

39. *Denní Hlasatel*, October 13, 1915, and March 5 and April 20, 1918. Because of their antipathy to the British, some Irish Americans were vociferous advocates for U.S. neutrality.

40. Matthew Frye Jacobson, *Special Sorrows: The Diasporic Imagination of Irish, Polish, and Jewish Immigrants in the United States* (Cambridge, Mass., 1995); Karen Majewski, "Crossings and Double-Crossings: Polish-Language Immigrant Narratives of the Great Migration," in Werner Sollors, ed., *Multilingual America: Transnationalism, Ethnicity, and the Languages of American Literature* (New York, 1998), 247, 253. According to "Preserving Polonia in America: The Polish-American Experience," a Web site of the Balch Institute for Ethnic Studies (<http://www.libertynet.org/balch/polonia>), "an estimated 3 out of 10 Polish immigrants arriving between 1906 and 1914 returned to Poland. . . . Given the opportunity to return when Poland regained independence in 1918, no mass exodus ensued."

41. "Polish American Veterans the Proof of Loyalty," *Dziennik Zjednoczenia*, September 3, 1927, emphasis added.

42. John Higham, *Strangers in the Land: Patterns of American Nativism, 1860–1925*, 2d ed. (New York, 1963), 196–97.

43. Non-Jewish newspapers also used these statistics from the Bureau of Jewish War Records. On June 3, 1919, the *Daily Jewish Courier* quoted them from an editorial in the *(Chicago) Herald-Examiner* of that date; on February 25 they were used in an editorial in the German-American *Abendpost*, "American Jews' Participation in the War."

44. Another aspect of the history of American immigrants and the First World War—the manner in which the army accommodated the large number of immigrant soldiers and their various religions, cultures, and languages—has been studied by Nancy Gentile Ford. See Ford's "'Mindful of the Traditions of His Race': Dual Identity and Foreign-Born Soldiers in the First World War American Army," *Journal of American Ethnic History* 16 (Winter 1997): 35–57.

45. "Greek Soldier, George Dilboy, Killed in the Battle of Belleau Woods, Proclaimed as One of the World's Greatest Heroes," *Saloniki*, November 10, 1923. His corpse was sent to his parents' hometown, Alatsata, in Turkey, but after the American flag and his coffin were desecrated, his parents asked that it be sent to the United States.

46. Hellenic Association of Boston, *Souvenir Program Twelfth Annual Ball* (Boston, 1919).

47. *Greek Press*, April 23, 1930; *Saloniki*, September 26, 1931; and *Saloniki-Greek Press*, May 16, 1935.

48. "Address Delivered by Sotirios Nicholson on Decoration Day at Tomb of the Unknown Soldier," *Greek Star*, June 19, 1931. Greek Americans were of course not alone in reminding each other and the nation of their sacrifices during the world war more than a decade after it was over. A monument for the Polish-American "Deceased Heroes of the World War" was unveiled at the Saint Adalbert Cemetery in Niles, Illinois, on July 4, 1928, and in its notice the preceding day the *Dziennik Zjednoczenia* introduced the event with glowing words about "our national heroes Casimir Pulaski and Thaddeus Kosciuszko" and the participation of "people of Polish descent" in other wars. Some months earlier (February 27, 1929) the same newspaper had celebrated the "three hundred thousand boys of Polish descent who showed in action, and not in speech, the quality of their patriotism."

49. "Greeks for America," *Loxias*, August 8, 1917. As evidence of Greek patriotism, there is also a reference to "the naval battle of Manila, [where] Greeks played a brilliant role as gunners. Greeks were the first to die for their country, and the first to storm the forts."

50. John G. Moses, *Annotated Index to the Syrian World, 1926–1932* (St. Paul, Minn., 1994), 42–46.

51. The best brief account of the Americanization drive, its organization as well as its influence, is Higham, "Crusade for Americanization," *Strangers in the Land*, 234–63.

52. Carl Chrislock, *Watchdog of Loyalty: The Minnesota Commission of Public Safety During World War I* (St. Paul, Minn., 1991), 222.

53. I have not seen any Liberty Loan pamphlet addressed specifically to immigrants from Britain.

54. *Svenska Kuriren*, May 2, 1918. A similar editorial had been published on April 18.

55. Frederick Luebke, *Bonds of Loyalty: German-Americans and World War I* (De Kalb, Ill., 1974), 235, 273.

56. The novel was originally published in Norwegian as *To tullinger: Et billede fra idag* (Two idiots: A contemporary portrait) (Minneapolis, 1920).

57. Chrislock, *Watchdog of Loyalty*, 275; Luebke, *Bonds of Loyalty*, 273.

58. Curti, *Roots of American Loyalty*, 227.

59. Henry (Yoshitaka) Kiyama, *The Four Immigrants Manga: A Japanese Experience in San Francisco, 1904–1924*, trans. Frederik L. Schodt (Berkeley, Calif., 1999), 118–19.

Chapter 4: Ideology

1. The Kensington Stone is housed in the Runestone Museum in Alexandria. A cornerstone of the local conviction that the stone is authentic is the perception that Norwegians are incapable of fraud. See Odd S. Lovoll, *The Promise Fulfilled: A Portrait of Norwegian Americans Today* (Minneapolis, 1998), 5–6.

2. Matthew Frye Jacobson, *Special Sorrows: The Diasporic Imagination of Irish, Polish, and Jewish Immigrants in the United States* (Cambridge, Mass., 1995), 26, 126.

3. Victor R. Greene, *American Immigrant Leaders, 1800–1900: Marginality and Identity* (Baltimore, Md., 1987), 20–21, 28, 35–36, 40. O'Connor and Donahoe are quoted in Greene, who has added emphasis.

4. "A Resolution Made By the Holland Society of Chicago," in B. T. Van Alen, ed., *The Year Book of The Holland Society of Chicago, 1897, 1898, 1899, 1900* (Chicago, 1901), in *The Chicago Foreign Language Press Survey*, Dutch.

5. The confusion between the singular and the plural may be the translator's. This particular notice concludes with the admonishment to take part in the Liberty Loan drive and is signed by the president of the Holland Liberty Loan Co. Emphasis added.

6. *1609–1909: The Dutch in New Netherland and The United States*, Presented by The Netherland Chamber of Commerce in America on Occasion of the Hudson-Fulton Celebration in New York, September 25–October 9, 1909, pp. 45–47.

7. George Ford Huizinga, *What the Dutch Have Done in the West of the United States* (Philadelphia, 1909), 52.

8. Hans Mattson, *Reminiscences: The Story of an Emigrant* (St. Paul, Minn., 1891), 312–13; H. Arnold Barton, *A Folk Divided: Homeland Swedes and Swedish Americans, 1840–1940* (Uppsala, Sweden, 1994), 66–67. This Swedish-American view of their own excellence also found its way into Louis Adamic's *A Nation of Nations* (New York, 1945): "The Delaware Swedes were a friendly lot, partial to the ideal of freedom not only for themselves but for others as well. This traditional trait went back to their Scandinavian homeland. Planning new Sweden in the middle 1620s Gustavus Adolphus had stressed freedom as one of its main aspirations. The colony was to be an asylum for the persecuted everywhere, dedicated to the principle of security of person and property" (124).

9. Gary London, "The Delaware Finns and John Morton: Seeking to Legitimize the Immigrant Experience in America," *Siirtolaisuus/Migration*, no. 3 (1978): 16–18. London quotes and paraphrases Ilmonen and Louhi.

10. "Kosciuszko—Lincoln," *Dziennik Zwiazkowy,* February 12, 1915; Greene, *American Immigrant Leaders,* 106, 109.

11. Kellor's article, which is in the January issue of the *Yale Review* for 1919, is reprinted in Philip Davis, ed., *Immigration and Americanization: Selected Readings* (Boston, 1920). Quotations are from pages 630–33 and 637–38. She develops the same ideas in the concluding chapter, "Principles of Assimilation," of her *Immigration and the Future* (New York, 1920). Her use of gender is deliberate: "Americanization is also essentially a problem of men, since the women of old races in America still follow the leadership of their men" (627).

12. Wise is quoted in Lewis Fried, *Handbook of American-Jewish Literature: An Analytical Guide to Topics, Themes, and Sources* (Westport, Conn., 1988), 4. Wise's article was originally a Fourth of July sermon.

13. *(Chicago) Record-Herald,* November 25, 1905. A more extensive quote from Hirsch's statement appears in the prologue.

14. Max Goldberg, *The Contribution of the Chosen Race to Civic Progress in America: An Address Delivered Under the Auspices of the Essex Institute on February 10, 1930, at Academy Hall, Salem, Massachusetts,* 3, 21; Joseph Krauskopf, "The Jewish Pilgrim Fathers," *The Two Hundred and Fiftieth Anniversary of the Settlement of the Jews in the United States: Addresses delivered at Carnegie Hall, New York, on Thanksgiving Day MCMV . . .* (New York, 1906), 127; Emil G. Hirsch's address is in the book of anniversary addresses; Greene, *American Immigrant Leaders,* 87.

15. Georg Meyer, *Die Deutschamerikaner: Festschrift zur Feier des Deutschamerikanischen Tages in Milwaukee, Wisconsin, am 6. Oktober, 1890* (Milwaukee, 1890), 54; John G. Moses, *Annotated Index to the Syrian World, 1926–1932* (St. Paul, Minn., 1994), December 1926.

16. Vereinigten Deutschen Gesellschaften der Stadt New York, *Nachtrag zur Festschrift zur Feier des Zehnjährigen Bestehens der Vereinigten Deutschen Gesellschaften der Stadt New York* (New York, 1912), 17. A similar point was made by *Die Abendpost,* December 19, 1890, when it wrote on the "German influence on the American national character."

17. One of the points of particular interest to Lambros was the similarity between the two great men, Pericles and Lincoln, as it was expressed in the Funeral Oration of the former and the Gettysburg Address of the latter, "both masterpieces in eloquence, [that] stand out today as the most idealistic documents there are on the principles of democracy. It would take the pen of Thucydides, or the poetic talent of Homer, to sing the hymns of the two illustrious champions of the principles of freedom."

A speech given by A. A. Pantelis on the presentation of the flag of the Greek Republic to the State of Illinois on June 28, 1931, made a similar comparison: "Of all American statesmen, Lincoln's early career compares with the early struggles of Demosthenes, and his achievements are similar to those of the great Greek statesman Pericles" (see typescript included in *The Chicago Foreign Language Press Survey*).

18. Henry James, *The American Scene* (London, 1968), 128.

19. Leon Dominian, "Preface," in M. Vartan Malcom, *The Armenians in America* (Boston, 1919), x; "Lithuanians Were Among the Early Settlers of the New World," *Sandara,* October 10, 1930; *Die Abendpost,* October 6, 1906.

20. Pauline Maier, *American Scripture: Making the Declaration of Independence* (New York, 1997), 208.

21. Greene, *American Immigrant Leaders*, 116; Paul Prodis, "American Civilisation and the Culture of the Greeks," *Ahepa Magazine*, December 1932, pp. 11–13. On Mazzei, see the prologue.

22. *Denní Hlasatel*, May 31, 1911.

23. *Die Sonntagpost*, January 10, 1919; "The German in Public Offices," *Die Abendpost*, October 18, 1925. The article in *Die Sonntagpost* explains that the work for abolition was continued by "German idealists like Karl Follen, Franz Lieber, and later by Carl Schurz, until emancipation of negroes was effected by the Civil War." In *A Nation of Nations* Adamic says of the 1688 resolution from Germantown, "Rightly, no teller of the German saga in America neglects to mention this fact" (169).

24. "The Germans of 1848," *Die Abendpost*, April 16, 1924.

25. *Sentinel*, November 10, 1916, p. 6. At a time when increasing numbers of African Americans from the rural South were moving into Chicago and other northern cities, claims to have taken the initiative for racial equality in the United States may not have had an endearing effect on white middle- or working-class urban Americans. These German- and Jewish-American statements may therefore perhaps be interpreted as gestures of solidarity with black Americans as much as arguments for acceptance by fellow white Americans.

26. Meyer, *Die Deutschamerikaner*, 54; Arlow W. Anderson, *Rough Road to Glory: The Norwegian-American Press Speaks Out on Public Affairs, 1875 to 1925* (Philadelphia, 1990), 37. The 1854 story about Lincoln and nativism is in the *Illinois Staats-Zeitung* for January 29, 1901, and is discussed in chapter 3.

27. At the turn of the nineteenth century, the use of the hyphen was not yet to be taken for granted, and a contributor in the Norwegian-American newspaper, *Decorah-Posten*, published in Decorah, a small town in northeastern Iowa, urged its use, noting that "both native-born Americans and immigrants prefer to place a nationality indicator followed by a hyphen in front of the noun when speaking of naturalized Americans. . . . Norwegian-Americans should do the same and follow the others in cultivating their national heritage." See my *The Western Home: A Literary History of Norwegian America* (Northfield, Minn., 1996), 189.

28. Thomas J. Diven, "Is This an English Country?" *Der Zeitgeist*, October 23, 1917, pp. 35–36. Note that Diven, in 1917, and Georg Meyer, in 1890, both spoke of "the English yoke"—Meyer with reference to Americans demanding Anglo conformity, Diven with reference to Britain.

29. The editor's analysis of American "Anglomania" at the turn of the nineteenth century is in accord with the views of Marcus Lee Hansen and Horace M. Kallen. See Marcus Lee Hansen, *The Immigrant in American History* (New York, 1964), 148–49; Horace M. Kallen, *Culture and Democracy in the United States* (New Brunswick, N.J., 1998), 91.

30. The editorial concludes: "For America, a German victory would be a great blessing—would seem necessary for her welfare."

31. Andreas Ueland, *Recollections of an Immigrant* (New York, 1929). See chapter 5 on Anderson's ideas. Ueland argued that the maintenance of immigrant languages and the celebration of Old World traditions were "retarding influences." See his article, "A Minor Melting Pot," *Samband* 7 (June 1931): 47–55.

32. Mencken wrote "Die Deutschamerikaner" for *Die Neue Rundschau.* He is quoted in John A. Hawgood, *The Tragedy of German-America: The Germans in the United States of America During the Nineteenth Century—and After* (New York, 1940), 42.

33. Greene, *American Immigrant Leaders,* 140–41.

34. Louis Adamic, *From Many Lands* (New York, 1940), 298.

35. Nils. N. Rønning, *Fifty Years in America* (Minneapolis, 1938), 73; Ueland, *Recollections of an Immigrant,* 13. I am indebted to Øyvind T. Gulliksen for these two references.

36. Edward William Bok, *The Americanization of William Bok* (New York, 1924), 451. The reader may object that Bok's autobiography is more about being amazingly successful than about becoming American, and it may indeed be said that Bok seems to conflate the two: "'The sky is the limit' to the foreign-born who comes to America with honest endeavor" (450). He also seems to confuse the ideal of loyalty with an obligation to refrain from open criticism of government (445–46).

Chapter 5: Norwegian Americans Are Americans

1. *Saloniki,* September 20, 1919. A similar combination of all three genres in one narrative is evident in a speech made at a "Bohemian" celebration in Chicago in 1915 and reported in *Denní Hlasatel* (May 31) under the heading "National Festivals Succeed. Memorable Celebrations of the Narodni Hrbitov and the Ceska Utulna a Sirotcinec Draws Thousands."

2. For instance, in a discussion of an 1892 novel by Hans A. Foss, *Hvide Slaver,* I once gave a summary of what I now recognize is a version of a standard homemaking myth used by many ethnic groups. Nor did I fully see how the protagonist's marriage to a young woman of an Anglo-American family was an indication to the reader of the success of the homemaking argument. See *The Western Home: A Literary History of Norwegian America* (Northfield, Minn., 1996), 152, 155.

3. Odd S. Lovoll, *The Promise of America: A History of the Norwegian-American People* (Oslo, 1984), 9.

4. This was also observed by a perceptive contemporary immigrant: "The Norwegian immigration before the Civil War has had a far greater influence on the nationality's later development than one might believe by only looking at the relative numbers of those who came then and those who came later. Even though the latter are many times more in numbers, the first established and gave the still dominant tone to many important aspects of life." See David Monrad Schøyen, *Amerikas forenede Staters Historie. Anden Del: Unionen indtil Borgerkrigen,* part 2: (Chicago, 1875), 407.

5. Matthew Frye Jacobson, *Whiteness of a Different Color: European Immigrants and the Alchemy of Race* (Cambridge, Mass., 1998), 41.

6. In 1870, when the total Norwegian immigration to the United States since 1825 was not much more than eighty thousand, almost sixty thousand Norwegian immigrants were living in rather concentrated areas of Wisconsin, where they made up 5.6 percent of the state's population (Lovoll, *Promise of America,* 36).

7. The phrase is from Foss, *Hvide slaver* (Grand Forks, N.D., 1892), 246.

8. "Norwegian Mayflower" is Rasmus B. Anderson's term. See his *Life Story* (Madison, Wis., 1915), 176.

9. Ole Rynning, *Sandfærdig Beretning om Amerika, til Oplysning og Nytte for Bonde og Menigmand* (Christiania, Norway, 1838). It was translated and edited by Theodore C. Blegen as *Ole Rynning's True Account of America* (Minneapolis, 1926).

10. See my *Western Home,* 70–71. Svein Nilsson's pioneer history has been translated with an introduction by Clarence A. Clausen, *A Chronicler of Immigrant Life: Svein Nilsson's Articles in Billed-Magazine* (Northfield, Minn., 1982).

11. David Monrad Schøyen, *Amerikas forenede Staters Historie. Første Deel: Tidsrummet indtil Unionen,* part 1 (Chicago, 1874), 14–15.

12. On Schøyen's three-volume history and his correspondence with Anderson on his projected "saga," see my *Western Home,* 59, 71–72. Both Schøyen and Anderson knew that the word *Vesterheimen,* derived from Old Norse, meant the Western world or hemisphere. Among Norwegian Americans, however, it acquired the meaning "western home" and was used to describe their ethnic culture.

13. The University of Wisconsin was founded in 1848. When Anderson was member of the faculty from 1869 to 1883, the university, as his biographer has reminded us, "bore little resemblance to the huge, nationally respected institution of today." Indeed, the total enrollment in these years varied between a low of 316 to a "peak of 517." See Lloyd Hustvedt, *Rasmus Bjørn Anderson: Pioneer Scholar* (Northfield, Minn., 1966), 93. The information that Anderson was the first Wisconsin-born member of the faculty is from a conversation I had with one of his successors at the university, Einar Haugen.

14. Anderson, *Life Story,* 85–86. This autobiography is a rambling and not entirely reliable 671-page advertisement for himself. With its resentments and self-righteousness, however, it is an excellent source for my purposes. As a more balanced and also rather critical portrait, Hustvedt's 1966 biography, *Rasmus Bjørn Anderson,* is still unsurpassed. Copying seems to have been Anderson's main scholarly method.

15. Hustvedt, *Rasmus Bjørn Anderson,* 58.

16. The outlawed Erik the Red established the Norse settlement of parts of western Greenland in 985. This was his second migration; the first was from Norway to Iceland some years earlier. Leif Erikson, who centuries later acquired a mythic role in the imaginations of Norwegian Americans, was the son of Erik the Red. The Greenlanders had their own legal system and *ting,* or council of free men, based on systems of government in medieval Norway and Iceland and were a bishopric under the Church of Rome. Through much of their history they did, however, recognize the sovereignty of the king of Norway, as did the Icelanders. It may thus be a moot point whether Leif Erikson "really" was a Norwegian, an Icelander, or a Greenlander when he "discovered" America. The Greenlanders, as they referred to themselves, ceased to have regular communications with Europe around 1400, but archaeological evidence shows that their culture lived on with sporadic contacts with Europeans till some time in the first half of the sixteenth century, that is, after the voyages of Columbus. By that time they had had a longer history than the United States has had, including its colonial prehistory. The sagas of discovery and settlement are available in Einar Haugen, *Voyages to Vinland: The First American Saga* (New York, 1942). Farley Mowat, *Westviking:*

The Ancient Norse in Greenland and North America (London, 1965), offers a controversial but well-argued discussion of the records. All earlier accounts, however, have been superseded by the archaeological work of Helge and Stine Ingstad. See Finn Hødnebø and Jónas Kristjánsson, eds., *The Viking Discovery of America* (Oslo, 1991), and Anne Stine Ingstad, *The Norse Discovery of America*, 2 vols. (Oslo, 1985). The most recent study of the Greenlanders and medieval explorations of North America is Kirsten A. Seaver's carefully researched *The Frozen Echo: Greenland and the Exploration of North America ca A.D. 1000–1500* (Palo Alto, Calif., 1996). A fascinating fictional meditation on the late period of the Greenlander civilization is Jane Smiley's novel, *The Greenlanders* (New York, 1988).

17. Anderson, *Life Story*, 114, 141, 210. In his view of history, which highlighted the contributions of the Germanic peoples to European civilization, Anderson was inspired by the writings of the Danish scholar, bishop, and poet Nikolai F. S. Grundtvig.

18. Hustvedt, whose *Rasmus Bjørn Anderson* is quoted here, gives an excellent survey of American and European reviews (315–16) as well as of earlier literature on the Norse discoveries (312–14), showing that Anderson was hardly original. His biography is the main source for an understanding of the complex character of Anderson.

19. Rasmus B. Anderson, *America Not Discovered By Columbus* (Chicago, 1891). The book was also intended to raise money for a Leif Erikson statue in Madison. Nothing came of this, but his partner in the project, the violinist Ole Bull, took the idea with him to Cambridge, Massachusetts, and Boston, where it was taken up by both politicians and literati. The resulting statue may still be admired on Boston's Commonwealth Avenue.

20. The account of the 1870 Columbus Day celebration is in Odd S. Lovoll, *A Century of Urban Life: The Norwegians in Chicago before 1930* (Northfield, Minn., and Urbana, Ill., 1988), 130–31.

21. Arlow William Andersen, *The Immigrant Takes His Stand: The Norwegian-American Press and Public Affairs, 1847–72* (Northfield, Minn., 1953), 11, 26–27.

22. Jacobson, *Whiteness of a Different Color*, 70–71. I have found no evidence that Anderson read this particular lecture by Ullman, which was published as a pamphlet. The University of Wisconsin library has two pamphlets by Daniel Ullman, one from 1841 and one, *Amendments to the Constitution of the United States*, from 1876. For this information I am indebted to Asbjørn Grønstad.

23. Anderson, *Life Story*, 233.

24. See *Tale ved femti-aarsfesten for den norske udvandring til Amerika* (Chicago, 1875). With about 12,700 words the speech probably lasted much longer than the ninety minutes Anderson warned his listeners they were in for.

25. His speech has many references to "this day," meaning the Fourth of July. The title page of his pamphlet, however, gives the fifth as the date for the actual event in the park. Odd Lovoll explains that because the fourth was on a Sunday, the celebration "was postponed so as not to break the Sabbath." See Lovoll, *Century of Urban Life*, 330, note 48. The quotation from Anderson's pamphlet is from p. 3.

26. The passages quoted may be found on pp. 3–5, 8, 9, and 12 of Anderson's

pamphlet. The worst European weeds were later identified as "monarchism and aristocracy." They had infested Norway too in its postmedieval history.

27. The passages quoted appear on pp. 13, 14, 15, and 23 of Anderson's pamphlet. Anderson uses "American" in the sense of "Anglo-American."

28. The passages quoted appear on pp. 25 and 26 of Anderson's pamphlet. Langeland's editorial, also quoted in chapter 1, appeared in the *Skandinaven,* June 1, 1866; I used a microfilm copy of the weekly edition, not the *Chicago Foreign Language Press Survey,* which also includes selections from this newspaper.

29. For an interesting discussion of one aspect of this historiographical controversy, see Martin Thom, "Tribes Within Nations: The Ancient Germans and the History of Modern France," in Homi K. Bhabha, ed., *Narration and Nation* (London, 1990), 23–43.

30. For a convincingly devastating discussion of how Anderson's *Norse Mythology* (1875) was more or less copied from Petersen's *Nordisk Mytologi,* 2d ed. (Copenhagen, 1863), see Hustvedt, *Rasmus Bjørn Anderson,* 316–22.

31. The passage quoted appears on p. 25 of Anderson's pamphlet.

32. As I have observed in other chapters in this book, Anderson's version was also adopted by the Swedish Americans, especially through the efforts of Johan Enander, editor of the newspaper *Hemlandet* (Homeland).

33. That he would tell the same story again and again is suggested by an unkind comment in the Chicago newspaper *Skandinaven* in its report on the Seventeenth of May celebrations in 1893, a rather special event because it also marked the establishment of a Leif Erikson statue society. Anderson was not the main speaker: "Then R. B. Anderson spoke for Norway. Because he chose to give the same speech he has given each 17th of May for the past twenty years, we think it quite unnecessary to repeat any of it here. The readers of *Skandinaven* know it by heart" (Hustvedt, *Rasmus Bjørn Anderson,* 223).

34. Reidar Bakken, *Lad ingen sladdrelystne læse mine brever . . . Nordmenn blir amerikanarar: Brev hjemsendt frå norske emigrantar frå 1844–1930* (Fagernes, Norway, 1955), 107.

35. David Mauk, *The Colony That Rose from the Sea: Norwegian Maritime Migration and Community in Brooklyn, 1850–1910* (Northfield, Minn., 1997), 207.

36. Foss, *Hvide slaver,* 246.

37. Hustvedt, *Rasmus Bjørn Anderson,* 105. Hustvedt agrees that Peterson's novel has little literary merit but observes that "as a journalistic account of pioneer life and of the life of a Norwegian boy at an American university, it has considerable value for historians" (105–6).

38. For the report of Rølvaag's speech, see Kristine Haugen, "Syttende mai i Sioux City," in the June 1926 edition of the journal *Norsk Ungdom* (Norwegian Youth). Although all his earlier books were published in Norwegian in Minneapolis, Rølvaag's first books to be published in Norway were *Giants in the Earth,* published in two volumes in 1924 (*I de dage*) and 1925 (*Riket grundlægges*); *Peder Victorious,* published in 1928 as *Peder Seier*);, and *Their Father's God,* published in 1931 as *Den signede dag.* Publication in a European capital rather than in Minnesota also made them visible in New York and led to their publication there in English translation—*Giants* in 1927, *Peder Victorious* in 1929, and *Their Father's God* in 1931.

39. Kaldahl's reference to the Bill of Rights is, of course, to the British act of

1689, which, along with other acts after the reign of the Stuarts, was a central document in the development of British democracy. See Rølvaag, *Their Father's God*, 205–10. The long quotation is on pp. 209–10.

40. Michael A. Musmanno, *Columbus Was First* (New York, 1966), 112.

41. The origin of this notion is a book by Albert Welles, president of the American College for Genealogical Registry and Heraldry, *The Pedigree and History of the Washington Family Derived from Odin, the Founder of Scandinavia, B.C. 70, Involving a Period of Eighteen Centuries, and Including Fifty-Five Generation, Down to General George Washington, First President of the United States* (New York, 1879). For an example of how this story lived on in the imagination of some Norwegian Americans, see Simon Johnson, "Glimt av norsk foreningsliv i Amerika," *Nordmands-Forbundet* 18 (April 1925): 191. Occasional references to the idea that Washington was Norwegian appear in Norwegian-American publications. *The Northern Review: Cultural Magazine for Northwest* [*sic*], a journal that during World War I attempted to forge an alliance—first pro-German, then neutral—between the German and the Scandinavian groups in the upper Midwest, featured extracts from Welles's book on Washington in its January 1918 issue.

42. Articles in *Skandinaven almanak og kalender* (Chicago, 1926) include "Norse Words Used by White Indians" (reprinted from the *Literary Digest*) and "Norse Explorers Ahead of Columbus" (reprinted from the *New York World*), which give both material and linguistic "evidence" for Nordic visitors to the Pacific Northwest in medieval times. The Kensington rune stone, believed by all professional scholars to be a hoax, was discovered in 1898 by a farmer of Swedish descent and is kept in Alexandria, Minnesota. The most prominent advocate of the Kensington Stone as evidence of Viking explorations was Hjalmar Holand, and he has an article on Norse antiquities in Minnesota ("Norske oldfund i Minnesota") in *Skandinaven almanak og kalender* (Chicago, 1927). Among Holand's many publications on this subject are *The Kensington Stone: A Study in Pre-Columbian American History* (Ephraim, Wis., 1932), and *America, 1355–1364: A New Chapter in Pre-Columbian History* (New York, 1946). As promoter of the rune stone, he has been succeeded by another amateur historian, O. G. Landsverk, *The Kensington Runestone: A Reappraisal of the Circumstances Under Which the Stone Was Discovered* (Glendale, Calif., 1961). Another who carries on this tradition is W. R. Anderson, who founded the Leif Ericson Society in 1962 and whose most recent publication is *Norse America: Tenth Century Onward* (Evanston, Ill., 1997); his book presents "evidence" for an extensive Viking presence in both North and South America. A balanced scholarly study of the stone and the controversy is Theodore C. Blegen, *The Kensington Rune Stone: New Light on an Old Riddle* (St. Paul, Minn., 1968).

43. Olson is quoted in *Skandinaven almanak og kalender* (1927), 42; Hansen's article appeared in the 1928 edition of the almanac (the quote is from p. 14). Olson's use of the first-person plural illustrates how easily the immigrant could be proud of two identities. In the first instance, "our instruments of government" refers to the American institutions and "our" means "American." The second "our" refers to the specific Norwegian-American ethnic group. There is no conflict here; the loyalty to "our instruments of government" was undivided.

44. See Peter Thoresen Reite, *Fra det norske Normandi* (Moorhead, Minn., 1912), and Ditlef Ristad, *Fra det nye Normandi: Kvad* (Edgerton, Wis., 1922), re-

spectively. The titles cited in the text are translations of Reite's and Ristad's titles; no published translations of their books exist.

45. Johnson's poem was published in *Kvartalskrift*, July 1916, pp. 66–67.

46. C. A. Mellby, "New Norman Gothic 'Mount St. Olaf,'" *Viking*, 1926–1927, p. 104. See also Joseph M. Shaw, *History of St. Olaf College, 1874–1974* (Northfield, Minn., 1974), 288–94. According to Shaw, Lars Wilhelm Boe, who was then president of the college, met the architect Eliel Saarinen at the Cranbrook Academy near Detroit in 1939 and afterward declared, "I saw there a type of architecture that made me wish I had discovered this man twenty years ago." To another correspondent Boe wrote that "Saarinen has the right idea" but that it was too late to change course (294). I am indebted to Professor Todd W. Nichol of Luther Northwestern Theological Seminary for these references.

47. Hustvedt, *Rasmus Bjørn Anderson*, 242–43.

48. Sigurd Folkestad, "Leif Erikson," *Paa kongevei* (Strum, Wis., 1911), 109, my prose translation. The original reads: "Saa bor vi da her med den førstes ret, / vi folk af Leif Eriksons egen æt. / Han tændte for landet historiens dag. / At være dets lys er vor folkesag. / Vel er vi imod Millionerne faa. / Men slig skal en høvdingæt altid staa. / Som han var den første, der landet fandt, / skal vi bli den æt, som ved aand det vandt."

49. Julius Berg Baumann, *Samlede digte* (Minneapolis, 1924), 195–96, my prose translation. The original reads: "I statenes krige, før landet fik fred, / saa mange av fædrene kjæmpende stred, / mens forrest i linje de banneret bar / og døde som helter for landets forsvar. / . . . / Vort land, under stjernenes skinnende rad — / til dig har vi viet vort liv og vort kvad. / Her lyser vort haab som vor daad, vor tro, / og her vil i lykke og frihet vi bo."

50. John A. Johnson, *Det skandinaviske regiments historie* (La Crosse, Wis., 1869); Peter G. Dietrichson, *En kortfattet skildring af Det femtende Wisconsin regiments historie og virksomhed under borgerkrigen samt nogle korte træk af fangernes ophold i Andersonville* (Chicago, 1884); Kristofer Janson, *Femtende Wisconsin* (Minneapolis, Minn., 1887); Ole A. Buslett, *Det femtende Wisconsin frivillige* (Decorah, Iowa, 1894); and Waldemar Ager, *Oberst Heg og hans gutter* (Eau Claire, Wis., 1916), and *Gamlelandets sønner* (Oslo, 1926), translated by Trygve M. Ager and published as *Sons of the Old Country* (Lincoln, Neb., 1983).

51. The newspapers in which Johnson advertised were the February 12, 1866, editions of *Emigranten* (Emigrant) and *Fædrelandet* (Fatherland). He had good reason to fear that American historians would gloss over the immigrant contributions. Nor were American historians alone in neglecting the "Scandinavian character" of the Fifteenth Wisconsin. In a German history of Germans who fought in the Civil War, Heg is listed as a German officer whose regiment mainly consisted of German and Swedish soldiers. See Wilhelm Kaufmann, *Die Deutschen im amerikanischen Bürgerkriege* (München, 1911), 510.

52. Buslett, *Det femtende Wisconsin*, 7–8. The same statistical claim was of course also made by leaders of other immigrant groups.

53. Carl H. Chrislock, *Ethnicity Challenged: The Upper Midwest Norwegian-American Experience in World War I* (Northfield, Minn., 1981); April Schultz, *Ethnicity on Parade: Inventing the Norwegian American through Celebration* (Amherst, Mass., 1994), 121. The number of participants appears in *Skandinaven almanak og kalender* (1925), 66.

54. *Skandinaven almanak og kalender* (1926), 79.
55. Schultz, *Ethnicity on Parade*, 120.
56. The Dayton advertisement, the medal, and the two stamps appear as illustrations in Schultz, *Ethnicity on Parade*, 75, 80.
57. Ager, *Oberst Heg og hans gutter.*

Epilogue

1. The Amish Mennonites, who began to arrive before the nineteenth century, may be considered one exception. It may, however, be a moot point whether they should be considered a church or an ethnic group.
2. Herbert Gans, "Symbolic Ethnicity: The Future of Ethnic Groups and Cultures in America" (1979), reprinted with a new epilogue in Werner Sollors, ed., *Theories of Ethnicity: A Classical Reader* (New York, 1996), 425–59. An excellent study of the important role of ethnicity in the lives of many mainstream Americans is Odd S. Lovoll's *The Promise Fulfilled: A Portrait of Norwegian Americans Today* (Minneapolis, 1998).
3. John Bodnar, *Remaking America: Public Memory, Commemoration, and Patriotism in the Twentieth Century* (Princeton, N.J., 1992), 71–72. The disagreement between Scottish and Irish Americans about McKean may be compared to the disagreement between Finnish and Swedish Americans about John Morton. See chapter 2.
4. The precise year for the first Norse sighting of North America or the first landfall is difficult to determine on the basis of the accounts in the Icelandic sagas, which were written down several centuries after the events. Any indication of a day and month is of course arbitrary.
5. *Bulletin Order Sons of Italy of Illinois* 8, no. 11 (1936).
6. Rob Kroes, *The Persistence of Ethnicity: Dutch Calvinist Pioneers in Amsterdam, Montana* (Urbana, Ill., 1992).
7. Melvin G. Holli, "1938 Delaware Tercentenary: Establishing a Finnish Precence [sic] at the Three Hundredth Anniversary Celebration," in Auvo Kostiainen, ed., *Finnish Identity in America* (Turku, Finland, 1990), 41–42; Max Engman, "The Tug of War Over 'Nya Sverige,' 1938," *Swedish-American Historical Quarterly* 45 (April 1994): 99. These are the two main accounts of the conflicts between Finns and Swedes before the 1938 celebration.
8. H. Arnold Barton, *A Folk Divided: Homeland Swedes and Swedish Americans, 1840–1940* (Uppsala, Sweden, 1994), 5, 96–97, 282–83; Hans Mattson, ed., *250th Anniversary of the First Swedish Settlement in America, September 14th, 1888* (Minneapolis, 1889); Dag Blanck, "History at Work: The 1888 New Sweden Jubilee," *Swedish-American Historical Quarterly* 39 (April 1988): 5–20.
9. Engman, "Tug of War," 72, 79–80. The historian selected to be the secretary of the executive committee for the Swedish-American Tercentenary Committee was Amandus Johnson, one-time member of the department of Germanic languages at the University of Pennsylvania and someone who was in the filiopietistic Enander tradition. He was chosen rather than the prominent and respected historian George Stephenson, professor of history at the University of Minnesota. Barton characterizes Stephenson as "the first American academic historian of

Swedish origins to devote himself to the history of his ethnic group in the United States" (see Barton, *Folk Divided,* 309).

10. Auvo Kostiainen, "Delaware as a Symbol of Finnish Immigration," *Finnish Identity in America* (Turku, Finland, 1990), 50; Holli, "1938 Delaware Tercentenary," 37–42; Engman, "Tug of War," 88–89. Kostiainen refers to Berry's article, which was published in *Turun Sanomat,* July 30, 1988.

11. Olavi Koivukangas, "Conferences and Exhibitions Open the Delaware 350th Anniversary," *Siirtolaisuus/Migration,* no. 1 (1988): 23–36.

12. R. A. Skelton, Thomas E. Marston, and George D. Painter, *The Vinland Map and the Tartar Relation* (New Haven, Conn., 1965). The official invitation for the presentation of the book read: "An important occasion held at the Beinecke Rare Book and Manuscript Library, Yale University, New Haven, October 11, 1965." The "ceremonies" began at 9 P.M., followed by a black-tie reception.

13. After laboratory tests in 1974 suggested that the map might be a twentieth-century forgery, Yale University Press withdrew the book. In 1996, however, after new tests arrived at conclusions that argued for the authenticity of the map, the press published a new edition with an introduction by Wilcomb E. Washburn. In an article available to Washburn, Kirsten A. Seaver, probably the foremost authority on medieval Greenland and related explorations of North America, argues that the map is a forgery. See Seaver, *The Frozen Echo: Greenland and the Exploration of North America, ca. A.D. 1000–1500* (Palo Alto, Calif., 1996), 164–65. It may be added that after the publication of Anne Stine Ingstad, *The Norse Discovery of America* (Oslo, 1985), and the general acceptance of the archaeological analysis and interpretation of the excavations at L'Anse aux Meadows, Newfoundland, the Vinland map lost some of its value as the primary evidence—outside the Icelandic saga accounts—of Norse settlement in North America.

14. "Who Discovered America? New Evidence," *New York Times,* October 17, 1965.

15. *Martinsville* (Virginia) *Bulletin,* October 12, 1965.

16. *Boston Herald,* October 8, 1966. Gerry's Landing, not far from the present site of the marker, is where Eben N. Horsford, an amateur archaeologist (see chapter 2, note 25), and others believed that there had been a Norse settlement. According to an unidentified clipping in the Vinland map file in Yale's Beinecke Library, Vellucci also called for the removal of the marker, explaining that when it was first placed at Gerry's Landing, "there weren't any Italians around to protest."

17. Unidentified clipping, Beinecke Library.

18. *Chicago Tribune,* October 13, 1965.

19. "Cartography: The Map Flap," *Yale Alumni Magazine,* November 1965, pp. 15–16. Of course, many sent their reactions directly to the Yale University Press. Files relating to the publication of the Vinland map, however, were not available when I visited the Yale libraries in the spring of 1998.

20. Michael Musmanno, *Columbus Was First* (New York, 1966).

21. Vinland map file clipping, Beinecke Library.

22. Rosenthal is quoted in the *Chicago Tribune,* October 13, 1965.

23. The correspondent for the Spanish weekly is quoted in James Brooke, "An Anniversary Brings Pride and Resentment," *New York Times,* May 3, 1998. Al-

though twelve hundred "media outlets" were notified "in advance, coverage has been limited largely to reporters from New Mexico and Spain," the *Times* reported.

24. Judy Giannettino, "In Case You Missed It . . . The Week's News in Review," *Albuquerque Journal*, December 1, 1997. References to this newspaper and to the *New Mexican* are to the editions published by the respective papers' Web sites.

25. Ray Rivera, "Hero or Villain: How Should We Remember Don Juan de Oñate?" *New Mexican* January 11, 1998.

26. Ibid.

27. See Judy Giannettino, "The Week's News in Review," *Albuquerque Journal*, March 16 and 23, 1998. This did not happen without opposition. Millie Santillanes, an Albuquerque resident, organized the Hispanic Anti-Defamation League to erect a new monument that would honor Oñate and generated much local attention with her campaign against "people who aren't Hispanic rejecting our ancestors. . . . All we want to do is commemorate the moment in history when we arrived here." See Jim Belshaw, "Anger in a Warm Place," *Albuquerque Journal*, March 20, 1998. Again, note the use of "we."

28. Accounts of the reconciliation process are Hollis Walker, "Both Sides Worked Hard for Landmark Meeting," and Daniel J. Chacon, "Tribes, Spain Reach for Peace," *New Mexican*, April 23, 1998, and Brooke, "An Anniversary Brings Pride."

29. This material appears in the *New York Times* story of May 3, 1998. Gullón could also claim Aztec descent because his male ancestor married a granddaughter of Fernando Cortès and Isabel Moctezuma, daughter of the last Aztec emperor.

30. Consider, for instance, the distance traveled from Faulkner's McCaslins in *Go Down, Moses*—who could not bring themselves to say brother, sister, or cousin to relatives they called "niggers"—and the labors to reconstruct a divided family in Edward Ball's *Slaves in the Family* (New York, 1998).

31. Hamilton Holt, ed., *The Life Stories of Undistinguished Americans as Told by Themselves*, with an introduction by Werner Sollors (New York, 1990), 19, 20. Ernest Poole wrote this particular story for the *Independent*; that Poole also provided Upton Sinclair with information for *The Jungle* is well known. A comparison between the Lithuanian's life story and Sinclair's novel, however, reveals that Sinclair made use of more than mere information. It is evident that the novel follows the anonymous autobiography quite closely, both in many details and in its conclusion with a kind of conversion story set in the Socialist Party in Sinclair's novel rather than in a labor union.

Index

ORM ØVERLAND, a professor of American literature at the University of Bergen, Norway, received his Ph.D. degree in American studies from Yale University in 1969. He is the editor of a seven-volume edition of immigrant letters to Norway and the author of *The Western Home: A Literary History of Norwegian America* (1996), *Johan Schrøder's Travels in Canada, 1863* (1989), and numerous books and articles on American literature and history. His main research interests at present are immigration and the uses of languages other than English in the United States.

The Immigrant World of Ybor City: Italians and Their Latin Neighbors in
  Tampa, 1885–1985 *Gary R. Mormino and George E. Pozzetta*
The Butte Irish: Class and Ethnicity in an American Mining Town,
  1875–1925 *David M. Emmons*
The Making of an American Pluralism: Buffalo, New York, 1825–60
  David A. Gerber
Germans in the New World: Essays in the History of Immigration
  Frederick C. Luebke
A Century of European Migrations, 1830–1930 *Edited by
  Rudolph J. Vecoli and Suzanne M. Sinke*
The Persistence of Ethnicity: Dutch Calvinist Pioneers in Amsterdam,
  Montana *Rob Kroes*
Family, Church, and Market: A Mennonite Community in the Old and
  the New Worlds, 1850–1930 *Royden K. Loewen*
Between Race and Ethnicity: Cape Verdean American Immigrants,
  1860–1965 *Marilyn Halter*
Les Icariens: The Utopian Dream in Europe and America
  Robert P. Sutton
Labor and Community: Mexican Citrus Worker Villages in a Southern
  California County, 1900–1950 *Gilbert G. González*
Contented among Strangers: Rural German-Speaking Women and
  Their Families in the Nineteenth-Century Midwest
  Linda Schelbitzki Pickle
Dutch Farmer in the Missouri Valley: The Life and Letters of Ulbe Eringa,
  1866–1950 *Brian W. Beltman*
Good-bye, Piccadilly: British War Brides in America *Jenel Virden*
For Faith and Fortune: The Education of Catholic Immigrants in Detroit,
  1805–1925 *JoEllen McNergney Vinyard*
Britain to America: Mid-Nineteenth-Century Immigrants to the
  United States *William E. Van Vugt*
Immigrant Minds, American Identities: Making the United States Home,
  1870–1930 *Orm Øverland*

Typeset in 9.5/12.5 Trump Mediaeval
Composed by Jim Proefrock
at the University of Illinois Press
Manufactured by Thomson-Shore, Inc.

University of Illinois Press
1325 South Oak Street
Champaign, IL 61820-6903
www.press.uillinois.edu